MW01519429

Shared Beliefs, Honest Differences

A Biblical Basis for Comparing the Doctrines of Mormons and Other Christians

Shared Beliefs, Honest Differences

A Biblical Basis for Comparing the Doctrines of Mormons and Other Christians

Dwight E. Monson

First Printing: November 1998

International Standard Book Number:
0-88290-633-X

Horizon Publishers' Catalog and Order Number:
1091

Printed and distributed
in the United States of America by

Horizon
Publishers
& Distributors, Incorporated

Mailing Address:
P.O. Box 490
Bountiful, Utah 84011-0490

Street Address:
50 South 500 West
Bountiful, Utah 84010

Local Phone: (801) 295-9451
WATS (toll free): 1 (800) 453-0812
FAX: (801) 295-0196

Internet: www.horizonpublishers.com

Contents

Introduction

One day a few years ago, I came home from work to find my wife and daughter engaged in serious discussion. At that time, our daughter, Marianne, was a senior at Naperville North High School in Naperville, Illinois. Among her friends were several born-again Christians with whom she had conversations regarding religion from time to time. One of her friends, Betsy, was consistently more open in her challenges to Marianne and our Latter-day Saint faith. This led to periodic discussions in our home, but nothing more significant than other issues that arise in the course of getting a child through high school.

On this occasion, Marianne came home very upset by a conversation that had occurred earlier in the day. It seems that Betsy had just completed a unit in her Bible study program about the Mormons. She shared the overview and handwritten notes from the unit with Marianne. (See *Appendix One.*)

The tone of Betsy's interaction with Marianne, from our daughter's perspective, had been condemnatory and intolerant. The overview of Mormonism that Betsy had been given, from my perspective, was prejudiced and unflattering, stating half-truths as fact and intending to mislead rather than to inform.

Marianne asked for the counsel of her parents to know how to respond in a positive but forceful manner. That night as we discussed different options, the thought occurred to me to write a letter to my daughter that she could share with her friends clarifying our teachings and providing a different perspective on Latter-day Saint teachings in relation to those of our Christian friends.

The next day, I composed the response found in *Appendix Two.* It was shared with Betsy, who apparently read it. Her comment to Marianne after studying the letter was that she could better understand our faith and that she would have more respect for our beliefs in the future.

The letter had served its purpose. It provided a sense of peace to our daughter who had felt the condemnation of uninformed opinion but was at a loss to know how to respond in an appropriate manner. It was perceived by her as an act of kindness on the part of her father who cared about her feelings and wanted to help her feel comfortable, despite differences in our religious tenets.

The contents of the letter were discussed within our family and shared with an investigator or two with whom I had contact at the time in the capacity of my church calling as Ward Mission Leader. Nothing more came of the episode with Betsy and her born-again friends or of the letter for about eighteen months.

Then a series of events occasioned my sharing the letter with four people: two members of The Church of Jesus Christ of Latter-day Saints and two non-members. As I interacted with each individual who came in contact with the letter, I was struck that, while the reception was different for each person, the reaction was deeply felt and engaging. There was genuine interest and excitement for the subject at hand. It occurred to me that there might be a wider audience of members and non-members who would have a similar reaction.

As I pondered this possibility, an amazing number of specific incidents flooded into my mind where it would have been helpful to have had a relatively concise statement of my Latter-day Saint beliefs juxtaposed to the teachings of more traditional Christian doctrines and discussed in the light of Biblical evidence. In the future when similar situations arise, I will have a more thoughtful response to share with other Christians.

The purpose of this book is not to condemn or tear down another's faith. My personal belief, consistent with the teachings of Latter-day Saint prophets and apostles, is that the world, in general, and the Christian community, specifically, is richly blessed and benefitted by its diversity as well as by its strength of numbers, regardless of denomination.

Neither is my purpose to argue the correctness of different positions. The existence of thousands of Christian denominations and sects, all claiming to be founded on the teachings of the Bible, provides definitive proof of the futility of such an undertaking.

The purpose of this book is to set forth a compelling and accessible case for the teachings of Latter-day Saints and to do so in a manner relevant to other Christians. The World Council of Churches defines Christians as "those (who) confess the Lord Jesus Christ as God and

Savior according to the scriptures." Accepting this definition, the intent of this book is to demonstrate that The Church of Jesus Christ of Latter-day Saints is undeniably Christian based on teachings of the Bible. This does not imply that doctrines of Latter-day Saint Christians conform completely to those of Catholic, Protestant and Eastern Orthodox Christians. These other members of the Christian community cannot agree among themselves, yet all are acknowledged as Christians. It is simply inconsistent and intellectually dishonest to impose a different standard on Latter-day Saints in qualifying as part of the Christian community.

Other books, such as Stephen E. Robinson's *Are Mormons Christians?* and *Offender For A Word* by Daniel C. Peterson and Stephen D. Ricks, make this case against the highly biased and inconsistent treatment of Latter-day Saints by those who would discredit the doctrines of our faith. This book serves as a complement to their efforts and others in presenting the affirmative, strong doctrinal position of Latter-day Saints as Christians. *Shared Beliefs, Honest Differences* is unique in its focus on the standard that other Christians accept universally, namely the Bible. Using this sacred volume of scripture as one measure of Christian devotion, Latter-day Saints have much to celebrate and to share with others.

Finally, this book is written for those lovers of truth who have sufficient courage to examine the faith of another. It is my sincere prayer that those who read this book will do so with an open mind and a sincere heart, seeking to understand the differences and similarities that make Latter-day Saints a vibrant part of the Christian community. As William George Jordan has written:

> The man who has a certain religious belief and fears to discuss it, lest it may be proved wrong, is not loyal to his belief; he has but a coward's faithfulness to his prejudices. If he were a lover of truth, he would be willing at any moment to surrender his belief for a higher, better and truer faith. (as cited in Richards, p. 438)

This book is addressed to such brave souls.

1

Pagan Gods and Divine Potential

At the heart of doctrinal differences separating The Church of Jesus Christ of Latter-day Saints from other Christian denominations lie two dramatically different conceptions of God. Almost two thousand years ago, the Apostle Paul stood on Mars' hill in Athens and proclaimed the true and living God to those who ignorantly worshiped the unknown God of their time. In our day, the dialogue has taken an intriguing twist, with traditional Christians and Latter-day Saints declaring very different views of the same God, whom both claim to worship in knowledge and truth. In no small part, our salvation will depend on identifying and emulating the only true God. So the Savior taught, "And this is life eternal, that they may know thee the only true God, and Jesus Christ, whom thou hast sent." (John 17:3)

Some Christians teach that Latter-day Saints worship a pagan god. This claim seems to be based on the charge that the God of Latter-day Saints is both anthropomorphic (i.e., God has a glorified body that is similar in form to man's) and polytheistic (i.e., God the Father, God the Son, and God the Holy Ghost are separate and distinct beings who have attained the same nature of deity). (Ankerberg, pp. 98-111, 118-9; Bray, p. 57; Reed and Farkas, p. 81) They charge that these teachings are non-biblical. A careful examination of the Bible will be necessary to test these claims.

Without intending offense, there is great irony in the charge by some Christians that the deity of Latter-day Saints is a pagan, non-biblical God. Most credible scholars of Christian theology acknowledge that the traditional conception of Trinity derives from Greek philosophy and human reasoning, rather than from revelation or the Bible, as some Christians profess.

TRINITY: A NON-BIBLICAL GOD

Historically, the doctrine of Trinity (one divine substance, three divine persons, namely the Father, the Son and the Holy Ghost) attained orthodox status in 325 AD at a council of Christian leaders convened by Emperor Constantine in the city of Nicaea in what is now northwest Turkey. The purpose of the council was to unify teachings of the Christian churches. The primary points of controversy centered around the attributes and nature of God. The dilemma before the council is described by one Christian writer, Dr. John Lawson, in the *Comprehensive Handbook of Christian Doctrine*:

> The primitive Church went before the world preaching two imperative religious interests—from its Jewish background in the Scriptures, that there is but one sovereign God; and from its experience of salvation, that Jesus Christ is divine. . . . Thus the fathers of the Church had to construct a doctrine of God which would enable them to say that their Lord was a divine Saviour, in the full and proper sense of the word, and at the same time make it plain that there is only one God. The fruit of this admittedly exacting intellectual quest is the doctrine of the Trinity . . . In summary, the doctrine of the Holy Trinity is the logical background in speculative thought for the devotional doctrine that God is love. (Lawson, pp. 121-4)

In this statement, Dr. Lawson acknowledges that the doctrine of the Trinity is a product of human reason, trying to reconcile two seemingly contradictory positions: (1) God is one God and (2) Jesus Christ is also God, equal in stature to the Father. In its deliberations, the council of Nicaea resolved these seemingly conflicting positions by creating the doctrine of Trinity which was issued in a statement known as the Nicene creed. In its original form, the Nicene creed states:

> We believe in one God, the Father Almighty, maker of all things, both visible and invisible; and in one Lord, Jesus Christ, the Son of God, Only begotten of the Father, that is to say, of the substance of the Father, God of God and Light of Lights, very God of very God, begotten, not made, being of one substance with the Father, by whom all things were made, both things in heaven and things on earth; who, for us men and for our salvation, came down and was made flesh, was made man, suffered, and rose again on the third day, went up into the

heavens, and is to come again to judge both the quick and the dead; and in the Holy Ghost. (*World Book Encyclopedia*, Vol. N, pg 318)

Dr. Lawson observes, "the basis for the Nicene creed was an eastern baptismal creed, into which was inserted the Greek word, *homoousios*, 'of the same substance,' despite the objection of some that this was a novel and non-biblical word." (Lawson, p. 51) However, this "novel and non-biblical" addition is the fundamental premise of the doctrine of the Trinity.

Christian scholars generally agree, "*homoousios* owed its insertion to [Emperor] Constantine's express wish [and] caused embarrassment at the council." (Kelly, p. 232; see also Erickson, p. 83, Rusch, pp. 19-21) This word was a concession to political compromise and appearances of unity. Dr. William Rusch, director of ecumenical relations for the Lutheran Church of America explains:

> One of the assets of the word *homoousios*—and this led to its acceptance—was that different groups were able to interpret it in ways compatible with their own theology. As far as Constantine was concerned, this was acceptable. Constantine was amenable to tolerating a variety of groups, as long as they accepted his creed and each other. (Rusch, p. 20)

It is unclear what the council actually intended by injecting the word, *homoousios* into the creed. According to Dr. Rusch, "The word was selected at Nicaea to express that the Son was fully God. This agrees with what all the historical sources convey: the issue at Nicaea was the Son's co-eternity, not the [physical] unity of the Godhead." (Rusch, p. 20)

Fifty-six years later (381 AD, the Council by Constantinople attempted to clarify the doctrine of the Trinity by attributing physical unity to the Godhead. Two scholars, Gregory of Nazzianzus and Gregory of Nyssa, provided the intellectual construct for this novel teaching. Speaking of these two influential scholars, Dr. Rusch observes, "Their debt to Aristotelian and Neoplatonic thought is undeniable." (Rusch, p. 23)

Of even greater significance was the secular support of the emperor. Beginning in Nicaea, a new chapter in church and state relations was opened. Neither Nicaea nor Constantinople ended the trinitarian controversy, but history confirms, "the changing convictions of successive emperors became increasingly significant for the theology of the church." (Erickson, p. 84; see also Barker, pp. 272-327) After several major reversals by successive heads of church and state, the non-biblical concept of the Trinity eventually won broad support as the orthodox doctrine of the church.

There is little doubt the doctrine of the Trinity evolved from human philosophies and not from the Bible. Most Christian scholars agree with Dr. Bruce N. Kaye, "Scripture had an indirect role in forming the doctrine of the Trinity." (Kaye, "The New Testament," OGT) After conducting a thorough examination of the concepts of Trinity as found in the Bible, the Jesuit scholar, Edmund J. Fortman, concludes:

> There is no formal doctrine of the Trinity in the New Testament writers, if this means an explicit teaching that in one God there are three co-equal divine persons. . . . The Biblical witness to God, as we have seen did not contain any formal or formulated doctrine of the Trinity . . . (as quoted in Robinson, S., p. 74)

This conclusion is echoed again and again by traditional Christian theologians and Biblical scholars. For example, "Nowhere in the Bible do we find the doctrine of the Trinity clearly formulated . . . There is no formal statement of trinitarian doctrine in the Bible." (Keeley, p. 164) "Careful reading of the Old Testament shows no indication of the trinity itself." (*Ibid.*, p. 166) "Neither the word nor the doctrine of trinity appears anywhere in the New Testament." (Cantelon, p. 75) "The Trinity is not really a biblical doctrine." (Erickson, p. 97) "Trinity does not appear in the Bible." (Marty, p. 80) "The doctrine of the Trinity is not a biblical doctrine in the sense of being specifically found in the New Testament writings. It is a creation of the fourth century church." (Richardson, p. 100) It is worth noting that the doctrine of the Trinity is also absent in all extant writings of the Apostolic Fathers from the first and early second centuries. (Rusch, p. 3; 37-42)

Since this doctrine is not found in the Bible, then from whence did it spring? The doctrine of the Trinity was the culmination of processes fully evident by the second century, incorporating prevailing philosophies of the time.

> The desire [of Christian scholars] to show that Christianity was the true philosophy may at times have led them to adapt their theology to the prevailing culture more than some might be inclined to do. Yet they

did so because they wanted to relate the doctrine that they held to the broader streams of thought." (Erickson, p. 12)

Early creeds of Christianity are a product of philosophical ruminations by such scholars. Dr. Arthur W. Wainwright observes, "It could be argued that the doctrine [of the Trinity] emerged when Christian writers began to use philosophical methods of investigation." (Wainwright, p. 5; see also Erickson, p. 54) Other Christian writers concede the doctrine of the Trinity and its evolved notions of an invisible God without form and shape sprang from popular philosophies of the times.

In his *History of Christian Doctrine*, renowned author Dr. William G. T. Shedd states, "Plato, Aristotle and Cicero exerted more influence than all other philosophical minds united, upon the Christian Fathers: upon the greatest of the Schoolmen; and upon the theologians of the Reformation. . ." (as quoted in Roberts, MDD, p. 118) Much evidence suggests that Greek philosophers and their teachings about an invisible, immaterial God were more influential than the authors of the New Testament or any other source in the development of the doctrine of the Trinity.

A prominent historian of the early Christian period, Robert Wilkens, has written of attempts by early Christian thinkers to reconcile Christian doctrine with concepts in Greek philosophy.

Indeed, Christians adopted precisely the same language to describe God as did pagan intellectuals. The Christian apologist Theophilus of Antioch described God as "ineffable . . . inexpressible . . . uncontainable . . . incomprehensible . . . inconceivable . . . incomparable . . . unteachable . . . immutable . . . inexpressible . . . without beginning because he was uncreated, immutable because he is immortal." (Ad Autolycum 1.3-4) This view, that God was an immaterial, timeless, and impassable divine being . . . served to establish a link to the Greek spiritual and intellectual tradition. (as quoted in Peterson and Ricks, p. 81)

In *A History of Christian Theology*, William C. Placher, Professor of Philosophy and Religion at Wabash College draws a similar conclusion:

Israel worshiped a God who could grow angry, who changed his mind, a God involved in history . . . The greatest philosophers of Greece spoke of an unchanging divine principle, far removed from our world, without emotion, unaffected by anything beyond itself. Improbably enough, Christian theology came to identify these two as the same God . . . A number of theologians of the second and third centuries, confronted with Greek culture, undeniably tried to reinterpret Christian faith in terms of the most important ideas of that era. (Placher, p. 55)

Finally, Dr. Gerald L. Bray concludes, "It is beyond dispute that Christianity took on the dress of a particular, and fundamentally alien, culture in the course of its early development . . . Hellenism corrupted Christianity in its development of dogma." (Bray, "The Patristic Dogma," OGT, p. 73)

Protestant and Catholic theologians acknowledge that the process of arriving at the doctrine of the Trinity was messy and convoluted, but they believe that God's truth eventually emerged in the deliberations at Nicaea and subsequent councils. Latter-day Saints claim their concept of Deity was revealed by God to modern prophets and apostles and is plainly taught in the Bible. It should not be surprising that these teachings diverge on several specifics.

CONTRASTING CONCEPTS OF GOD

Fundamental points of variance between traditional Christians and Latter-day Saints regarding the nature of God can be summarized as follows:

Table 1

Traditional Christians	Latter-day Saints
Physical Attributes	
God is unembodied Spirit, invisible and without form	God is a Spirit with a glorified and resurrected physical body; man's body is in the image of God
Unity of Godhead/Plurality of Gods	
Father, Son and Holy Ghost are one physical substance but three persons fulfilling different roles of Deity	Father, Son and Holy Ghost are separate and distinct personages who are exactly similar, being one in purpose and attributes, having attained a perfect God-nature
Man's Potential to Become Like God	
God is never changing and has always been God; man can never become like God	The God-nature is never changing and has always been; man can become like God and attain the perfect God-nature by following the pattern of the Son in becoming God

The question before us is how to judge between these two bodies of doctrine. The Apostle Peter admonishes against using personal interpretations of scriptures rather than relying on inspired teachings and interpretations of living apostles and prophets. Referring to himself and his fellow apostles, Peter writes,

> We (the apostles) have also a more sure word of prophecy; whereunto ye do well that ye take heed, as unto a light that shineth in a dark place, until the day dawn, and the day star arise in your hearts; Knowing this first that no prophecy of the scripture is of any private interpretation. (2 Pet 1:19-20)

Most traditional Christians believe this more sure word of prophecy ended with the death of the apostles around the end of the first century, AD. Latter-day Saints embrace the teachings of inspired leaders as recorded in the Bible. In addition, they proclaim that Christ leads his church through living apostles and prophets called again in these latter days. The common ground between Latter-day Saints and traditional Christians is confined to the inspired writings of past prophets as contained in the Bible. With an appropriate humility inspired by the Apostle Peter's note of caution, we turn to the Bible to examine the doctrines of traditional Christians and Latter-day Saints regarding the concept of Deity.

PHYSICAL ATTRIBUTES OF GOD

While many denominations record their own official statement regarding the description of God, Catholics or Protestants are in fundamental agreement regarding the Trinity. A typical example of orthodoxy is the *Presbyterian Church Confession of Faith*: "There is but one living and true God, who is infinite in being and perfection, a most pure spirit, invisible, without body, parts or passions . . ." (*Encyclopedia of American Religions*, pg. 218)

Many Christians point to passages in the Bible to support their conception of God. (Ankerberg, pp. 81-8; Chafer/ Walvoord, pp. 39-42; Vander Donkt in Roberts, MDD, pp. 45-51; Swinburne, pp. 125-7; Bray, p. 97; MacArthur, Glory, pp. 193, 220) Chief among them is John's statement that "God is a Spirit." (John 4:24) Writing to the Saints in Corinth, Paul states, "Now the Lord is that Spirit: and where the Spirit of the Lord is, there is liberty." (2 Cor 3:17) To establish the physical properties of a spirit, some Christians refer to the words of the resurrected Christ when he appeared to his disciples. The scriptures record that:

> they [the disciples] were terrified and affrighted, and supposed that they had seen a spirit.
>
> And he [Jesus] said unto them, Why are ye troubled? and why do thoughts arise in your hearts?
>
> Behold my hands and my feet that it is I myself: handle me, and see; for a *spirit hath not flesh and bones, as ye see me have.* (Luke 24:37-39; emphasis added)

The preceding passages provide an excellent example of potential pitfalls of scriptural interpretation. While the statement that God is a spirit has been used to support the doctrine of Trinity, it does not follow that God is *only* a spirit and therefore without a body. The physical properties of a spirit without a body are clear from the Savior's description, above. However, it does not follow that all spirits are unembodied. For instance, the Bible teaches that man is a spirit with a mortal body in this life (1 Cor 6:20, James 2:26, Num 16:22, Eccl 12:7, Job 32:8, Acts 7:59, Rom 8:16) and will be resurrected with an immortal body in the future. Most Christians would agree that Christ's spirit was clothed in flesh while in mortality (Luke 23:46) and in a glorified body when he appeared as a resurrected being. In both instances, his spirit was joined with a body.

GOD AS INVISIBLE SPIRIT

In support of their position, many Christians insist the Bible teaches that God is invisible. (Ankerberg, p. 88; Vander Donkt in Roberts, MDD, pp. 45-51, Rahner, Trinity, p. 81) They often cite Paul's letter to Timothy: "Now, unto the King eternal, immortal, *invisible*, the only wise God, be honour and glory for ever and ever." (1 Tim 1:17; emphasis added) They also refer to the words of John: "No man hath seen God at any time." (John 1:18)

However, these passages are only a portion of what the Bible records regarding the attributes of God. Many other passages of scripture make it apparent that under proper circumstances holy men have seen God. The Apostle John almost seems to contradict his own statement above when he writes, "Not that any man hath seen the Father, *save he which is of God, he hath seen the Father."* (John 6:46; emphasis added) The Bible is very clear that God has appeared to holy men in all dispensations of time. Jacob saw God face to face. (Gen 32:30) God was seen by Moses (Ex 33:11), by Aaron, Nadab, Abihu and seventy of the elders of Israel (Ex 24:9-11), by Isaiah (Isa 6:1-5), by Ezekiel (Ezek 1:28), by Stephen (Acts 7:56) and by John the Beloved (Rev 1:17).

Likewise, it does not follow that because God is referred to as invisible that He is invisible in all circumstances. Bacteria are invisible to the naked eye. One could accurately state that bacteria are invisible. But under certain conditions such as magnification under a microscope, bacteria become visible, revealing their shape, form and physical properties. This may be an explanation for the apparent contradiction in the gospel of John, noted above. It is perfectly reasonable that under most circumstances God is invisible and under those circumstances, "No man hath seen God at any time." (John 1:18) But under sacred circumstances, holy men are permitted to see a God of shape and form, and "he which is of God, he hath seen the Father." (John 6:46) This is consistent with the teachings of Paul in his epistle to the Hebrews: "Follow peace with all men, and holiness, without which no man shall see the Lord." (Heb 12:14) Likewise, the Savior taught, "Blessed are the pure in heart, for they shall see God." (Matt 5:8)

GOD AS A GLORIFIED PHYSICAL BEING

The preponderance of biblical passages suggests that God, far from being without shape or form, is a Spirit with a glorified body and that man was made in the image of God. There are more than thirty references to specific body parts of God. These passages refer to God's face (Gen 32:30, Ex 33:11; Rev 22:4), His mouth (Num 12:5-8), His hand (Ex 33:21, Acts 7:56 and Heb 1:13), His finger (Deut 9:10), His feet (Ex 24:10), His back parts (Ex 33:21-23) and to functions associated with a body such as sitting (Psalms 46:8), walking (Gen 3:8, 5:24) and standing (Acts 7:56). There are numerous passages referring to God's image (Gen 1:27, Gen 9:6, and 2 Cor 4:4), form (Philip 2:6), and person (Heb 1:3). The inspired writers inform us that man was made in God's image (Gen 1:27 and Gen 9:26), likeness (Gen 5:1) and similitude (James 3:9).

As though to remove all question regarding the similarity between the form of God and the form of man, the writer of Genesis records this amazing parallel between God and man and between a man and his son: "In the day that God created man, *in the likeness of God* made he him . . . and Adam . . . begat a son *in his own likeness*, after his image and called his name Seth." (Gen 5:1,3; emphasis added)

Some Christians claim Latter-day Saints are too literal in their interpretations of the Bible and maintain passages referring to the body parts, form and person of God are symbolic. According to this line of thought, symbolic images are used to provide a point of reference to which mortals can relate when discussing a being incomprehensible to the finite mind. (Vander Donkt in Roberts, MDD, pp. 45-51; Marty, p. 79; Rahner, Trinity, pp. 72-8)

There is no question the inspired writers of the Bible often use symbols and images to communicate their sacred truths, but it seems more than a stretch to attribute all mention of God's glorified body to mere symbolism.

For example, Isaiah, a master of language and the use of symbols, records his own vision of the Lord in these words, "I saw also the Lord sitting upon a throne, high and lifted up, and his train filled the temple . . . mine eyes have seen the King, the Lord of hosts." (Isa 6:1,5) Details in this passage of the Lord sitting, of the throne and of the train filling the temple have the sound of an eyewitness account. Certainly, Isaiah's description seems far removed from the formless, shapeless God of traditional Christians.

ANTHROPOMORPHISM

Some Christians also charge that one of the results of what they regard as Latter-day Saints' interpreting the Bible too literally is a concept of God that is anthropomorphic, that is conceived in the image of man. (Ankerberg, p. 88; Vander Donkt in Roberts, MDD, pp. 45-51; Marty, p. 79; Bray, pp. 57, 95-97; Little, p. 26) On this point the Bible is perfectly clear: It is not God who is in the image of man, rather it is man who is in the image of God. "And God said, Let us make man in our image, after our likeness . . . So God created man in his own image, in the image of God created he him." (Gen 1:26-27) It is a strange interpretation indeed that begins with man created in God's image and concludes that God is without shape or form.

If man is in the image of God, then passages referring to God's body parts are not symbolic but are simply a revelation that God made man, his highest creation, in the image and likeness of his own glorified body that is eternally joined with his Spirit.

Perhaps the most definitive revelation of the physical attributes of God is the resurrected Christ. As noted previously, when the Savior revealed himself to his disciples, he taught them that he had a body of flesh and bones. (Luke 24:37-39) They saw the nail prints in his hands and feet and witnessed with their natural senses the reality of his resurrection. He walked with his disciples. He partook of food. He stood, and he sat. His actions mirrored those of his mortal ministry, only his body was resurrected, refined and immortal. In this resurrected state, he was able to transport his body instantaneously and pass through physical barriers without constraint. (Luke 24:31,36) However, the body of the resurrected Lord was clearly defined and identifiable in each encounter. When he had taught his disciples sufficiently for them to carry on his ministry, he ascended into heaven:

> And while they (his disciples) looked stedfastly toward heaven as he went up, behold two men stood by them in white apparel;
>
> Which also said, Ye men of Galilee, why stand ye gazing up into heaven? this same Jesus, which is taken up from you into heaven, shall so come in like manner as ye have seen him go into heaven. (Acts 1:10-11)

Most Christians do not dispute that the resurrected Christ had an immortal body of flesh and bones as reported in the Bible. Some have reasoned that this body was necessary to manifest God to man but that it does not constitute a permanent physical attribute of Deity. Rather, they teach that Christ's resurrected body was set aside after his ascension to be retrieved again when the Savior returns to earth so that Jesus "shall come in like manner as ye have seen him go into heaven." (Vander Donkt in Roberts, MDD, p. 46)

There are problems with this assertion by some Christians. First, these teachings are not supported by the Bible; in other words, they are non-biblical. These precepts are the "logical extension" of theologians attempting to justify the non-biblical doctrine of the Trinity. In this case, one non-biblical precept is used to make sense of another non-biblical precept.

In addition, what is the resurrection if not the permanent reuniting of the body with the spirit? If the Savior laid aside his immortal body following his ascension, then Jesus Christ, who proclaimed himself "the resurrection and the life" (John 11:25), is resurrected only temporarily. Yet Paul taught that, "we shall be also in the likeness of his resurrection." (Rom 6:5)

John the Revelator, years after the ascension of Jesus, beheld the resurrected Savior, felt his body and heard reaffirmation of the reality of Christ's resurrection:

> And when I saw him [the Savior], I fell at his feet as dead. And he laid his right hand upon me, saying unto me, Fear not; I am the first and the last:
>
> I am he that liveth, and was dead; and, behold, I am alive for evermore, Amen; and have the keys of hell and death. (Rev 1:17-18)

Jesus Christ, "who is the image of God" (2 Cor 4:4) "being in the form of God" (Philip 2:6), "being the brightness of his [Father's] glory and the express image of his [Father's] person" (Heb 1:3), is the revelation of God the Father to his children, and he "shall change our vile body, that it may be fashioned like unto his glorious body. . . ." (Philip 3:21)

The resurrection of man's body is so central to the gospel of Jesus Christ that Paul taught:

> If the dead rise not, then is not Christ raised:
>
> And if Christ be not raised, your faith is vain . . .
>
> But now is Christ risen from the dead, and become the first fruits of them that slept." (1 Cor 15:16-17,20)

Paul's statement suggests a pivotal question. Why is our faith vain unless man is resurrected, receiving a glorified body? If God is only a Spirit, then why is it essential for man to be resurrected? As taught by the Savior, a spirit can exist without a body. (Luke 24:37-39) So why is man's faith vain without the resurrection? Traditional Christian doctrines offer no reasonable explanation to these queries. Latter-day Saints teach the resurrection is necessary precisely because it is the only means of obtaining a glorified body similar to those possessed by God the Father and His Son, Jesus Christ. Without a resurrected, immortal body, man's faith is vain; never attaining the highest purpose for which God placed him on this earth.

God's perfected body, having the exact form of man's mortal body which was fashioned in its image, has been seen by holy prophets and their accounts are recorded in the Bible. Man's resurrection, as well as Christ's, testifies of the physical attributes of God the Father, as a glorified personage with a perfected and immortal body.

THE ONENESS OF GOD

The second major point of variance between the traditional Christian concept of Deity and that of Latter-day Saints concerns the unity of the Godhead. Protestants and Roman Catholics adhere to the triune concept of the Trinity, that God is three persons "of the same substance." As discussed above, this notion of three members of the Godhead being of the same substance is a novel and non-biblical innovation adopted by early Christian councils. This has not deterred many Christians from justifying the doctrine of the Trinity by referring to selective passages in the Bible. (Chafer/ Walvoord, pp. 39-42; Vander Donkt in Roberts, MDD, pp. 58-66; MacArthur, Glory, p. 22; Martin, R., p. 98; Bray, p. 53)

Among those scriptures most frequently cited are Moses' declaration to Israel: "Hear, O Israel, The Lord our God is one Lord" (Deut 6:4) and the statement by the Savior, "I and my Father are one" (John 10:30). Other passages of scripture referring to the oneness of the Godhead include Paul's expression, "there is none other God but one," (1 Cor 8:4) and the Savior's teachings, "he that hath seen me hath seen the Father . . . Believe me that I am in the Father and the Father in me." (John 14:9-11) Finally, John the Beloved records, "There are three that bear record in heaven, the Father, the Word, and the Holy Ghost: and these three are one." (1 John 5:7)

Traditional Christians and Latter-day Saints are in complete agreement that the Bible teaches God the Father, Jesus Christ, His Son, and the Holy Ghost are one. The divergence of doctrine revolves around the assertion that this oneness is a physical unity, rather than a oneness of purpose and spiritual attributes.

Commenting on Deuteronomy 6:4, "Hear, O Israel, the Lord our God is one Lord," Millard J. Erickson, a Protestant scholar, writes:

> There are two Hebrew words for one. The first is *yakid*, which means unique, the only one of a class . . . If this were the word used here, it would simply be telling us of the uniqueness of God, the fact

that he is the only one in his class . . . There is another Hebrew word for one. It is the word *ehad*. It is derived from a verb form meaning to unify . . . It is this word that is used of God in Deuteronomy 6:4. It is also used in Genesis 2:24, which says that 'a man will leave his father and mother and be united to his wife, and they become one flesh.' There the unity is not uniqueness, but the unity of diversity. It speaks of union, rather than aloneness. (Erickson, pp. 174-5)

It is worth noting that writers of scripture, in both Hebrew and Greek texts, consistently use the second term, *ehad*, or its equivalent in referring to the oneness of God. This is important since a triune God would be unique (*yakid*), indeed, different from all human experience and without a counterpart in the universe.

Baptist scholar, Ralph P. Martin, writing about the use of *ehad* to refer to both the oneness of God and of marriage, observes, "Obviously, the unity of and in marriage is a unity which contains a plurality—that is a duality . . . The unity of God is not that of a simple monad, but is a oneness which allows for and contains a plurality." (Martin, R., p. 98) Martin and Erickson seize upon this plurality to support the concept of the Trinity, three persons in one being. They fail to acknowledge the separateness of beings in the unity of marriage and its perfect parallel to three separate God-beings, unified in oneness of purpose and spiritual attributes but not of the same substance.

Another passage of scripture used to provide a scriptural basis for the concept of the Trinity is John 1:1, "In the beginning was the Word, and the Word was with God, and the Word was God." In John 1:14, the Word is identified as Jesus Christ who "was made flesh and dwelt among us." According to some interpretations, John 1:1 demonstrates the separate Beings of two members of the Trinity (the Word was with God) while affirming the singular identity of the two Beings as "of the same substance" (the Word was God).

However, examination of the Greek texts of the New Testament not only discredits this interpretation but points again to the separateness of two God-beings sharing a unity of purpose and attributes. In the first phrase, "the Word was with God," a definite article is used in the Greek to denote 'the God,' or to state it more precisely, "the Word was with 'the God.'" In the second phrase, "and the Word was God," the definite article is absent. Without a definite article in front of it, the second use of God denotes "a property or a relation" and identifies "several members of a class." (Erickson, p. 240) A more appropriate rendering of John 1:1 might be, "The Word was with 'the God,' and the Word was of the same nature as 'the God.'" (Erickson, p. 201)

Clearly, the scriptures speak of spiritual oneness that does not require a physical unity. For example, Paul addressing the Saints of Rome writes, "So we, being many, are one body in Christ, and every one members one of another." (Rom 12:5). Likewise to the Hebrews, Paul states, "For both he that sanctifieth and they who are sanctified are all of one." (Heb 2:11) It is apparent this oneness is not "of the same substance." So which kind of oneness applies to the Godhead?

SEPARATE AND DISTINCT BEINGS, ONE GOD

Fortunately, we are not left to speculate as to the nature of the oneness of God. Scripture records the prayer of the Savior with his disciples prior to leaving the upper room and walking to Gethsemane. In this prayer, the Son addressed the Father in these words,

> keep through thine own name those whom thou hast given me, that they may be one, as we are.
> Neither pray I for these alone, but for them also which shall believe on me through their word;
> That they all may be one; as thou, Father, art in me, and I in thee, that they also may be one in us:
> that they may be one as we are one: I in them and thou in me that they may be made perfect in one. (John 17:11,20-23)

Just as disciples of Jesus and those who believe on their words will remain separate and distinct, so are the Father, the Son and the Holy Ghost. The parallels are clearly drawn in the Savior's prayer, precluding a oneness of the same substance.

The oneness and indwelling spoken of in the Bible is a unity of purpose and spirit. The Savior taught his disciples, "I am in my Father, and ye in me, and I in you." (John 14:20) Paul writes, "he that is joined unto the Lord is one spirit." (1 Cor 6:17)

The scriptural accounts of the Father, the Son and the Holy Ghost manifesting themselves as distinct and separate beings are almost as numerous as those attesting to the glorified, physical body of God. At the Savior's baptism, the Son came up out of the waters, the Father spoke his approbation from heaven and the Holy Ghost descended as a dove. (Matt 3:16-17, Mark 1:10-11, Luke 3:21-22) On numerous occasions Jesus knelt on earth in prayer addressing his God, "Our Father which art in heaven" (Matt 6:9, Matt 14:23, Matt 26:39, Luke 9:29, John 17:1). Are we to believe that a being 'of the same substance' on earth was praying to Himself 'of the same substance' in heaven?

The scriptures teach that Jesus was begotten as the first born of the Father. (Rev 3:14, John 1:14; see also Heb 1:5, Col 1:15, Ps 89:27, Rom 8:29 and Heb 1:6) In addition, Jesus was foreordained by the Father (1 Pet 1:20), sent into the world by the Father (John 3:16-17, John 5:24), raised by the Father (Acts 2:24,32, Gal 1:1, Eph 1:20), glorified by the Father (Acts 3:13), exalted by the Father (Acts 2:33, Acts 5:31), anointed by the Father (Heb 1:8-9, Ps 45:6-7), made Lord and Christ by the Father (Acts 2:36) among many other specifics where the Father acted upon the Son.

In Gethsemane, the Son submitted his will to the separate will of his Father, "nevertheless not my will, but thine, be done" (Luke 22:42, Matt 26:39, Mark 14:36). On the cross, the Savior cried out, "My God, my God, why hast thou forsaken me?" (Matt 27:46) During the three days while his body was in the tomb, Jesus was separated from the Father, having not yet ascended to Him. (John 20:17) The Savior taught he did not have all knowledge possessed by the Father. "But of that day and hour knoweth no man, no, not the angels in heaven, but my Father only." (Matt 24:36) In the parable of the vine and the branches, the Father is the vine dresser and the Son is the vine, clearly separate and distinct entities. (John 15:1-8) The disciple, Stephen, as he was being stoned,

> being full of the Holy Ghost, looked up steadfastly into heaven, and saw the glory of God, and Jesus standing on the right hand of God,
> And said, Behold, I see the heavens opened, and the Son of man standing on the right hand of God. (Acts 7:55-56)

This should suffice, though much more could be cited, to demonstrate that the members of the Godhead are separate and distinct.

Latter-day Saints are not unique in teaching that the Father, the Son and the Holy Ghost are separate and distinct beings. The earliest Christian writers, generally referred to as Apostolic Fathers, were consistent in identifying the Father, the Son and the Holy Ghost as three separate beings, united in spirit but separate in body or essence. (Kelly, pp. 88-95; Robinson, S., pp. 76-7)

It is clear that in our day some Protestants are more comfortable with a concept of God as three distinct beings. In a pamphlet entitled "What is Meant by the Trinity? And When We Get to Heaven Will We See Three Gods?," fundamentalist preacher, Jimmy Swaggert, has written that the three members of the Godhead are one in unity and will appear as separate beings. (as quoted in Peterson and Ricks, p. 68) Another traditional Christian scholar observes, "While relatively few theologians have held this view (the Father, the Son and the Holy Ghost are separate and distinct beings) in any official way, it is likely that a fairly large percentage of ordinary Christians have taken this position in an informal fashion." (Erickson, p. 132; see also Bray, p. 111)

Mainstream writers within the Christian community have a difficult time explaining the traditional concept of Trinity. Virtually any book dealing with the Trinity will include a phrase similar to the following by Reverend Billy Graham: "The Bible teaches that God is actually three Persons. This is a mystery that we will never be able to understand." (Graham, PWG, p. 92; see also Chafer/ Walvoord, pp. 40-1 and Rahner, Trinity, pp. 77-8) As Dr. Erickson, a prominent Baptist theologians, acknowledges, "There is a fundamental difficulty that lies at the heart of the discussion of the doctrine of the Trinity: the doctrine seems to be impossible to believe, because at its core it is contradictory." (Erickson, p. 130.)

MONOTHEISM AND WORSHIPING GOD

Despite difficulties in comprehending or believing the triune concept of the trinity, some Christians contend that a doctrine depicting the three members of the Godhead as physically separate is a form of polytheism (more than one God) and is therefore paganistic. (Ankerberg, pp. 81-2; Decker/Hunter pp. 22-31). Largely, this reaction is due to such teachings conflicting with entrenched notions of deity. As one evangelical theologian acknowledges: "To a Jew or to a Muslim, (the doctrine of the Trinity) appears to be a denial of monotheism." (Bray, p. 111)

While it is true Latter-day Saints maintain there is more than one God-being, they equally hold that there is only one God-nature which is completely unified and perfect in knowledge, power, wisdom, love, mercy and justice. Those who attain to this perfect God-nature are one in purpose, mind and spiritual attributes. Presented with a similar set of circumstances, those who attain the perfect God-nature will always act in a similar manner, manifesting attributes that characterize all God-beings. Thus John the Beloved can write, "For there are three that bear record in heaven, the Father, the Word, and the Holy Ghost: and these three are one." (1 John 5:7) And Moses can rightfully proclaim, "Hear, O Israel; The Lord our God is one Lord" (Deut 6:4), even though there are three separate and distinct beings who comprise the Godhead.

In traditional Christianity, the triune God of the Trinity consists of three persons of equal power comprising the same substance. (Toon in OGT, p. 9; Erickson, p. 84; Bray, p. 53; Tillich, ST, pp. 288-92) As a result, other Christians are likely to assume the Godhead as taught by Latter-day Saints consists of three separate and autonomous entities, equal in power and organized horizontally. This conception of the Godhead might suggest man is free to address his petitions to any of three Deities or pay his devotions to one member of the Godhead while ignoring the others. Such practices would surely produce confusion, for "no man can serve two masters." (Matt 6:24) This scenario conjures images of pagan gods competing with each other for dominance and supremacy and evincing motives of human passion and self-interest. None of this harmonizes with Biblical teachings.

The Latter-day Saint conception of the Godhead, supported by teachings in the Bible, consists of a single divine will organized and administered in a vertical line of authority and accountability. From on high, God the Father presides over all the affairs of His children. All prayers are addressed to Him, and His will is the highest authority of all creation. (Matt 6:10, John 5:30) He is 'the God' referred to in John 1:1. According to his command, all things pertaining to God's kingdom are to be done in the name of Jesus Christ. He is the great mediator of all mankind. Prayers are offered and sacred ordinances performed in the name of Jesus Christ. "For there is none other name under heaven given among men, whereby we must be saved." (Acts 4:12) The Holy Spirit acts in accordance with the will of the Father and serves as the messenger of the Father and the Son in his sacred role as comforter, revelator, sanctifier, testator, etc.

Paul spoke of this vertical line of authority through which heaven and earth are organized and administered under one God in describing a scene from the final judgment.

> Then cometh the end, when he [Christ] shall have delivered up the kingdom to God, even the Father; when he shall have put down all rule and all authority and power.
>
> For he [the Father] hath put all things under his [Christ's] feet. But when he [the Father] saith all things are put under him [Christ], it is manifest that he [the Father] is excepted, which did put all things under him [Christ].
>
> And when all things shall be subdued unto him [Christ], then shall the Son also himself be subject unto him [the Father] that put all things under him [Christ], that God may be all in all. (1 Cor 15:24,27,28)

No doctrine could be farther removed from pagan notions of polytheism. The order of heaven and the divine nature of God-beings assure perfect unity among three God-beings who perform different roles in bringing to pass the divine purposes of an all-loving, all-knowing, all-powerful Father. As one Latter-day Saint author has stated, "This single authority in which the three act in unity, which is proclaimed by the Bible and taught in Mormon theology, is the characteristic that makes Mormonism, of all Christian religions, most clearly monotheistic." (Hopkins, pp. 95-6)

BIBLICAL EVIDENCE OF MULTIPLE GOD-BEINGS

But what of the charge regarding plural Gods? What evidence can be called forth from the Bible to support the idea of more than one God-being? There are numerous scriptural references to God as "God of Gods" by Moses (Deut 10:17), Joshua (Josh 22:22), David (Ps 136:2-3), and Daniel (Dan 11:36) and "Lord of Lords" by John the Revelator. (Rev 17:14) The Psalmist records: "God standeth in the congregation of the mighty; he judgeth among the gods." (Ps 82:1)

Paul writes that:

> there be that are called gods, whether in heaven or in earth, (as there be gods many, and lords many,)
> But to us there is but one God . . ." (1 Cor 8:5-6).

Some Christians have argued these other Gods refer to false gods of pagan nations and do not imply anything about the number of true

God-beings. However, there are other passages suggesting some references are, in fact, to other God-beings similar to our Father in Heaven, though "to us there is but one God."

For instance, it is a widely recognized fact among Biblical scholars that the word translated "God" in the first chapter of Genesis, "in the Hebrew, is Elohim—plural for Eloah—and should be rendered 'Gods'—so as to read 'In the beginning the Gods created the heaven and the earth . . . The Gods said, Let there be light. . . . The Gods said, Let us make man, etc.'" (Roberts, p. 139) This point is acknowledged by writers from mainstream Christian traditions. (Keeley, p. 166 and Cantelon, pp. 72-4; Erickson, pp. 166-9)

Those who performed the work of translating the Bible into English were not anxious to preserve references to plural Gods. Accordingly, they altered their translations of the holy word so as to refer to a single God. Another example of this is Ecclesiastes 12:1 which in the King James translation reads: "Remember now thy Creator . . ." In the original Hebrew, the word translated Creator is plural, so that this passage should read, "Remember now thy Creators . . ." (Roberts, MDD, p. 143)

Likewise in Psalms, David's inspired verse is rendered:

What is man, that thou art mindful of him? . . .
For thou hast made him a little lower than the angels, and hast crowned him with glory and honour." (Ps 8:4-5)

Examination of the Hebrew text shows that the translators substituted "angels" for "Gods," so that the passage should read, "What is man, that thou art mindful of him? . . . For thou hast made him a little lower than the *Gods*, and hast crowned him with glory and honour." (Cantelon, pp. 72-4)

Despite liberties taken in altering the word of God, some references to plural Gods have come through the translation process without modification. The most significant examples are found in connection with the creation where the words of the Creator are preserved. "And God said, Let *us* make man in *our* image . . ." (Gen 1:26; emphasis added) and "the Lord God said, Behold, the man is become as one of *us* . . ." (Gen 3:22; emphasis added) In both of these passages, we have the word "Elohim" (Gods) associated with the plural pronoun, "us" or the plural possessive, "our" or both. Surely, other Christians will not contend that these "Gods" involved in the creation of this world are pagan gods.

Some have asserted that references to plural entities at the time of the creation result from God addressing his angels, not other Gods. (Erickson, pp. 168-69) This attempt to explain away the obvious has problems. First, this explanation would have God, the Creator, placing himself on the same level as his angels. "Behold, the man has become as one of us," (Gen 3:22) meaning God and his angels. Nowhere in sacred writ does God, in his majesty and exalted state, suggest parity between himself and inferior beings. Second, the subsequent verse in the first chapter of Genesis makes it clear man was created in the image of God and not in the image of angels. "So God created man in his own image, in the image of God created he him." (Gen 1:27) In the preceding verse when God says, "Let *us* make man in *our* image" (Gen 1:26; emphasis added), he can only be addressing himself to other Gods having a similar image.

Later in Genesis, the inspired word speaks of Gods acting in unison to confound the language of the people at the time of the tower of Babel:

And the Lord said,

Go to, let *us* go down, and there confound their language . . ." (Gen 11:6-7; emphasis added)

Isaiah refers to a discussion among plural God-beings involved in organizing the world. "Whom shall I send and who shall go for us?" (Isa 6:8) In the Hebrew text of the Old Testament, plural verbs, obscured in English translations, clearly refer to multiple God-beings in Genesis 20:13 and 35:7. Other references to a plurality of God-beings can be found in Psalms 110:1, Mark 12:35 and Hosea 1:7, as acknowledged by mainstream Christian scholars. (Cantelon, pp. 72-5) As one of these has observed, "The implications of trinity in the Old Testament are more accurately implications of plurality." (*Ibid*, p. 75)

The Bible provides much evidence of plural God-beings who act in perfect harmony and oneness of purpose, "But to us there is but one God, the Father, of whom are all things, and we in him; and one Lord Jesus Christ, by whom are all things, and we by him." (1 Cor 8:6)

T<small>HE</small> D<small>IVINE</small> P<small>OTENTIAL OF</small> M<small>AN</small>

On the preceding points relative to physical attributes of God, some have charged that Latter-day Saint doctrine is paganistic. An even more serious indictment—blasphemy—is leveled at Latter-day Saints by some Christians with regard to the proposition that man can become like God.

The religious tradition of orthodox Christianity teaches that God is so fundamentally different from man that the finite mind is incapable of comprehending the Trinity. The idea that man can become like his Creator is sufficiently radical as to be judged by some as an offense to God. It brings man too close to Deity. The contention is that this proposition demeans God by making Him too accessible and too familiar to man while overstating the importance of man relative to the God of heaven and earth. (Tillich, ST, Vol. I., pp. 235-9, 271-2)

In recent years, Latter-day Saints have faced a strident barrage of propaganda and denunciation by various Christian denominations for adhering to this point of doctrine, with much of their propaganda utilizing the techniques of slanted, "yellow" journalism. Visible tools in this assault include the film and books, *The God Makers* and *The God Makers II*, which have been distributed to thousands of congregations with condemnation of Latter-day Saints and their beliefs as blasphemous and satanic. Organizations like Saints-Alive and Christian Apologetics and Research Ministry fill the Internet with similar charges.

R<small>ESPONDING TO</small> C<small>HARGES OF</small> B<small>LASPHEMY</small>

Of course, this is not the first time that the charge of blasphemy has been leveled against those who teach a doctrine so bold that it challenges a tradition of the ages. Jewish leaders accused the Savior of making himself equal to God, contrary to their religious traditions, as recorded in the gospel of John:

> Then the Jews took up stones again to stone him.
> Jesus answered them, Many good works have I shewed you from my Father; for which of those works do ye stone me?
> The Jews answered him saying, For a good work we stone thee not; but for *blasphemy*; and because that thou, being a man, *makest thyself God*. (John 10:31-33; emphasis added)

What better opportunity for Jesus Christ to proclaim the doctrine of the Trinity to his believers and detractors, if that were a true doctrine? Why not explain that he and the Father are of the same substance and are equal? Instead, the Savior's reply suggests that a doctrine placing man close to God is not such a novel concept:

> Jesus answered them, Is it not written in your law, I said, Ye are gods?
>
> If he called them gods, unto whom the word of God came, and the scripture cannot be broken; Say ye of him, whom the Father hath sanctified, and sent into the world, Thou blasphemest; because I said, I am the Son of God? (John 10:34-36)

Latter-day Saints answer those who accuse them of blasphemy with a similar response. If there is support for this doctrine in the scriptures, then the accusation of blasphemy is clearly unfounded. Let us examine the Bible to see if this is such a novel notion, or if it is rejected by other Christians because it differs from their traditions.

NO OTHER GODS, ONE GOD-NATURE

Some Christians place significant weight on Isaiah 43:10 to "prove" what they regard is the error of Latter-day Saints. "Ye are my witnesses, saith the Lord . . . before me there was no God formed, neither shall there be after me." (Ankerberg, p. 119; also see Martin, R., p. 99) Other scriptures cited to supposedly demonstrate the impossibility of man progressing to become like God include: "For I am the Lord, I change not." (Mal 3:6; see also Ps 102:27, Heb 1:12) Also Jesus Christ is "the same yesterday, and to day, and for ever." (Heb 13:8) The reasoning goes something like this: If no other God was formed before God and none will be formed after Him and if God is unchanging, how can man hope to progress and become like God?

From the perspective of Christians who embrace the triune doctrine of Trinity, the conclusion seems inescapable. They reason that since the three personages of the Godhead are of the same substance, there can be only one God-being. No other God-being was formed before the Trinity of the same substance and none will be formed after Him. To some, it is insulting to believe that man could remotely resemble his trinitarian creator. (Ankerberg, p. 119 and Chafer/ Walvoord, p. 42)

However, this logic obviously breaks down if three separate and distinct God-beings comprise the Godhead, as taught in the Bible and discussed above. Since God is not a Trinity of the same substance, the words of the Lord as cited by Isaiah cannot apply to a single God-being. Clearly, more than one Being has attained Godhood, namely, the Father, the Son and the Holy Ghost.

An alternative explanation of the citation in Isaiah might suggest that the spiritual attributes and perfect unity of purpose, or in other words, the God-nature, never changes and cannot be altered or added upon; not the number of God-beings. According to this interpretation, there is only one God-nature, unchanging; the same yesterday, today and forever. There never was a time when the God-nature was different. Before this one God-nature, there was no other God-nature formed, and none will be formed after it.

A complimentary way of understanding this passage in Isaiah is in the context of Paul's teachings concerning "gods many, and lords many." Paul instructs us that though there be gods many, and lords many, as pertaining to this creation and the deity who directs its course, "to us there is but one God." (1 Cor 8:5-6) As it pertains "to us" and who we worship, "there was no God formed" before the God of this creation; "neither shall there be after [this one God]" (Isa 43:10), as it pertains to us.

Both interpretations are compatible with Isaiah's teachings while harmonizing with numerous passages in the Bible that refer to more than one God-being. Both interpretations leave open the possibility of more than one God-being fully personifying the single God-nature. It also suggests that God-beings can attain the God-nature at different points in time, since it is the God-nature, not the number of God-beings, that never changes nor is enlarged. Under these circumstances, the possibility of man, as a child of God, attaining this one God-nature through Jesus Christ cannot be ruled out.

In evaluating the soundness of these interpretations, it would be most compelling to find an example in the Bible of one who progressed in relation to God the Father and became a God. In this regard, Latter-day Saints ask other Christians, "What think ye of Christ?" (Matt 22:42)

CHRIST: AN EXAMPLE OF PROGRESSING TO GODHOOD

Paul writes, "Jesus Christ (is) the same yesterday, and to day, and for ever." (Heb 13:8) It is clear in the Bible that this sameness refers only to his spiritual, not his physical attributes. Jesus Christ, the Word, existed with his Father and was the principle creator, under the direction of his Father. (John 1:1-3, Eph 3:9) At his mortal birth, the Word was made flesh, undergoing a physical change. (John 1:14) The scriptures inform us that while on the earth, "yet learned he obedience by the things that he suffered" (Heb 5:8) and "Jesus increased in wisdom and stature, and in favour with God and man." (Luke 2:52) Dare one say that Jesus progressed in his standing with man and with God? After setting a perfect, God-like example for all mankind, Jesus laid down his life, allowing his spirit to separate from his body, another physical change. (Luke 23:46) Three days later, Jesus resurrected. His spirit was reunited with his body, which had undergone a change to become immortal, never to die again. (Luke 24:3-6, 1 Cor 15:42-44)

What think ye of Christ? Is he God? Traditional Christians and Latter-day Saints agree: the answer is yes. Did he change in physical attributes? The scriptures are very clear: he did. Did he change in his spiritual attributes? The account is equally clear. Jesus Christ was unwavering in his devotion and obedience to the Father, without sin or spiritual blemish. He was God-like before his mortal life, and he exhibited the perfect God-nature in all his dealings on earth. (John 1:1) Jesus Christ, who is the same yesterday, today and forever in spiritual attributes (his God-nature), still changed in physical attributes and increased in favor with man and with God.

Did Christ progress? In other words, did he gain power and authority and stature that he did not possess prior to his resurrection? During his earthly ministry, Jesus often acknowledged his subordinate position to God the Father. For example, "my Father is greater than I" (John 14:28), and "there is none good but one, that is God." (Matt 19:17) Later, Paul writes, "Christ Jesus . . . thought it not robbery to be equal with God." (Philip 2:5-6) He who was less than the Father, thought it not robbery to be equal with the Father. This was the very charge the Jews leveled at Jesus, as referenced above. (John 10:31-38; see also John 5:15-18)

Did Jesus Christ, who acknowledged himself less than the Father, become equal to the Father? Paul writes of a time when Jesus Christ was anointed heir of all things and was exalted to sit on the right hand of God:

> God . . .
>
> hath in these last days spoken unto us by his Son, whom he hath appointed heir of all things, by whom also he made the worlds;
>
> Who being the brightness of his glory, and the express image of his person, and upholding all things by the word of his power, when he had by himself purged our sins, sat down on the right hand of the Majesty on high. (Heb 1:1-3)

To be appointed heir of all things and to sit down on the right hand of God begins to approach equality with God the Father.

Paul continues to describe this amazing scene in which Jesus Christ is ordained to be a God:

> But unto the Son he [God the Father] saith, Thy throne, O God, is for ever and ever: a sceptre of righteousness is the sceptre of thy kingdom.
>
> Thou hast loved righteousness, and hated iniquity; therefore God, even thy God, hath anointed thee with the oil of gladness above thy fellows. (Heb 1:8-9)

Here we have it from the ultimate source. God the Father, addresses the Son and calls the Son, God. The Father declares that He has anointed the Son with oil and has given to the Son a throne, a sceptre and a kingdom forever and ever. The Son was not previously exalted to this status, but only after "he had by himself purged our sins" because he "hath loved righteousness, and hated iniquity." (Heb 1:9; see also Heb 1:1-3)

Paul is not alone as a prophetic witness to this blessed event. The Psalmist describes the identical scene beheld in vision. In the Psalmist's account, God the Father anoints His Son as a God and gives him power to exalt others.

> Thy throne, O God, is for ever and ever: the sceptre of thy kingdom is a right sceptre.
>
> Thou lovest righteousness, and hatest wickedness: therefore God, thy God, hath anointed thee with the oil of gladness above thy fellows.
>
> Instead of thy fathers shall be thy children, whom thou mayest make princes in all the earth.

> I will make thy name to be remembered in all generations: Therefore shall the people praise thee for ever and ever. (Ps 45:6-7, 16-17)

These accounts are consistent with the Savior's own declarations. After his resurrection, Jesus declared to his disciples, "All power is given unto me in heaven and in earth." (Matt 28:18)

If given, then this power must have been conferred by another possessing all power, as described by Paul and the Psalmist. If conferred or anointed, then there must have been a time when this power had not been given, which occasioned the anointment or conferral. If this is so, then Christ progressed from a state of possessing limited power to one of receiving all power in heaven and in earth. Is this not progression? Is this not a change of stature by Jesus Christ who is the same yesterday, today and forever? Is this not the forming of another God-being, though the God-nature changes not?

MAN: POTENTIAL JOINT-HEIRS WITH CHRIST

Still, one may protest, Jesus becoming like God is one thing. Though Christ was not given all power and did not possess an immortal body until after his resurrection, still he was of the God-nature from the beginning. (John 1:1) While on earth, he was perfect and overcame all things. It is one thing to believe that Jesus was able to progress and become like God. It is a far different thing to imagine that man, with all of his foibles and weaknesses, is capable of the same.

On this point, it must be admitted that the mind will need to stretch to comprehend eternity. It is almost too good to be true. Except, that man has the potential to do so is the witness of prophets in all times, including the prophets of the Bible. Paul testifies of this reality:

> The Spirit itself beareth witness with our spirit, that we are the children of God:
>
> And if children, then heirs; heirs of God, and joint-heirs with Christ; if so be that we suffer with him, that we may be also glorified together. (Rom 8:16-17)

Also,

> And because ye are sons, God hath sent forth the Spirit of his Son into your hearts, crying Abba, Father.
>
> Wherefore thou art no more a servant, but a son; and if a son, then an heir of God through Christ. (Gal 4:6-7)

As "children of God," literally His sons and daughters, man has inherited qualities and traits from the Father of our spirits, (Heb 12:9), imbuing [man] with the potential to be like his heavenly parent, or "partakers of his holiness." (Heb 12:10) Further evidence of this is found in the teachings of Paul where he refers to man as the "offspring" of God.

> For in him we live, and move, and have our being; as certain also of your own poets have said, For we are also his offspring.
>
> Forasmuch then as we are the offspring of God, we ought not to think that the Godhead is like unto gold, or silver, or stone, graven by art and man's device. (Acts 17:28-29)

Paul refers to man "as the offspring of God." The English word "offspring" is translated from the Greek word "*genos*," meaning "race." As one scholar has noted, "This word forms the basis for such English words as 'genetics' and 'genes,' and indicates unequivocally that Men are the same species as God." (Hopkins, p. 98)

Being of the same race or species, man is "no more a servant, but a son!" As a son, it is his rightful position "through Christ" to inherit all God has, "if so be that we suffer with him, that we may be also glorified together." (Rom 8:17) This is the whole purpose of the atonement and resurrection of Jesus Christ.

> For it became him [God], for whom are all things, and by whom are all things, *in bringing many sons unto glory*, to make the captain of their salvation perfect through sufferings.
>
> For *both he that sanctifieth and they who are sanctified are all of one*. (Heb 2:10-11; emphasis added)

Likewise, John the Revelator leaves his solemn witness to this marvelous truth as he quotes the Resurrected Lord: "To him that overcometh will I grant to sit with me in my throne, even as I also overcame, and am set down with my Father in his throne." (Rev 3:21) "He that overcometh shall inherit all things; and I will be his God, and he shall be my son." (Rev 21:7) "Be thou faithful unto death, and I will give thee a crown of life." (Rev 2:10)

Finally, the chief apostle, Peter, speaks of the saints' ultimate reward:

> Ye shall receive a crown of glory that fadeth not away. (1 Pet 5:4)

[Christ] hath given unto us all things that pertain unto life and god-liness . . . Whereby are given unto us exceeding great and precious promises: that by these ye might be partakers of the divine nature (2 Pet 1:3-4),

that he may exalt you in due time. (1 Pet 5:6)

What could be more clear? The Lord Jesus Christ promises to share his throne, which is the Father's throne, with those who overcome as he overcame. He covenants that those who overcome will inherit all things. As cited above, Jesus has received "all power . . . in heaven and in earth" (Matt 28:18) and is "set down . . . in his (Father's) throne." When man "inherits all things," including "all power in heaven and in earth" and sits with the Lord in his Father's throne, will he not be like God? Will he not be "one" with Christ who sanctified him? Will he not be a partaker of the divine nature? Will he not possess the very title of the Father and the Son; even God? The promises of our Savior are sure.

Beloved, now are we the sons of God, and it doth not yet appear what we shall be: but we know that, when he shall appear, *we shall be like him;* for we shall see him as he is.

And every man that hath this hope in him purifieth himself even as he is pure. (1 John 3:2-3; emphasis added)

But as many as received him, to them gave he power to become the sons of God . . . (John 1:12)

CLARIFYING THE SIN OF LUCIFER

Some Christians recoil in horror at this bold doctrine which they do not understand. To them it is too much to imagine man can be like God! According to their perspective, this is the sin that caused Lucifer to fall from the heavens and become the devil. (Decker/ Hunt, p. 28; Gibbs, p. 25; Lutzer, SP, p. 60) They like to quote this passage from Isaiah:

How art thou fallen from heaven, O Lucifer, son of the morning!

For thou has said in thine heart, I will ascend into heaven, I will exalt my throne above the stars of God . . . I will ascend above the heights of the clouds; I will be like the most High. (Isa 14:12-14)

The inference drawn from this passage by these Christians is that Lucifer desired something totally inappropriate, to "be like the most High," and therefore, he was cast out of heaven. However, it is equally reasonable to conclude from this passage that Lucifer's sin consisted of an unwillingness to submit to the Father's will as a means of attaining the desires of his heart. (see MacArthur, *Glory*, p. 158)

In trying to understand the cause of Lucifer's fall, it is worth noting the repeated use of "I will . . ." in reference to the son of the morning. Four times, Isaiah begins his phrases with the same words, "I will." This technique of repeating the most important idea in a passage was frequently used by Isaiah and other Jewish poets to focus attention on the key point.

Lucifer's willfulness stands in stark contrast to the example of Jesus Christ. The Savior always subordinated his will to the Father's. He received all things from the Father in humility of spirit.

Lucifer's "heart" was filled with a spirit of "my will be done." This constitutes rebellion against the Father and will never qualify one to "inherit all things." It is far removed from the attitude commended by John: "And every man that hath this hope in him [to be like Christ] purifieth himself, even as he [Christ] is pure." (1 John 3:3)

Later in the same chapter of Isaiah, the Lord identifies the means provided for attaining all things. "Surely as I [God] have thought, so shall it come to pass; and as I have purposed, so shall it stand." (Isaiah 14:24) The blessings of God can only be received in his own way, and that way is through Jesus Christ. (John 14:6)

Jesus is the way. He is our supreme exemplar. Paul informs us the Savior did not think it too bold "to be equal with God." (Philip 2:6) But Jesus always submitted to his Father's will and purpose. "He humbled himself, and became obedient unto death, even the death of the cross. Wherefore God also hath highly exalted him . . ." (Philip 2:8-9)

In like manner, if we submit our will to God, He will highly exalt us through Jesus Christ. Then, "when he [Christ] shall appear, we will be like him." (1 John 3:2)

It would appear that Lucifer's sin is more appropriately attributed to his rebelliousness in not submitting to the thoughts and purpose of the Father. It is a righteous desire to be like the Father as evidenced by the aspirations of Jesus Christ to be equal with God. But all things must be done in God's own way and according to his purposes.

GOD'S DESIRES FOR HIS CHILDREN

It was the Savior who commanded us, "Be ye therefore perfect, even as your Father which is in heaven is perfect." (Matt 5:48)

It must be possible to be perfect like our Father in Heaven through Jesus Christ, unless we take the Savior's words to be absurd and nonsensical.

To say that this is impossible is to question God's word and power, not man's potential. Only through Christ can man receive forgiveness for all of his sins and become pure, as he is pure. Once man is made pure in Jesus Christ, he is pure forever and ever—like God. Will other Christians claim that God, who is omnipotent, is incapable of exalting man to be like Himself? This is indeed blasphemous.

The issue ultimately comes down to the will of God and His desires for His children. It must be possible for man to become like God unless God will not permit it. But what is more loving than to give to others all that brings the Father joy, all that the Father has? Is not this God-like?

We are his children. As earthly parents, would we desire for our children less than we ourselves enjoy and cherish? "If ye then, being evil, know how to give good gifts unto your children, how much more shall your Father which is in heaven give good gifts to them that ask him?" (Matt 6:11)

This proposition which at first blush is so bold, so incredible, so astounding, is upon further reflection so very reasonable, though awe-inspiring. God, who is all-loving, desires to give to his children all that He has, allowing them to experience all of the joy and peace and glory He knows as God.

Some Christians will see in this wonderful plan the pure love of our Father in Heaven. C. S. Lewis, a popular writer in the Protestant tradition, comes very close to grasping this amazing insight.

> The command 'Be ye perfect' is not idealistic gas. Nor is it a command to do the impossible. He (God) is going to make us into creatures that can obey that command. He said (in the Bible) that we were "gods" and He is going to make good His words. If we let Him—for we can prevent Him, if we choose—He will make the feeblest and filthiest of us into a god or goddess, dazzling, radiant, immortal creature, pulsating all through with such energy and joy and wisdom and love as we cannot now imagine . . . The process will be long and in parts very painful; but that is what we are in for. Nothing less. He meant what He said. (Lewis, pp. 174-5)

This glorious doctrine has the ring of truth. It is so amazing that man's finite mind could never have concocted it, yet it is so simple that it can be grasped by a child.

Other Christians can choose to take offense at this doctrine of Deity if they want. In doing so, they should be cautious not to repeat the mistake of those who took up stones when they heard Jesus proclaim himself the Son of God.

After conducting a thorough review of Biblical references and writings of the earliest Christian fathers, the Protestant scholar, Ernst Benz concludes:

> One can think what one wants of this doctrine of progressive deification, but one thing is certain . . . Joseph Smith (the Mormon Prophet) is closer to the view of man held by the Ancient Church than the precursors of the Augustinian doctrine of original sin were, who considered the thought of such a substantial connection between God and man as the heresy, par excellence." (Benz, as quoted in Madsen, Reflections, pp. 215-6)

A MODERN PROPHET REVEALS THE TRUE GOD

Latter-day Saints have been blessed with a more sure knowledge concerning this most essential doctrine. In these last days, the Lord has raised up a prophet, Joseph Smith. This prophet has spoken as one having authority. He has cut asunder the speculation and fallible reasoning of philosophers and theologians. In humility, he has proclaimed,

> Thus saith the Lord:
> "The Father has a body of flesh and bones as tangible as man's; the Son also; but the Holy Ghost has not a body of flesh and bones, but is a personage of Spirit. Were it not so, the Holy Ghost could not dwell in us." (D&C 130:22)
> God himself was once as we are now, and is an exalted man, and sits enthroned in yonder heavens! That is the great secret. If the veil were rent today, and the great God who holds this world in its orbit, and who upholds all worlds and all things by his power, was to make himself visible,—I say, if you were to see him today, you would see him like a man in form—like yourselves in all the person, image, and very form as a man. (Smith, TPJS, p. 345)

> God himself, finding he was in the midst of spirits and glory, because he was more intelligent, saw proper to institute laws whereby

the rest could have a privilege to advance like himself. The relationship we have with God places us in a situation to advance in knowledge. He has power to institute laws to instruct the weaker intelligences, that they may be exalted with himself, so that they might have one glory upon another, and all that knowledge, power, glory, and intelligence, which is requisite . . . (*Ibid*, p. 354)

Those who have ears to hear, will hear. All glory be to God. Truly, His ways are marvelous to behold.

2
Saving Grace and Good Works

T he second major area of doctrinal disagreement used by some
to contend that Latter-day Saints are not Christians concerns
requirements for salvation. In overly simplistic terms, these differences
are often represented as salvation by grace versus salvation by works.
In a more intolerant form, some Christians accuse Latter-day Saints of
denying the effects of the Savior's atonement. As will be shown, neither construct captures core differences in how Latter-day Saints and
some other Christians answer the question put to the Savior, "What
shall I do to inherit eternal life?" (Matt 19:16)

In the last chapter, Roman Catholics and Protestants were shown to
hold generally similar views about Trinity while the Latter-day Saints'
concept of Deity was distinctly different. However, this is not the case
regarding requirements for salvation. Several major positions have
emerged in mainstream Christianity. Of these, the tenets of Latter-day
Saints regarding roles of grace and works are more similar to those of
Roman Catholics and Eastern Orthodox Christians, and are at significant variance with those of many Protestants.

CONTROVERSY AMONG PROTESTANT FACTIONS

Prominent theologian Paul Tillich asserts, "The central doctrine of
the Reformation, the article by which Protestantism stands or falls, [is]
the principle of justification by grace through faith." (Tillich, ST, Vol.
2, p. 223) Despite the pre-eminence of this doctrine, Protestant denominations are divided in their teachings about how salvation is secured.
Core differences within the Protestant community lie in divergent
views about man's relationship to God and the degree to which one is

free to exercise moral agency. Historically, Protestant denominations have tended to segregate into two major camps.

Presbyterians, most Baptist sects, Lutherans and those in the Reformed tradition embrace doctrines of predestination (sometimes referred to as foreordination or election), which teach that all events are determined in advance by the will of God. (Evans, pp. 54-6; see also Mead) These doctrines, generally associated with John Calvin, the 16th-century reformer, maintain that God predetermines all things, even the exercise of an individual's moral agency.

In its application to salvation, predestination holds that some are destined in advance for heaven while others are foreordained to damnation. The elect, chosen by the will of God, find grace and salvation "irresistible." For these fortunate souls, personal rebellion against God and his teachings inevitably give way to the saving grace of the Lord. In matters of salvation or damnation, one's choices and efforts are relatively inconsequential. Individual salvation is foreordained according to God's will and foreknowledge. (Evans, pp. 54-6; also Berkhof, HCD, pp. 147-9) Calvinist influences permeate teachings of Dr. Paul Tillich when he writes, "It should be regarded as the Protestant principle that, in relation to God, God alone can act and that no human claim, especially no religious claim, no intellectual or moral or devotional 'work,' can reunite us with him." (Tillich, ST, Vol. 2, p. 224)

In contrast, members of Methodist congregations, Evangelical Churches, Episcopalian/Anglican Churches, Pentecostal denominations including Assemblies of God, Free Will and General Baptists, Mennonites, Church of God congregations and some sects in the Brethren traditions reject many Calvinist notions of predestination in favor of teachings attributed to Jacob Arminius and John Wesley. (Evans, pp. 54-6; also see Mead) Arminius was a Dutch theologian (1560-1609) who argued forcefully against Calvinist doctrine, declaring that man is free to choose good or evil and salvation is available to all. John Wesley and his followers later embraced these teachings, weaving them into the fabric of Methodist theology. From there, they found acceptance within a broader cross-section of Protestantism.

According to Arminian precepts, salvation is available to all mankind, not just the elect of God. Man can exercise moral agency in choosing to follow the promptings of grace There is individual accountability in man's choices. However, in modern Arminianism, grace, not the exercise of moral agency, justifies man and qualifies him for salvation. It is possible to withstand grace and salvation, but grace alone determines salvation when one gives in to its promptings. Good works are present as a natural consequence of grace, but works have no role in determining salvation. (MacArthur, Gospel, pp. 37-9; Berkhof, HCD, pp. 150-1; Marty, pp. 109-110) Arminian precepts are evident in the teachings of Pentecostal theologian John F. MacArthur when he writes: "Though divine initiative is ultimately responsible for redemption—although men and women are elected, predestined, chosen from the foundation of the world—there must still be on our part a submissive response of personal faith in Jesus Christ." (MacArthur, Gospel, p. 81)

Some trends within modern Protestantism tend toward minimizing historical differences between Calvinists and Arminianists by emphasizing salvation by grace alone. However, implications of the two bodies of doctrine are difficult to reconcile, creating a major schism within the Protestant community; what one Protestant scholar calls "the debacle in contemporary evangelism." (MacArthur, Gospel, p. 66) Some denominations adopt a position sometimes referred to as Lordship salvation while others support its counterpart, No Lordship salvation. (MacArthur, Gospel, pp. 28-37 and 104-5; also see Hopkins, pp. 130-6; Marty, p. 111; Berkhof, HCD, pp. 188-190; Chafer/Walvoord, pp. 220-4, 232-3)

DIFFERENT POSITIONS: REQUIREMENTS FOR SALVATION

Some differences resulting from this schism as they affect requirements for salvation are discussed below. Others can only be appreciated in shades and nuances that go far beyond the scope of this effort. General threads running through most Protestant teachings can be summarized under the following headings:

Man is saved by grace alone through the atonement of Jesus Christ. God's grace is a gift that man cannot earn or merit.

Salvation is not universal. *To be saved, man must have a personal experience with grace*, sometimes referred to as "the moment of faith" in which he becomes aware of his complete inability to lay hold of salvation on his own and accepts Jesus Christ as his personal Savior. At that moment, he feels God's grace and power indwell him. This experience with grace is what Protestants mean by being born again.

Outward ordinances such as baptism are unnecessary for salvation because salvation is secured at the moment of faith when one experiences baptism of the Spirit.

Having experienced God's grace, salvation is guaranteed without further conditions, according to the teachings of No Lordship denominations. On the other hand, *Lordship denominations insist that salvation is assured provided additional signs of true discipleship follow the moment of faith.* A small minority of Protestant sects teach that salvation is guaranteed provided man continues to walk in righteousness.

Good works are not a condition of salvation. For No Lordship denominations, salvation is irresistible and works are immaterial. According to Lordship teachings, good works will be evident among the recipients of grace. However, these good works are not the result of individual effort, rather they flow from grace. Man must surrender to grace which produces a longing to obey. *Little or no personal effort or sacrifice is required or appropriate* since Christ has accomplished all that is necessary for salvation.

Teachings of Roman Catholics, Eastern Orthodox Christians and Latter-day Saints regarding the role of grace and good works in salvation bear significant similarities to each other while they vary substantially from those of most Protestant denominations. Explanations and descriptions of the process by which salvation is secured differ to some degree among Roman Catholics, Eastern Orthodox and Latter-day Saints with greater emphasis placed on liturgical requirements by the non-LDS churches. These variances will not be explored here. For our purposes, it is sufficient to acknowledge basic similarities of doctrine regarding roles of grace and works among these members of the Christian community and to contrast their precepts with those of most Protestant denominations.

The following summary of doctrine regarding salvation by grace and works utilizes terms and explanations familiar to Latter-day Saints and parallels the headings used to describe Protestant teachings, above:

Man is saved by grace alone through the atonement of Jesus Christ. God's grace is a gift that man cannot earn or merit.

Salvation is available to all but will not be universal. To be saved, *man must enter into the new covenant of grace and be born again through baptism of water and of the Spirit. Salvation is granted to those who continue in the new covenant of grace and strive to follow the Savior's example of righteousness;* coming to know him and love him through emulation. This requires ongoing repentance and submission to his will. As man repents and perseveres in righteousness, the sanctifying influence of the Spirit changes his desires, reshaping him in the image of Christ.

Once one enters into the path of salvation through proper baptism, salvation is guaranteed conditionally provided one continues striving to live a righteous life after the example of Jesus Christ. The promises of salvation become unconditional only after one's calling and election are made sure, an event preceded by much diligence and the thorough testing of one's faith.

Works will be used by the Savior to judge all mankind and to select those who will receive the full measure of his mediation and advocacy. *Because of man's carnal nature, persevering in righteousness is a struggle.* Despite inadequacies and shortcomings, those who strive to keep their covenants in righteousness are promised the Savior's mediation on their behalf. By exercising faith in this promise and with assistance of the Spirit, man finds strength to persevere and endure to the end.

POINTS OF AGREEMENT AMONG CHRISTIANS

The first point evident in comparing teachings of Latter-day Saints to those of Protestant denominations is the quintessential role of Jesus Christ in providing salvation. There is absolute agreement among members of the Christian community that salvation comes only through the grace of God made possible by the atonement of Jesus Christ. All parties embrace the expression of the writer of Acts, "But we believe that through the grace of the Lord Jesus Christ we shall be saved." (Acts 15:11) All rejoice in the proclamation of the Savior, "I am the way, the truth, and the life: no man cometh unto the Father, but by me." (John 14:6)

Those who attempt to label Latter-day Saints as non-Christian seem to ignore the most fundamental requirement for membership in the Christian community, accepting Jesus Christ as one's personal Savior. By this measure, Latter-day Saints are most certainly Christians. The first prophet of the latter-days, Joseph Smith, wrote,

The fundamental principles of our religion are the testimony of the Apostles and Prophets, concerning Jesus Christ, that He died, was buried, and rose again the third day, and ascended into heaven; and all other things which pertain to our religion are only appendages to it. (Smith, TPJS, p. 121)

Along with Protestant, Catholic and Eastern Orthodox Christians, Latter-day Saints rejoice in Christ and the good news.

In addition, there is agreement that salvation is not the result of good works. No amount of effort can save man. No rigid set of prescribed rules and no checklist of merits and demerits can bring man to salvation. In all of creation, only one being, Jesus Christ, qualified for salvation on the merits of his own works. For all others, salvation is possible through the grace of God, alone. It is a gift that cannot be earned by any amount of good works. "There is none righteous, no, not one." (Rom 3:10) "Therefore by the deeds of the law there shall no flesh be justified . . ." (Rom 3:20)

Protestants often attempt to represent Latter-day Saints as relying solely or at least primarily upon their good works to attain salvation. Nothing could be further from the truth. An oft-quoted Latter-day Saint Apostle, Bruce R. McConkie, has written regarding the role of grace in man's salvation:

Does salvation come by grace, by grace alone, by grace without works? It surely does, without any question, in all its parts, types, kinds, and degrees. We are saved by grace, without works; it is a gift of God. How else could it come? In his goodness and grace the great God ordained and established the plan of salvation. No works on our part were required. In his goodness and grace he created this earth and all that is on it, with man as the crowning creature of his creating— without which creation his spirit children could not obtain immortality and eternal life. No works on our part were required . . .

In his goodness and grace—and this above all—he gave his Only Begotten Son to ransom man and all life from the temporal and spiritual death brought into the world by the fall of Adam . . .

And finally, there neither has been, nor is, nor ever can be any way nor means by which man alone can, by any power he possesses, redeem himself." (as recorded in Millet, p. 8; also see 'grace' in LDS Bible Dictionary)

Finally, there is agreement among Latter-day Saints and most Protestants that salvation is not universally attained. On the day of judgment, there will be a sorting out of sheep on the right hand of God and of goats on the left. Rewards and punishments will be appointed in the divine wisdom of the eternal judge, Jesus Christ. Some will come forth to salvation while others will experience the chastisement of the damned.

CORE DIFFERENCES IN DOCTRINE

Despite areas of agreement, teachings of Latter-day Saints and Protestants are at variance on several specific points of doctrine. These include the following:

Table 2

Protestants	Latter-day Saints
Entering into God's Kingdom through the New Covenant	
Moment of Faith; Baptism of the Spirit	Baptism by Immersion and conferral of the Holy Spirit by one having proper authority
Promises of Salvation	
Guaranteed unconditionally at moment of faith (*No Lordship denominations*);	Guaranteed conditionally at baptism;
Guaranteed at moment of faith provided evidence of true discipleship follows (*Lordship denominations*)	Unconditionally only after calling and election are made sure
The Role of Good Works in the New Covenant	
Not used in determining who will receive mediation of Jesus and be justified unto salvation; Works used to condemn those not justified by grace;	Essential in determining who abides in the new covenant and qualifies for mediation of Jesus at the last judgment;
Flow naturally from grace requiring little or no effort by man; present among the recipients of grace but not resulting from human effort;	Flow from grace but requiring man to struggle and sacrifice while growing from grace to grace;
Obedience, repentance and submission classified as works (*No Lordship denominations*); as part of saving faith (*Lordship denominations*)	Obedience, repentance and submission included as part of saving faith and righteous works; invite an increase of the Spirit which sanctifies man

Each of these areas of doctrinal divergence is significant. Salvation hangs in the balance and the scales tip according to Jesus' response to the question put to him on more than one occasion: "What shall I do to inherit eternal life?" (Luke 18:18). The soundness of Protestant and Latter-day Saint positions deserve to be tested by examining each body of doctrine in the light of Biblical teachings.

ENTERING INTO GOD'S KINGDOM

Anyone who has been queried by a Protestant faithful, "Are you saved?," will recognize the sincerity with which these believers maintain that salvation is assured in an experience with grace. According to Protestant teachings, this moment of faith constitutes baptism by the Spirit and the rebirth of man as a new creature in Christ. (Evans, pp. 33-5; MacArthur, Gospel, pp. 47 and 83; Gibbs, pp. 37-41) As popular evangelist, Tony Evans, states,

> When you understand that Christ died on the cross in your place for your sins and rose bodily from the dead; when you respond to the truth and put your complete trust and confidence in Him; when you rest your eternal destiny on Jesus Christ alone for salvation; then the Holy Spirit comes to indwell you; you are baptized into the body of Christ . . . (Evans, p. 57)

It may come as a surprise to some that Latter-day Saints acknowledge and rejoice in their personal experiences with grace, similar to the moment of faith described in Protestant theology. These epiphanies are sacred, providing a spiritual anchor in the life of each member. Differences in doctrine are not related to the reality of a grace experience. Rather, disagreement centers on the significance attached to these experiences.

SUDDEN GRACE: THE THIEF ON THE CROSS

The scriptural precedent most often cited to support the position of spiritual baptism at the moment of conversion is the thief on the cross. As the Savior hung between two robbers, "one of the malefactors . . . railed on him saying, If thou be Christ, save thyself and us." (Luke 23:39) The other condemned man reprimanded his fellow thief, testifying of the righteousness of Jesus. Then:

he said unto Jesus, Lord, remember me when thou comest into thy kingdom.

And Jesus said unto him, Verily I say unto thee, Today shalt thou be with me in paradise." (Luke 23:42-43)

The Biblical account indicates both men were deserving of their punishment for previous criminal acts. (Luke 23:40-41) Most Protestants believe that, despite this unworthiness, the second malefactor was assured salvation in the final hours of his life without baptism and good works. According to this interpretation, the Savior's statement that the thief would be with him in paradise was tantamount to declaring the thief's salvation. He was saved in his moment of faith by confessing the righteousness of Jesus.

The basis for this interpretation relies on an assumption that paradise and heaven are one and the same. In this case, the text suggests otherwise. Three days after the crucifixion, the resurrected Lord appeared to Mary Magdalene at the garden tomb. After tenderly speaking her name, Mary recognized her master and approached him. He admonished her, "Touch me not; *for I am not yet ascended to my Father.*" (John 20:17; emphasis added) Assuredly, Jesus and the thief departed mortality and communed together in "paradise," as promised by the Savior, but this was somewhere other than heaven. Though the Savior had been in paradise for three days, he had not ascended to his Father—*in heaven.*

An epistle of Peter informs us that after suffering death, "[Jesus] went and preached unto the spirits in prison which sometime were disobedient . . ." (1 Pet 3:18-20; see also 1 Pet 4:6) Peter's description of a location visited by Jesus following his crucifixion in which the spirits of those who have departed mortality are taught the gospel seems consistent with promises of the Savior to the thief. It is also consistent with the statement of the resurrected Lord to Mary that he had not ascended to heaven where the Father dwells. Only after his resurrection did Christ ascended to his Father, where he "is gone into heaven, and is on the right hand of God; angels and authorities and powers being made subject unto him." (1 Pet 3:22) Paradise is a location separate from heaven. This is discussed further in the next chapter.

Since paradise is not heaven, then the promise to the thief as he hung on the cross was *not* one of unconditional salvation, as suggested by most Protestants. The thief on the cross does not qualify as a clear example of salvation by sudden grace.

OTHER GRACE EXPERIENCES IN THE BIBLE

Other examples of sudden grace recorded in the Bible include the conversion of Cornelius, the gentile centurion (Acts 10), a dramatic outpouring of the spirit upon many of the Jewish nation on the day of Pentecost (Acts 2), and the vision of Saul, later called Paul, as he traveled the road to Damascus (Acts 9). In all of these accounts, the spirit of the Lord descended upon individuals in a sudden experience similar to the moment of faith.

Based on most Protestant doctrine, one would expect to find in these accounts assurances of salvation for the recipients of grace without further requirements. However, in each case, the scriptures are silent regarding such assurances, and no subsequent passage in the Bible refers to one of these moments of faith as the point in time when salvation was secured by those present.

In each case, these accounts identify additional actions required of the recipients of grace to lay hold on promises of salvation. In the case of Cornelius, he and his household were commanded to be baptized (Acts 10:48). Likewise, the Jewish converts on the day of Pentecost were given the following instructions, "Repent, and be baptized in the name of Jesus Christ for the remission of sins, and ye shall receive the gift of the Holy Ghost." (Acts 2:38) Saul was told by the Lord, "Arise, and go into the city, and it shall be told thee *what thou must do*." (Acts 9:6; emphasis added) Three days later, Ananias informed him,

> Brother Saul, the Lord, even Jesus, that appeared unto thee in the way as thou camest, hath sent me, that thou mightest receive thy sight, and be filled with the Holy Ghost.
>
> And immediately there fell from his eyes as it had been scales: and he received sight forthwith, and arose, and was baptized. (Acts 9:17-18)

Apparently, one of those things that Saul and all others "must do" even after the moment of faith is to be baptized.

BAPTISM: THE DOOR

In most Protestant denominations today, baptism by immersion is an optional ordinance. At most, it provides some assistance to individuals in developing spirituality but is deemed unnecessary for salvation. (Berkhof, HCD, p. 248; Marty, pp. 157-8,162; Chafer/Walvoord, pp. 269-271; Hopkins, p. 265; Barth, Teachings, pp. 23-5; MacArthur, Gospel, p. 47; Gibbs, pp. 49-50, 99; Bowman p. 97; Lucado, p. 115) According to some Protestant teachings, baptism is a requirement for discipleship but not for salvation. (Marty, p. 162; Berkhof, HCD, p. 251; Hopkins, p. 169)

Most Protestant denominations have replaced water baptism with baptism of the Spirit, teaching that spiritual conversion at the moment of faith is the only baptism required for salvation. (Chafer/ Walvoord, p. 240; MacArthur, Gospel, p. 47; Evans, pp. 35-53; Gibbs, pp. 37-40) This doctrine is an extension of Protestant teachings emphasizing justification by grace alone, though some refer to First Corinthians 12:13 for scriptural support: "For by one Spirit are we all baptized into one body." As one Protestant theologian has put it, "religious rituals—including baptism—cannot give eternal life." (MacArthur, Gospel, p. 47)

Latter-day Saints acknowledge that the act of being baptized does not "give eternal life." Only Jesus Christ can provide salvation. However, Latter-day Saints teach baptism by immersion as an essential ordinance by which one enters into the covenant of grace with his or her Savior. Baptism is the ordinance appointed by God that opens the door leading to His kingdom. There is no other way.

> He that entereth not by the door into the sheepfold, but climbeth up some other way, the same is a thief and a robber.
> But he that entereth in by the door is the shepherd of the sheep . . . *he goeth before them and the sheep follow him:* for they know his voice. (John 10:1-4; emphasis added)

Jesus Christ entered through the door of baptism by immersion "to fulfil all righteousness." (Matt 3:15) True believers enter his "sheepfold" by following the shepherd. "The disciple is not above his master: but every one that is perfect shall be as his master." (Luke 6:40) The Savior taught, "My sheep hear my voice, and I know them, and they follow me." (John 10:27)

During his mortal ministry, Jesus spoke of the necessity of being baptized. John records a clandestine meeting between the Savior and Nicodemus, a member of the Sanhedrin. During this encounter, Jesus taught of rebirth. "Except a man be born again, he cannot *see* the kingdom of God." (John 3:3; emphasis added) According to the Savior, an experience with the Spirit, of being born again, is necessary to glimpse or "see the kingdom of God." However, seeing the kingdom of God is not the same as entering the kingdom of God. Christ taught that more is required to enter his kingdom.

Jesus continued, "Verily, verily, I say unto thee, Except a man be born of water and of the Spirit, he cannot *enter* into the kingdom of God." (John 3:5) As specified by the Savior, requirements for *entering* God's kingdom include two additional steps or commitments: (1) to be born of water (baptism) and (2) to be born of the Spirit (receiving the gift of the Holy Ghost by the laying on of hands).

Paul leaves no doubt regarding how rebirth in Christ occurs. Through the ordinance of baptism by immersion, one participates in a perfect likeness of the death and resurrection of Jesus Christ. "Therefore we are buried with him by baptism into death: that like as Christ was raised up from the dead by the glory of the Father, even so we also should walk in newness of life." (Rom 6:4) By following his example of being baptized by immersion, we complete the process of rebirth, being raised from the waters as a new creature in Christ and fit to enter into the kingdom of God.

Other passages in the Bible make it clear that the gift of the Holy Ghost as a continuing presence is bestowed upon the new creature after being raised from the waters of baptism.

> Now when the apostles which were at Jerusalem heard that Samaria had received the word of God, they sent unto them Peter and John:
>
> Who, when they were come down, prayed for them, that they might receive the Holy Ghost:
>
> (For as yet he was fallen upon none of them: only they were baptized in the name of Jesus Christ.)
>
> Then laid they their hands on them and they received the Holy Ghost. (Acts 8:14-17)

Thus they are born of the water and of the Spirit. (see also Acts 2:38; Matt 3:11; Mark 1:8; and Luke 3:16) It is worth noting the same pattern was observed at the Savior's baptism. The spirit descended following baptism. (Matt 3:16, Mark 1:10, Luke 3:21-22)

Elsewhere, Paul taught that baptism is the means of entering into a relationship with Christ which brings forth the promises of salvation:

> For ye are all the children of God by faith in Christ Jesus.
> For as many of you as have been baptized into Christ have put on Christ.
> And if ye be Christ's, then are ye Abraham's seed, and heirs according to the promise. (Gal 3:26-27)

This relationship with Christ is the new covenant spoken of in both the Old and New Testaments. (Jer 31:33-36; Heb 8:10-13) The old covenant, sealed in the flesh by circumcision, is supplanted by the new covenant, sealed in the act of baptism by immersion.

> In whom [Christ] also ye are circumcised with the circumcision made without hands, in putting off the body of the sins of the flesh by the circumcision of Christ:
> Buried with him in baptism, wherein also ye are risen with him through the faith of the operation of God, who hath raised him from the dead." (Col 2:11-12)

There should be no mistake that the baptism spoken of by Paul is by immersion in water. The symbolic parallels are straightforward and purposeful. As prominent theologian Karl Barth observes,

> Primitive baptism (carried out by complete immersion in water) had in its mode, exactly like the circumcision of the Old Testament, the character of a direct threat to life, succeeded immediately by the corresponding deliverance and preservation, the raising from baptism. (Barth, Teachings, p.10)

We become the seed of Abraham and "the children of God by faith in Christ Jesus" (Gal 3:26) by being baptized, even as he was.

The linkage between baptism and salvation is plainly evident in the teachings of the Savior and his apostles as recorded in the Bible. For example, the resurrected Christ commanded his apostles to take the gospel to the world. "*He that believeth and is baptized shall be saved;* but he that believeth not shall be damned." (Mark 16:16) The Savior's words indicate that both requirements—believing and being baptized—are necessary for salvation.

Other writers in the Bible also teach that baptism in water is inextricably linked to salvation. Peter wrote to members of the church, likening baptism to the floods in the days of Noah which separated the righteous from the unrighteous. "The like figure where unto even baptism doth also now save us . . ." (1 Pet 3:21) Paul also taught that salvation comes by being born of the water and of the Spirit, "according to his mercy he saved us, by the washing of regeneration, and renewing of the Holy Ghost." (Titus 3:5) Ezekiel indicates water plays a role in cleansing our sins and preparing us to receive a new heart and a new spirit. (Ezek 36:24-26)

Paul wrote of baptism as one of the essential elements of the foundation of the gospel.

> Therefore leaving the principles of the doctrine of Christ, let us go on unto perfection; not laying again the foundation of repentance from dead works, and of faith toward God,
> Of the doctrine of baptisms, and of laying on of hands, and of resurrection of the dead, and of eternal judgment. (Heb 6:1-2)

Baptism is so fundamental to the doctrine of Christ that Paul identifies it as part of the foundation along with repentance, faith, the laying on of hands for the gift of the Holy Ghost, the resurrection and the judgment. These are not optional principles of the gospel. Certainly, most Protestants would not suggest that faith toward God is non-essential to salvation. By the same logic, neither can baptism be considered optional. Along with these other principles, baptism is an essential part of the foundation of the gospel from which mankind can go on unto perfection. There is no other way.

BIBLICAL PATTERN OF REQUIRING BAPTISM

The pattern of requiring baptism to enter Christ's kingdom is evident throughout the scriptures. As noted above, Christ showed the way by submitting to baptism, though he was perfect and in no need of a remission of sins. (Matt 3:14-17; Mark 1:9-11) This act of righteousness invoked a marvelous manifestation of heavenly approbation as the spirit descended in the form of a dove and the Father spoke from heaven: "This is my beloved Son, in whom I am well pleased." (Matt 3:17) Those who deny the necessity of following the Savior into the waters of baptism would do well to ask themselves the question put forth by the Lord: "The baptism of John, whence was it? from heaven, or of men?" (Matt 21:25, Mark 11:30; Luke 20:4)

Throughout his mortal ministry, believers in Christ were baptized. Under the Savior's direct supervision, more believers were baptized by his apostles than by John the Baptist. (John 4:1) Among other things, Pharisees and lawyers were condemned because they "rejected the counsel of God . . . being not baptized of him." (Luke 7:30) On the other hand, publicans and sinners were commended for being baptized. (Luke 7:28)

The resurrected Lord commanded his disciples to preach the gospel and to baptize in the name of each member of the Godhead:

> Go ye therefore, and teach all nations, baptizing them in the name of the Father, and of the Son, and of the Holy Ghost:
> Teaching them to observe all things whatsoever I have commanded you." (Matt 28:19-20)

Thereafter, the chief apostle, Peter, preached the gospel of Jesus Christ to the Jews.

> Now when they heard this, they were pricked in their heart, and said unto Peter and to the rest of the apostles, Men and brethren, what shall we do?
> Then Peter said unto them, Repent, and be baptized every one of you in the name of Jesus Christ for the remission of sins, and ye shall receive the gift of the Holy Ghost. (Acts 2:37-38)

The commandment of the Savior was to teach baptism to all. Peter taught there was no other way. "Be baptized every one" was the commandment he had received from the master, and he imparted it to all who believed.

As noted above, this pattern was followed in the conversion of Cornelius and his household as the gospel was taken to the gentile nations. (Acts 10) Likewise, Saul, later known as Paul, followed this same pattern. (Acts 9:1-18) In both accounts, baptism opened the door to salvation for these believers in Christ.

Elsewhere in the record of the Bible, this pattern repeats itself; all believers come unto Christ through the ordinance of baptism. For example, citizens of Samaria, "when they believed Philip preaching the things concerning the kingdom of God, and the name of Jesus Christ, they were baptized, both men and women." (Acts 8:12) On condition of believing "with all thine heart," Philip baptized an Ethiopian eunuch who confessed Jesus Christ as the Son of God. (Acts 8:35-38) In the city of Philippi, a woman by the name of Lydia believed the teachings of Paul and was baptized along with the rest of her household. (Acts 16:14-15) Likewise, a jailer was baptized with his family, accepting Jesus Christ after the walls of the prison shook and doors of the cells flew open during the incarceration of Paul and Silas. (Acts 16:26-33) Many citizens of Corinth hearing the gospel of Jesus Christ as taught by Paul "believed and were baptized." (Acts 18:8)

As further evidence of the necessity of baptism, Paul re-baptized some when questions arose about the validity of the original ordinance. (Acts 19:1-6) If baptism were an optional ordinance, why would Paul deem it necessary to re-baptize believers? Paul understood and taught in word and deed that believers enter Christ's kingdom through the door of baptism by one having proper authority.

BAPTISM AND "MERITORIOUS WORKS"

Some Protestant writers have pointed to Paul's statement to the Corinthians: "For Christ sent me not to baptize, but to preach the gospel" (1 Cor 1:17), suggesting that "to baptize" is not an essential part of "the gospel." (MacArthur, Gospel, p. 208) However, Paul's words do not draw a distinction between baptizing and the gospel. Rather, the distinction is between baptizing and preaching. These are two separate offices or functions within the church, but both are part of the same church and the same gospel. At times, Christ baptized. (John 3:26) At other times, he presided over the activities of his disciples as they performed the sacred ordinance (John 4:1-2), and he preached the gospel. Christ commanded his disciples to teach all nations and to baptize. Paul baptized believers (Acts 19:1-6 and 1 Cor 1:14-16), and he made no distinction between baptism and the gospel. For him, it was all one whole: "One Lord, one faith, and one baptism." (Eph 4:5)

Most Protestants reject baptism as a requirement for salvation, in part, because their predecessors classified it as a "good work," sometimes referred to as "meritorious works." (MacArthur, Gospel, pp. 47 and 120; Lutzer, HYCBS, pp. 110-111) Despite this unwillingness to acknowledge baptism as necessary for salvation, most Protestant denominations require some practice or ritual in its place. (MacArthur, Gospel, p. 214) For example, many Protestant denominations teach that one must confess Jesus Christ. Paul's writings support this practice:

> That if thou shalt confess with thy mouth the Lord Jesus, and shalt believe in thine heart that God hath raised him from the dead, thou shalt be saved. For with the heart man believeth unto righteousness; and with the mouth confession is made unto salvation. (Rom 10:9-10)

However, confessing Jesus Christ is a good work in the same way that baptism is a good work. Protestant teachings seem inconsistent in requiring the good work of confession while denying the necessity of baptism.

This inconsistency extends to other outward ordinances substituted for baptism in Protestant practices. A ritual similar to the following is employed in many Protestant congregations when accepting Christ:

> The auditorium was as hot with emotion as with the breath and the sweat of six thousand devotees who had shouted and sung and praised through the night at every call from the temporary pulpit on stage. The evangelist had reached the climax of his final exultation from the Word. In tones the more electric for their hushed energy, he calls for all who will accept Christ to come forward. Those who respond are assisted by an aide who leads them in a short written prayer. They are given information on how they can grow in Christ and a list of local churches where they can be discipled. Those who say the prayer sincerely are assured that they have received Christ and have been saved. The joy of the moment is one the penitent will cherish for years to come. (Hopkins, p. 165)

Responding to the evangelist's call and reciting a prescribed prayer are examples of ritual and good works. Despite Biblical evidence of baptism being the ordinance required by the Lord to enter his kingdom, Protestants deny its efficacy and substitute other outward symbols. In making these substitutions, they risk being the means of fulfilling the prophecy of Isaiah, "The earth also is defiled under the inhabitants thereof; because they have transgressed the laws, *changed the ordinance*, broken the everlasting covenant." (Isa 24:5; emphasis added)

THE NATURE OF GOD'S PROMISES

The second point of Protestant variance on requirements for salvation involves the nature of God's promises concerning salvation, specifically the degree to which they are unconditional. In some Protestant theology, when one enters into Christ's kingdom at the moment of faith, salvation is guaranteed unconditionally. This doctrine has been referred to as "positionalism" because they believe that those who receive the Lord's grace have a permanent "position" in Christ that cannot be altered. (Chafer/Walvoord, pp. 206-7; MacArthur, Gospel, pp. 157, 162-3; Hodges, p. 14; Thieme, p. 23; Evans, pp. 55-62, 70; Gibbs, p. 51; Lutzer, HYCBS, pp. 113 and 193)

UNCONDITIONAL GUARANTEES

Protestants often cite passages in the Bible that refer to being sealed as evidence of positionalism or unconditional salvation. For example, Paul writes,

In whom [Christ] we have obtained an inheritance, being predestinated according to the purpose of him who worketh all things after the counsel of his own will.

In whom ye also trusted, after that ye heard the word of truth, the gospel of your salvation: in whom also after that ye believed, ye were sealed with that holy Spirit of promise,

Which is the earnest [or pledge] of our inheritance . . . (Eph 1:11,13-14; "pledge" is used in the NASB translation)

Some Protestants see in this passage unconditional promises of "inheritances . . . sealed with that holy Spirit of promise." All is assured by God who elects or "predestinates" those who will be saved. (Chafer/Walvoord, pp. 227-34; Evans, p. 62; Little, p. 84; Gibbs, p. 41; Lutzer, HYCBS, pp. 193-4)

However, in this and similar citations, Paul does not define the nature of these "promises" or "inheritances" as either conditional or unconditional. While many Protestants assert they are unconditional, it is not necessarily so. For example, legal contracts containing "promises" and "inheritances" are attested to, witnessed, often notarized and "sealed," but many of these contracts contain provisions and conditions that must be met to qualify for promised benefits.

A related line of reasoning often used in Protestant writings is drawn from comforting teachings of the Apostle Paul:

And we know that all things work together for good to them that love God, to them who are the called according to his purpose.

Moreover whom he did predestinate, them he also called: and whom he called, them he also justified: and whom he justified, them he also glorified.

What shall we then say to these things? If God be for us, who can be against us? (Rom 8:28, 30-31)

The reasoning follows a line something like this. Since "all things work together for good" and "God be for us," then it would be impossible for one to lose the ultimate "good,"—salvation, once attained. God has chosen or "predestinated" those who will be "justified" and "glorified," and nothing can alter His fixed determination to save His elect.

The logic of the argument is inescapable when applied to God's part in salvation. God is perfect and unchanging. He has established conditions which work together for good. He is immutable in his desire to bless and glorify his children. He is always for us. God will do his part to bring man to salvation. He will call man. He will justify man. He will glorify man. And nothing can overrule his will to save us.

However, this does not translate into an unconditional promise of salvation without regard to man's choices and actions. Throughout sacred writ, the Savior promises to confirm us (1 Cor 1:8-9) and not forsake us. (Heb 13:5) However, these promises speak only of his steadfastness, not of ours. Christ will not forsake us, but we may forsake him. He stands at the door and knocks, but we must listen to his voice and open the door. (Rev 3:20) Likewise, his sheep hear his voice and follow their master. (John 10:27-28) Though he remains the shepherd, many will refuse to understand or to follow. God will not force one to be saved, destroying man's moral agency.

A few verses later in this same epistle to the Romans, Paul records:

I am persuaded, that neither death, nor life, nor angels, nor principalities, nor powers, nor things present, nor things to come,

Nor height, nor depth, nor any other creature, shall be able to separate us from the love of God, which is in Christ Jesus our Lord. (Rom 8:38-39)

In his list of forces incapable of separating us from Christ, Paul omits personal rebellion and sin. Death, life, angels, principalities, powers, etc. will not come between us and our Lord, but personal sin will, if we remain unrepentant. "For the wages of sin is death." (Rom 6:23)

Further evidence put forth by some Protestant faithful that salvation is a "*fait accompli*," places particular emphasis on the use of the past tense in key passages of scripture. (Evans, p. 67; MacArthur, Gospel, pp. 73-3; Hopkins, pp. 150-2) For some, Paul's wording provides evidence of unconditional salvation, for in Christ we *have obtained* an inheritance. The same logic is employed relative to passages identifying those who have been saved. For example, "the preaching of the cross is to them that perish foolishness; but *unto us which are saved* it is the power of God." (1 Cor 1:18; emphasis added; see also 2 Tim 1:9)

An alternative way of understanding Paul's teachings is illustrated through the use of an analogy. Suppose a woman is adrift at sea and struggling to survive when she is thrown a life preserver. The moment she lays hold of the preserver, it is perfectly accurate to say she has been saved. Her salvation no longer depends primarily on her own efforts to stay afloat. Provided she clings to the preserver as it is reeled into the safety of the waiting ship, she is certain of deliverance.

However, if she lets go of the preserver and proceeds on her own, she will relinquish the promise of salvation. Furthermore, even when she is safely on board the ship, there is no absolute certainty she will not fall back into perilous waters unless she avoids circumstances that might endanger her. She "has been saved" as long as she does her small but essential part.

In a similar way, Paul would be perfectly accurate in referring to inheritances and being saved in the past tense after one has entered Christ's kingdom through the new covenant of baptism. However, this does not necessarily imply the absence of conditions by which these promises can be forfeited.

Such a conclusion fits Protestant theology without establishing the correctness of the underlying doctrine. Many other Biblical passages plainly reveal conditional provisions of God's promises regarding the salvation of his children.

MAKING ONE'S ELECTION SURE

The Apostle Peter wrote of the promises of salvation, imploring the faithful to be diligent in making their calling and election sure.

Whereby are given unto us exceeding great and precious promises: that by these ye might be partakers of the divine nature . . .

Wherefore the rather, brethren, give diligence to make your calling and election sure: for if ye do these things, ye shall never fall:

For so an entrance shall be ministered unto you abundantly into the everlasting kingdom of our Lord and Saviour Jesus Christ. (2 Pet 1:4, 10-11)

When individuals enter Christ's kingdom, they become recipients of precious promises. Peter indicates these precious promises of salvation are given unto us; that is, to all members of the church. However, Peter is clear that these precious promises are conditional at first. Only following another event, when one's calling and election are made sure, does Peter indicate that "ye shall never fall." (2 Pet 1:10) The reception of precious promises and one's calling and election being made sure occur at separate occasions divided by time. Hence, Peter's appeal to "give diligence to make your calling and election sure." (2 Pet 1:10) Only "if ye do these things" (2 Pet 1:10) do believers in Christ receive assurances they "shall never fall." And what are "these things" to which Peter refers in verse ten? They are those things cited in the preceding verses (2 Pet 1:4-9) which include escaping the corruption of the world, being diligent in faith, virtue, knowledge, temperance, patience, godliness, kindness and charity. According to these teachings, the promises of salvation are conditional until one's calling and election are made sure.

Consistent with Peter's teachings, Paul points to future promises available only to those who obey Gods' will: "Cast not away therefore your confidence, which hath great recompense of reward. For ye have need of patience, *that, after ye have done the will of God*, ye might receive the promise." (Heb 10:35-36; emphasis added) According to Paul, it is appropriate to cling with confidence to assurances of a great reward, but the guarantee, or more sure promise, of that reward is not granted when one enters Christ's kingdom. It is received only after much patience in doing the will of God.

As further evidence, Paul revealed in his epistle to the Philippians that he had not yet attained this more sure promise for himself, at that time. Rather, he was striving to have his calling and election made sure.

I have suffered the loss of all things, and do count them but dung,
that I may win Christ,

And be found in him . . .

That I may know him, and the power of his resurrection, and the
fellowship of his sufferings . . .

Not as though I had already attained, either were already perfect:
but I follow after, if that I may apprehend that for which also I am
apprehended of Christ Jesus.

Brethren, *I count not myself to have apprehended:*

But this one thing I do, forgetting those things which are behind,
and reaching forth unto those things which are before,

*I press toward the mark for the prize of the high calling of God in
Christ Jesus.* (Philip 3:8-10,12-14; emphasis added)

If Paul did not count himself as having attained the prize in Jesus
Christ, it seems presumptive for some Protestants to insist on permanent salvation secured in the moment of faith. Promises of eternal life
gave Paul hope and sustained him through his suffering and losses.
However, these promises did not include more sure assurances that he
had already apprehended the prize. Rather, it was the desire of Paul's
heart to attain that more certain assurance. For this cause, he pressed
forward in Christ.

This humble admission by Paul follows his counsel to the
Philippian saints to "work out your own salvation with fear and trembling." (Philip 2:12) If salvation were guaranteed at the moment of
faith as taught by many Protestants, Paul's exhortation would be
unnecessary and confusing. If salvation were assured, there would be
no place for fear and trembling and no need to work. Paul's words only
make sense if promises of salvation are conditional until after one's
calling and election are made sure.

This conditional state that appropriately invokes fear and trembling
on our part is obviously different from the secure state of unconditional guarantees in Protestant theology. At the same time, it is distinctly
different from the rigid justice of Mosaic law. Perfect adherence to
every fine point of the law is not required. Rather, the Lord requires
perseverance, or in other words, a striving to walk in his footsteps and
abide in the covenant. This will require regular repentance and continued effort.

Accordingly, Paul taught we can "[forget] those things which are behind" (Philip 3:13) or past, once we repent. Christ has atoned for past sins. Our attention should be on the future "reaching forth unto those things which are before" us. (Philip 3:13) Striving to obtain the prize which Paul and all other faithful saints desire above all else: the pearl of great price spoken of by the Savior for which man must be willing to sell all he has. (Matt 13:46)

The Savior entreated his followers:

> Come unto me, all ye that labour and are heavy laden, and I will give you rest.
>
> Take my yoke upon you, and learn of me; for I am meek and lowly in heart: and ye shall find rest unto your souls.
>
> For my yoke is easy, and my burden is light. (Matt 11:28-30)

Compared to the unbending justice of the law and the weight of personal sin, Christ's yoke is easy and his burden is light. However, there is a yoke that we take upon ourselves which keeps us in his way, and there is a burden which we bear in persevering to follow his example and abide in the new covenant.

The teachings of many Protestant faithful would suggest no yoke and no burden; that salvation is guaranteed without condition beyond accepting Christ at the moment of faith. The teachings of the Bible make it clear that man has a yoke and a burden to work out his salvation with fear and trembling before God. Only after much diligence is the promise of salvation made unconditional; when one has his calling and election made sure.

A FALL FROM GRACE

One of the clearest indications that salvation is conditional after entering Christ's kingdom is the doctrine plainly evident in the Bible regarding a fall from grace. For example, in his second epistle, Peter implores his readers to stay unspotted from the sins and corruption of the world so as to not violate the conditions of the promise and lose their reward.

> For if after they [believers] have escaped the pollutions of the world through the knowledge of the Lord and Savior Jesus Christ, they are again entangled therein, and overcome, the latter end is worse with them than the beginning.

For it had been better for them not to have known the way of righteousness, than, after they have known it, to turn from the holy commandment delivered unto them. (2 Pet 2:20-21)

Again, Peter's words stand in stark contrast to teachings of positionalism or unconditional salvation. Those who become entangled in
the ways of the world after receiving a knowledge of the Lord Jesus
Christ are worse off than if they had never known of their Savior and
his way of righteousness.

Peter's teachings parallel Jesus' parable of the sower:

And some [seed] fell upon a rock; and as soon as it was sprung up,
it withered away, because it lacked moisture.

And some fell among thorns; and the thorns sprang up with it, and
choked it. (Luke 8:6-7)

Later, the Savior provided his own interpretation as to the meaning of
this parable:

They on the rock are they, which when they hear, receive the word
with joy; and these have no root, which for a while believe, and in time
of temptation fall away.

And that which fell among thorns are they, which, when they have
heard, go forth, and are choked with cares and riches and pleasures of
this life, and bring no fruit to perfection. (Luke 8:13-14)

In both cases, believers received the good word with joy; one might
suppose they experienced the moment of faith. However, in both cases,
these believers eventually fell. Their moment of faith did not secure
salvation unconditionally.

Paul also wrote about falling from grace after accepting Jesus
Christ. Twice, in his letter to the Hebrews, Paul refers to the destiny that
awaits those who fall away after embracing truth:

For it is impossible for those who were once enlightened, and have
tasted of the heavenly gift, and were made partakers of the Holy Ghost,

And have tasted the good word of God, and the powers of the world
to come,

If they shall fall away to renew them again unto repentance . . .

But that which beareth thorns and briers is rejected, and is nigh unto
cursing; whose end is to be burned." (Heb 6:4-6,8)

Later in the same epistle, Paul taught:

> For if we sin wilfully after that we have received the knowledge of the truth, there remaineth no more sacrifice for sins,
>
> But a certain fearful looking for of judgment and fiery indignation, which shall devour the adversaries. (Heb 10:26-27)

John the Beloved also instructed believers of his day that they could lose their reward by not abiding in the teachings of the Savior after having accepted them:

> Look to yourselves, that we lose not those things which we have wrought, but that we receive a full reward.
>
> Whosoever transgresseth, and abideth not in the doctrine of Christ, hath not God. He that abideth in the doctrine of Christ, he hath both the Father and the Son. (2 John 1:8-9)

To be saved is to return to the Father and the Son, but one who languishes in transgression will never dwell with the Father, or as John puts it, he "hath not God."

Teachings in the Bible regarding the possibility of losing salvation have been addressed to some extent by Protestant theologians. Lordship Protestants are clearly more comfortable with this doctrine than their No-Lordship counterparts. (Chafer/Walvoord, pp. 220-8)

According to Lordship Protestants, a fall from grace will occur when an individual's works do not demonstrate the effects of true conversion at the moment of faith. When good works do not follow, Lordship Protestants insist that the individual never really received the Lord's grace in the first place. A leading Lordship proponent writes:

> The point is not that God guarantees heaven to everyone who professes faith in Christ, but rather that those whose faith is genuine will never totally or finally fall away from Christ . . . True believers will persevere. Professing Christians who turn against the Lord only prove that they were never truly saved. (MacArthur, Gospel, p. 105)

No-Lordship Protestants have been generally unwilling to entertain the possibility of a fall from grace for believers. According to this school of thought, "there is no salvation purposed, offered, or undertaken under grace which is not infinitely perfect and that does not abide forever." (Chafer/Walvoord, p. 228, also see Gibbs, pp. 83-4; Lutzer, HYCBS, p. 150) Instead, No-Lordship Protestants have suggested that a fall from grace refers only to blessings forfeited in this life or the next, without jeopardizing one's ultimate salvation. "Believers can fall away, but not to eternal damnation." (Lutzer, HYCBS, p. 151; see also Chafer/Walvoord, pp. 285-6; Connelly, pp. 118-9)

Neither position adequately addresses teachings in the Bible concerning a fall from grace because neither accepts the Biblical precept that true believers can lose salvation after experiencing God's grace. On this point, it is hard to imagine how Paul could have been any clearer in describing those at risk of losing their salvation. They include:

> those who were once enlightened, and have tasted of the heavenly gift,
> and were made partakers of the Holy Ghost, and have tasted the good word of God and the powers of the world to come. (Heb 6:4-5)

When such an individual falls, the result is loss of personal salvation. These fallen souls will not be renewed through repentance, but will be "rejected" and "burned" with the damned. If true believers can fall from grace, as is plainly taught in the Bible, then salvation must be conditional at the time one enters Christ's kingdom.

THE ROLE OF GOOD WORKS

This brings us to the third major difference in doctrine related to requirements for salvation, namely, the role of good works. Because Latter-day Saints maintain that good works and personal striving are necessary conditions for salvation, some Protestants have charged them with fixating on man's responsibility to work out his own salvation rather than humbly rejoicing in the redeeming gift of grace. (Ankerberg, pp. 88, 445) From the perspective of many Protestants, this produces self-righteous pride and an overstated sense of importance, which has the effect of devaluing the atonement. (Tillich, ST, pp. 79-86; Niebuhr, p. 105; Lutzer, HYCBS, pp. 110-1) The doctrine of justification by faith alone "insists that all needed to be done for salvation has been done, and done well, in and through Jesus Christ." (McGrath, p. 67)

Latter-day Saints agree with Protestants that some believers try to earn their way back into the presence of God, not understanding that only Christ's atonement can produce salvation. However, this does not mean that personal striving and good works necessarily involve pride or detract from the pre-eminent role of the atonement. As evident in Paul's teachings, above, good works can spring from hope of salvation made possible through Jesus Christ. They can be tempered with humility and gratitude, reflecting a spirit of grace which makes them God's works, not a hollow exercise in rigid conformity and self-abnegation.

To appreciate core differences in Protestant and Latter-day Saint teachings on this point, it is useful to refer to the judgment scene when each man or woman will stand before the Lord. At that moment, Protestants and Latter-day Saints agree that none will merit salvation on his own. When weighed in the balance of justice, all will be found woefully lacking. All will be unclean to varying degrees, but since no unclean thing can enter God's kingdom, (Deut 23:14; Gal 5:19-21), it will be immaterial whether one is more or less unfit to return to the Father.

Standing before God, it is not man's works but the Lord's mediation and grace alone that will save us. His perfect righteousness imputed to others is the only basis for salvation. The teachings of the Apostle Paul speak directly to this point.

> Therefore we conclude that a man is justified by faith without the deeds of the law. (Rom 3:28)
> And if by grace, then is it no more of works: otherwise grace is no more grace. (Rom 11:6)
> Jesus Christ "hath saved us, and called us with an holy calling, not according to our works, but according to his own purpose and grace . . ." (1 Tim 1:9)
> by grace are ye saved through faith; and that not of yourselves: it is the gift of God: not of works, lest any man should boast. (Eph 2:8-9)

In this sense, Latter-day Saints agree, "all needed to be done for salvation has been done, and done well, in and through Jesus Christ." (McGrath, p. 67)

However, this is not the totality of the answer given by the Savior when asked, "What shall I do to inherit eternal life?" (Luke 18:18) Since Christ is the author of our salvation, any conditions stipulated by him for receiving his mediation become requirements for salvation. Most Protestants agree with Latter-day Saints that such requirements exist and must be met to receive his mediation. In fact, these requirements constitute terms and conditions of man's part in the new covenant of grace. The basic disagreement between Latter-day Saints and Protestants lies in a different understanding of what Christ requires of man in the new covenant.

According to No-Lordship teachings, the only requirement of the new covenant is to accept Jesus Christ as our personal Savior at the moment of faith when God's elect are designated. "We must believe that Christ did all that is necessary and ever will be necessary for us to stand in the sight of God . . . If God is satisfied with the death of Christ, we should be, too. And when we are, we no longer owe God any righteousness." (Lutzer, HYCBS, pp. 113, 124)

Lordship Protestants, and other Christians, are troubled that people who do not repent are considered born again by No-Lordship Christians. According to Lordship teachings, "Genuine assurance [of salvation] comes from seeing the Holy Spirit's transforming work in one's life, not from clinging to the memory of some experience." (MacArthur, Gospel, p. 29)

Lordship teachings walk a fine line, insisting on obedience and submission to God, while denying the role of works. "Here is the test of true faith: Are you willing to do what (the Savior) wants you to do? . . . Repentance and submission are no more human works than faith itself. They are every bit the work of God." (*Ibid.*, p. 94; see also Bonheoffer, pp. 56, 168; Godsey, p. 154, 163) Following this line of reasoning:

> Salvation by faith does not eliminate works per se. It does away with works that are the result of human effort alone. It abolishes any attempt to merit God's favor by our works. (*Ibid.*, p. 39)

Latter-day Saints could almost agree with Lordship teachings except for two important caveats. *First*, the scriptures make it abundantly clear that *all mankind will be judged according to their works*. (2 Cor 5:10, Rom 14:12, Rev 20:12, 1 Pet 4:17-18) Those who accept Jesus Christ will be judged mercifully within the covenant of grace, but works will be used to determine if one has honored his part in the new covenant. Those who do not accept Jesus Christ by entering into the new covenant will also be judged according to their works, but without benefit of mercy. *Second*, contrary to Protestant teachings, personal effort and striving are necessary to persevere in righteousness, and they are commended by the Lord and his servants.

These two qualifiers then become the basis for judging the correctness of Latter-day Saint and Protestant doctrine related to requirements for salvation. If Protestant teachings are correct, good works are not part of the new covenant and will not be considered when the Savior bestows salvation on his followers. Good works may be in evidence among believers, but they will play no significant role in sorting the sheep from the goats in the final judgment. On the other hand, if doctrines of salvation as taught by Latter-day Saints are correct, then good works are a significant condition of the new covenant and will be featured prominently as a consideration used by the Savior to determine salvation on the day of judgment.

Likewise, if Protestant teachings are correct, personal striving is not commended in the scriptures, while the opposite would be true, if Latter-day Saint teachings are correct. Once again, we turn to the Bible seeking understanding of how the Savior will determine salvation for all individuals.

CHRIST: GOOD WORKS ESSENTIAL FOR SALVATION

Fortunately, the ultimate, authoritative source addressed this very issue head-on in the Bible. Twice the question was posed to the Savior, "Master, what shall I do to inherit eternal life?" (Luke 10:25-37 and Matt 19:16-22; see also Mark 10:17-22; Luke 18:18-23) In the first instance, the scriptures inform us that a "certain lawyer stood up and tempted [Jesus]." The Savior's response was to turn the query back to the questioner, "What is written in the law? How readest thou?" The lawyer summarized the law, "Thou shalt love the Lord thy God with all thy heart, and with all thy soul, and with all thy strength, and with all they mind; and thy neighbour as thyself." The Lord approved of this answer and said, "Thou hast answered right: this do, and thou shalt live. But [the lawyer], willing to justify himself, said unto Jesus, And who is my neighbour?" The Savior then expounded the parable of the good Samaritan. At the end of this parable, Jesus asked the lawyer, "Which now of these three, thinkest thou, was neighbour unto him that fell among the thieves? And he said, He that shewed mercy on him. Then said Jesus unto him, Go and do likewise." (Luke 10:25-37)

It is significant to note that the answer given by the Savior, from beginning to end, emphasizes the importance of good works. He referred to the law. He admonished the lawyer twice to do righteous works in loving and caring for his neighbor. The priest and the Levite were not commended, but only the doer of good works was held up as an example to answer the question: What shall I do to inherit eternal life.

The second instance of the Savior responding to this question is even more supportive of requirements of good works in qualifying for the gift of salvation. The one posing the question is described as a young man of great possessions. Jesus answered him, "If thou wilt enter into life, keep the commandments." (Matt 19:17) The young man asked for clarification about which commandments. The Savior proceeded to cite a number of the ten commandments. "The young man saith unto him, All these things have I kept from my youth up: what lack I yet?" (Matt 19:20)

If salvation is by grace alone, as taught by most Protestants, what could he possibly lack? He acknowledges the Savior as the "good master." His heart seems pure. His questions are sincere. His faith has produced a life of good works that proceed from true devotion to God. So what did he lack? Did he lack an experience with grace? Did he lack true conversion and a change of heart?

The answer from his Savior indicated none of these. "If thou wilt be perfect, go and sell that thou hast, and give to the poor, and thou shalt have treasure in heaven: and come and follow me." (Matt 19:21; see also Matt 19:16-22) For this young man of great possessions, the requirements for salvation included sacrificing all he possessed for the work of the Lord, a good work, indeed.

This sacrifice is somewhat reminiscent of the trial of Abraham. As the writer of the epistle of James explains:

> Seest thou how faith wrought with his works, and by works was faith made perfect?
>
> Ye see then how that by works a man is justified, and not by faith only. (James 2:22,24)

Unfortunately, the young man was not up to this trial of his faith, and accordingly, he did not receive the same promises as Abraham.

These two instances constitute only a portion of the teachings of Jesus Christ regarding requirements for salvation. In chapter 25 of Matthew, the Savior describes the day of judgment when all will be brought before him to be judged:

> When the Son of man shall come in his glory, and all the holy angels with him, then shall he sit upon the throne of his glory:

And before him shall be gathered all nations: and he shall separate them one from another, as a shepherd divideth his sheep from the goats:

And he shall set the sheep on his right hand, but the goats on the left.

Then shall the King say unto them on his right hand, Come, ye blessed of the Father, inherit the kingdom prepared for you from the foundation of the world. (Matt 25:31-34)

And what will be the basis for dividing those who are on the right hand from those on the left? The Lord's explanation clearly points to good works:

For I was an hungered, and ye gave me meat: I was thirsty, and ye gave me drink: I was a stranger and ye took me in:

Naked, and ye clothed me: I was sick, and ye visited me: I was in prison and ye came unto me.

Inasmuch as ye have done it unto one of the least of these my brethren, ye have done it unto me. (Matt 25:35-40)

In the Sermon on the Mount, the Savior describes those who will qualify for salvation in the kingdom of heaven. "Not every one that saith unto me, Lord, Lord, shall enter into the kingdom of heaven; *but he that doeth the will of my Father* which is in heaven." (Matt 7:21; emphasis added)

In addition, at least one parable taught by the Savior, the parable of the talents, clearly speaks to requirements for salvation. In this parable, the Lord entrusts five talents to the first servant, two to the second servant and a single talent to the third:

After a long time the lord of those servants cometh, and reckoneth with them.

And so he that received five talents came and brought other five talents, saying, Lord, thou deliveredst unto me five talents: behold I have gained beside them five talents more.

His lord said unto him, Well done, thou good and faithful servant: thou hast been faithful over a few things, I will make thee ruler over many things: enter thou into the joy of the lord. (Matt 25:19-21)

A similar response is elicited from the lord when the second servant brings forth two talents in addition to those entrusted to him. But the lord casts the third servant into outer darkness because he failed to act prudently in caring for the single talent placed in his care.

In this parable, qualifications for entering into the joy of the lord are directly related to works of the servants. Even the lord's statement of approbation places the emphasis on good works: "Well done."

The parable of the talents is an allegorical statement of doctrine taught more directly by the Savior in other passages of the Bible. "For the Son of man shall come in the glory of his Father with his angels; and then he shall reward every man according to his works." (Matt 16:27) Also, "If thou wilt enter into life, keep the commandments." (Matt 19:17; see also, Matt 10:38, John 15:14 and 14:15)

APOSTLES AND PROPHETS: GOOD WORKS REQUIRED FOR SALVATION

Other writers of the holy scriptures have pointed to good works as a requirement for receiving God's gift of salvation. The Apostle Paul writes, in the same epistle used by most Protestants as the cornerstone of their belief in salvation by grace alone, that:

> [God] will render to every man according to his deeds:
>
> To them who by patient continuance in well doing seek for glory and honour and immortality, [God grants] eternal life.
>
> glory, honour, and peace, to every man that worketh good . . ." (Rom 2:6,7,10)

The Psalmist records: "Also unto thee, O Lord, belongeth mercy: for thou renderest to every man according to his work." (Ps 62:12)

The Revelator saw in vision the day of judgment:

> And I saw the dead, small and great, stand before God; and the books were opened: and another book was opened, which is the book of life: and the dead were judged out of those things which were written in the books, *according to their works.*
>
> and they were judged every man according to their works. (Rev 20:12-13; emphasis added)

Other passages supporting the necessity of good works in attaining salvation include: "He that overcometh shall inherit all things . . ." (Rev 21:7) "Blessed are they that do his commandments, that they may have right to the tree of life . . ." (Rev 22:14) "Blessed is the man that endureth temptation: for when he is tried, he shall receive the crown of life . . ." (James 1:12) "but the doers of the law shall be justified." (Rom 2:13) "And being made perfect, he [Christ] became the

author of eternal salvation *unto all them that obey him.*" (Heb 5:9)
After calling on the Saints of Sardis to repent, the resurrected Lord
instructed the Revelator to write, "He that overcometh, the same shall
be clothed in white raiment; and I . . . will confess his name before my
Father and before his angels." (Rev 3:5) These passages of scripture
clearly suggest an essential role for good works in qualifying for the
Savior's greatest gift—salvation. They stand in stark contrast to asser-
tions by some Protestants that "A carnal Christian is as perfectly saved
as the spiritual Christian." (Chafer/Walvoord, p. 214)

The Old Testament prophet, Ezekiel, spoke of the Lord's judgment
and of the measure that would be used to determine salvation. These
writings seem to foretell teachings of many Protestants with prophetic
insight and relevance:

> When I shall say to the righteous, that he shall surely live; if he trust
> to his own righteousness, and commit iniquity, all his righteousnesses
> shall not be remembered; but for his iniquity that he hath committed,
> he shall die for it.
>
> Again, when I say unto the wicked, Thou shalt surely die; if he turn
> from his sin, and do that which is lawful and right;
>
> If the wicked restore the pledge, give again that he had robbed,
> walk in the statutes of life, without committing iniquity; he shall sure-
> ly live, he shall not die.
>
> None of his sins that he hath committed shall be mentioned unto
> him: he hath done that which is lawful and right; he shall surely live.
>
> When the righteous turneth from his righteousness, and committeth
> iniquity, he shall even die thereby.
>
> But if the wicked turn from his wickedness, and do that which is
> lawful and right, he shall live thereby.
>
> Yet ye say, The way of the Lord is not equal. O ye house of Israel,
> I will judge you every one after his ways. (Ezek 33:13-16,18-20)

In this passage, Ezekiel teaches eternal truths that will be operative
on judgment day. Those who take for granted promises of salvation and
do not continue in righteousness will lose their reward. Those who turn
from wickedness and repent of their sins in the Lord will live with the
Father eternally. The Savior will judge "every one after his ways," or in
other words, according to their works.

Ezekiel's teachings apply equally to those who have accepted
Christ. His words are echoed in the counsel of Paul to the Romans:

Let not sin therefore reign in your mortal body, that ye should obey it in the lusts thereof.

Neither yield ye your members as instruments of unrighteousness unto sin: But yield yourselves unto God, as those that are alive from the dead, and your members as instruments of righteousness unto God.

For sin shall not have dominion over you: for ye are not under the law, but under grace.

What then? shall we sin, because we are not under the law, but under grace? God forbid.

Know ye not, that *to whom ye yield yourselves servants to obey, his servants ye are to whom ye obey;* whether of sin unto death, or of obedience unto righteousness? (Rom 6:12-16; emphasis added)

There is nothing subtle or complicated about the measure to be used by the Lord in sorting his sheep from the goats. The Apostle John taught the straightforward test of righteousness:

Little children, let no man deceive you: he that doeth righteousness is righteous, even as [Christ] is righteous.

He that committeth sin is of the devil . . . Whosoever is born of God doth not commit sin . . .

In this the children of God are manifest, and the children of the devil. (1 John 3:7-10)

According to Paul, John and all apostles and prophets of Jesus Christ, the consequence of personal sin is death. Obedience to God in the pattern of the Savior is necessary for receiving and retaining promises of salvation.

THE BIBLE COMMENDS RIGHTEOUS STRIVING

Throughout the Bible, good works are inextricably linked to righteous striving. According to most Protestant doctrine, those touched by grace will naturally perform good works. Little or no effort is required on their part. By comparison, Latter-day Saints teach that salvation does not come easily. A popular saying captures the sense of personal sacrifice required by the Savior. "I never said it would be easy. I only said it would be worth it." Personal struggling and righteous striving are commended and necessary to attain salvation.

The Apostle Paul, he who expounded grace more than anyone else, acknowledged his own struggles with human weaknesses. "For the good that I would I do not: but the evil which I would not, that I do." (Rom 7:19) Despite lapses and failings, Paul continued to struggle and strive to overcome sin in his life. Good works required effort on his part.

This willingness to struggle with the "sin that dwelleth in me [man]" (Rom 7:20), is what separates the faithful and righteous from those who have been touched by the spirit but do not persevere. As in the parable of the sower, it is not just the seed (the gospel and God's grace), but it is also the condition of the ground (the submissiveness of the individual soul), that determines the harvest. (Mark 4:3-8)

The life of Paul provides a good case in point. Everyone will agree Paul was a recipient of grace, yet he continued to struggle with the "law in [his] members, warring against the law of [his] mind, and bringing [him] into captivity to the law of sin . . ." (Rom 7:23) Toward the end of his life, Paul wrote to Timothy from Rome, where he would be condemned to die. "For I am now ready to be offered, and the time of my departure is at hand. I have fought a good fight, I have finished my course, I have kept the faith." (1 Tim 4:6-7)

These are not the words of a man for whom good works naturally flow without significant personal effort. Paul is describing a "*war*," a "*fight*" to the finish. Paul believed in his heart that he would be honored and glorified by his Savior, in part, because he was working out his own salvation with fear and trembling.

Paul was earnestly striving for his salvation, not just following promptings of grace. His motivations were clear. "Henceforth there is laid up for me a crown of righteousness, which the Lord, the righteous judge, shall give me at that day." (1 Tim 4:8)

> Know ye not that they which run in a race run all, but one receiveth the prize? So run, that ye may obtain.
>
> Now they do it to obtain a corruptible crown; but we an incorruptible.
>
> But I keep under my body, and bring it into subjection: lest that by any means . . . I myself should be a castaway. (1 Cor 9:24-27)

In Paul's life, salvation was not assured without personal effort and sacrifice. He counseled to "strive for the mastery" (1 Cor 9:25), inviting others to participate in the race. "So run, that ye may obtain." (1 Cor 9:24) He endeavored to control his own "body, and bring it into subjection" (1 Cor 9:27), relying on the grace of God to secure a "crown," eternal life. Paul understood what one Lordship proponent calls "the twin truths": "salvation is a gift, yet it costs everything." (MacArthur, Gospel, p. 37)

The Savior invites us to "Strive to enter in at the strait gate." (Luke 13:24) "The Greek word for 'strive' is *agonizomai*, implying an agonizing, intense, purposeful struggle." (*Ibid.*, p. 206) Commending such purposeful efforts, the prophet Jeremiah recorded the words of the Lord, "And ye shall seek me, and find me, when ye shall search for me with all your heart." (Jer 29:13) The Apostle Peter also understood salvation does not come without personal effort and sacrifice. He taught, "if the righteous scarcely be saved, where shall the ungodly and the sinner appear?" (1 Pet 4:18)

This does not mean personal striving is the most important element in the process of working out our salvation. Without God's grace, man's efforts will be insufficient to turn away from sin and lay hold of salvation. Latter-day Saints resonate with the wisdom of Reverend Billy Graham when he writes, "The best resolution will not overcome the enemy . . . As long as you try by your own strength, you will fail." (Graham, Answer, p. 121) Consistent with Reverend Graham, Latter-day Saints counsel those dealing with temptation to pray, read the scriptures, avoid evil influences and adhere to true principles in obedience. (*Ibid.*, pp. 121-2) Striving alone is not enough, but righteous striving is never alone. The Lord's grace will change our desires and give us strength to overcome. However, man is expected to do his small part, abiding in the covenant of grace.

ALL PREREQUISITES SPECIFIED IN SCRIPTURE NECESSARY

In light of the many foregoing scriptures, one might wonder how it is possible for most Protestants to cleave to a doctrine of salvation by grace alone, denying an essential role for good works. This doctrine can only be supported by focusing on selected passages of scripture while ignoring many others requiring good works for salvation.

This will not surprise Protestants familiar with their own history. Martin Luther was well-acquainted with passages in the Bible that seem to contradict his notions of justification by faith alone. He referred to the Epistle of James, which clearly teaches the importance of good works, as "an epistle of straw" having "no gospel quality to it." (Peterson and Ricks, p. 125) "We should throw the Epistle of James out of this school (University of Wittenberg), because it's worthless." (*Ibid,*) He spoke of the Sermon on the Mount as "the devil's master-piece" (Ibid, p. 126) because of its clear references to the importance of works. His favorite epistle of Paul was Romans, the most supportive of his position, or so it would seem to some. As one Protestant theologian has stated, "Luther read the whole Bible as a corollary of the Pauline teachings of justification." (Marty, p. 105)

Like Martin Luther, many Protestants appear to support the doctrine of salvation by grace alone by referring to select passages that can be construed to provide support for cherished notions. It has been documented by one former minister that the number of "works" passages in the Bible far exceeds those referring to grace. (Morgan, p. 120)

But even if only one works passage appeared in the Bible, the teachings of Protestant denominations would still need to account for a requirement clearly taught in this sacred canon. All inspired scripture must harmonize. Certainly, grace passages do not nullify additional conditions for salvation set forth clearly in other portions of the Bible. Correct doctrines of Christ reconcile and unify requirements of grace and good works as taught in the complete canon of scripture.

On this crucial dimension, Protestant teachings of salvation by grace alone appear to miss the mark. When the Savior teaches, "if thou wilt enter into life, keep the commandments" (Matt 19:17), sound doctrine must account for the linkage between salvation and good works. When James proclaims, "by works a man is justified, not by faith only" (James 2:24), it must be acknowledged that good works play a role in salvation far beyond just being evident in the lives of believers. When Jesus informs his listeners, "the Son of Man . . . shall reward every man according to his works" (Matt 16:27), and this is the witness of Paul (Rom 2:6-13), the Psalmist (Ps 62:12), and John (Rev 20:12-13), it should be evident to seekers of truth that more is required following the moment of faith. When Paul teaches, "[Christ] became the author of eternal salvation *unto all them that obey him*" (Heb 5:9; emphasis added) and the Savior admonishes, "Not every one that saith unto me, Lord, Lord, shall enter into the kingdom of heaven; *but he that doeth the will of my Father* which is in heaven" (Matt 7:21; emphasis added), one would be wise to believe that obedience to God's commandments is more than an optional provision for salvation.

Indeed, the only logical conclusion is that conditions for salvation must include all qualifications specified in scripture, including: grace (Eph 2:8-9), faith (Rom 3:28), confession (Matt 10:32), baptism (Mark 16:16), a change of heart (John 3:3-7), sacrifice (Matt 19:16-19), keeping the commandments (Heb 5:9), well doing (Rom 2:6-10), and enduring to the end (Matt 24:13).

One might inquire with Paul, "Do we then make void the law through faith?" Paul's response was emphatic, "God forbid: yea we establish the law." (Rom 3:31) And so it is when roles of grace and good works are both accounted for properly.

RECONCILING PAUL AND JAMES REGARDING FAITH AND GOOD WORKS

The need to harmonize inspired scripture points to apparent contradictions long recognized by Bible scholars in the writings of Paul and James. Reconciling these teachings provides insight into roles of grace and works in salvation.

Both authors used the example of Abraham to illustrate important teachings regarding personal salvation. On the surface, Paul and James seem to be at odds relative to roles of faith and works. For example, Paul wrote to the Romans:

> For if Abraham were justified by works, he hath whereof to glory; but not before God.
>
> For what saith the scripture?
>
> Abraham believed God, and it was counted unto him for righteousness.
>
> Now to him that worketh is the reward not reckoned of grace, but of debt.
>
> But to him that worketh not, but believeth on him that justifieth the ungodly, his faith is counted for righteousness. (Rom 4:2-5)

By contrast, James seems to offer a different explanation of the means by which Abraham was able to secure salvation:

> Was not Abraham our father justified by works, when he offered Isaac his son upon the altar?

Seest thou how faith wrought with his works, and by works was faith made perfect?

And the scripture was fulfilled which saith, Abraham believed God, and it was imputed unto him for righteousness: and he was called the Friend of God.

Ye see then how that by works a man is justified, and not by faith only. (James 2:21-24)

As a reader of scripture, the natural tendency is to apply a single definition to the same word used elsewhere in the Bible. However, James and Paul clearly define "works" and "faith" somewhat differently. The key to harmonizing their teachings lies in understanding what each inspired writer meant by "faith" and "works."

James makes a distinction between faith separated from works or mental assent, and works flowing from a vibrant commitment to Christ. For James, saving faith is perfected in good works. "By works was faith made perfect." (James 2:22) Mere acceptance of Christ is insufficient to secure salvation. "Thou believest that there is one God; thou doest well: the devils also believe, and tremble." (James 2:19) For James, the condemnation of some believers is that, like devils, they do not act on their beliefs. This kind of superficial faith without works "is dead, being alone." (James 2:17)

By contrast, "Abraham believed God, and it was imputed unto him for righteousness." (James 2:23) Abraham was justified by works because he acted on his beliefs, obeying the will of God. Abraham's faith and good works are an example to all. "Ye see then how that by works a man is justified, and not by faith only." (James 2:24)

For Paul, "works" refer to the dead rituals of the Mosaic law. After describing forgiveness of sin in Christ, Paul asks:

Cometh this blessedness then upon the circumcision only, or upon the uncircumcision also? for we say that faith was reckoned to Abraham for righteousness.

How was it then reckoned? when he was in circumcision, or in uncircumcision? (Rom 4:9-10)

Paul wants us to understand that circumcision and other works of the Mosaic law are no longer necessary to lay hold on promises of salvation. In conforming to the law, man's reward is given as payment of debt. "Now to him that worketh is the reward not reckoned of grace, but of debt." (Rom 4:4) Using this standard, Abraham and all others, excepting only Jesus Christ, fall short, and "the law worketh wrath." (Rom 4:15) Abraham received God's grace because he believed God and exercised faith in performing righteous works.

"Faith," as used by Paul, is not the superficial faith condemned by James. For Paul, faith includes an inner conviction and commitment that produce works of righteousness.

> [Abraham] who against hope believed in hope . . .
>
> staggered not at the promise of God through unbelief; but was strong in faith, giving glory to God
>
> And being fully persuaded that, what [God] had promised, he was able also to perform.
>
> And therefore it was imputed to [Abraham] for righteousness. (Rom 4:18, 20-22)

It is this type of faith which brought salvation to Abraham and will bring salvation to all who exercise it unto righteousness. Paul never taught that the basis for salvation was mere belief or acceptance, separate from action.

The teachings of James and Paul are harmonized only when different definitions for the same words are understood as the inspired writers intended them. When proper definitions are applied, scriptural passages used to defend salvation by grace alone are consistent with other citations in the Bible requiring good works.

> Being justified freely by his grace through the redemption that is in Christ Jesus.
>
> Therefore we conclude that a man is justified by faith [including righteous works] without the deeds of the law [Mosaic rituals and Pharisaic fanaticism]. (Rom 3:24,28)

> For by grace are ye saved through faith [including righteous works]; and that not of yourselves: it is the gift of God:
>
> Not of works [Mosaic ritual and Pharisaic exactness], lest any man should boast. (Eph 2:8-9)

During the Savior's ministry, the Pharisees were uninspired in emphasizing the law above the lawgiver. In our day, the pendulum has swung to the opposite extreme, with Protestants emphasizing grace to the exclusion of good works. A divine balance is struck between God's grace and man's faith, including good works, when man performs his small but essential part. Protestants will be blessed by holding fast to their core beliefs in the redeeming power of Jesus Christ and his grace alone to save mankind. But the Bible clearly informs us there is more. "And every man that hath this hope in him purifieth himself, even as [Christ] is pure." (1 John 3:3)

3

God's Plan
For His Children

From earliest recorded times, men and women have gazed in utter awe at starry heavens and marveled at the order and expanse of the universe. In our day, many of us continue to resonate in reverence with ancestors who have pondered the relative nothingness of man:

> When I consider thy heavens, the work of thy fingers, the moon and the stars, which thou hast ordained;
> What is man, that thou art mindful of him? (Ps 8:4)

Groping for context that gives meaning to our lives and provides direction and relevance to our daily existence, each of us, in his or her own way, poses the most profound questions:

- Where did I come from?
- Where will I go after I die?
- Why am I here on earth?

Latter-day Saints offer a unique perspective in answering these questions and addressing many of the classic problems about human suffering and divine justice that have troubled theologians and philosophers through the ages. The teachings of Latter-day Saints, revealed through modern-day prophets, are consistent with the Bible while contrasting in significant ways with many traditional teachings of other Christian denominations. These inspired doctrines provide insights into passages of scripture and precious truths found in the Biblical record that other Christians cannot explain or fit into their theological framework. The revelation of man's relationship to a loving God offers meaning and eternal hope in a world that too often seems cold and absurd.

WHERE DID I COME FROM?

In answer to this question, traditional Christian theologians expound their dogma of ex nihilo creation. This dogma maintains that man, this world, and all things that comprise the universe, were brought into existence from nothing by God, the creator. Ex nihilo means "from nothing."

TRADITIONAL CHRISTIANS: EX NIHILO CREATION

The *Catholic Encyclopedia* defines ex nihilo creation as "God bring[ing] the entire substance of a thing into existence from a state of nonexistence . . . What is peculiar to creation is the entire absence of any prior subject matter." (R. Appleton, p. 470) Protestant scholar, Paul E. Little, writes, "God created matter ex nihilo (out of nothing). He then formed matter into living objects—plants, animals, and man." (Little, p. 62)

According to this doctrine, there was never a moment in time previous to conception or birth, when man or his soul existed in any way or shape. At the moment of conception or birth, God breathes life into an otherwise lifeless form. "All souls are created by God directly and are infused by being created, and so are produced ex nihilo apart from any pre-existent matter . . . New souls are created daily by God out of nothing." (Heppe, pp. 228-9) The traditional Christian answer to the question of where did we come from is: "We came from nothing; created in an instant by God, our existence began at conception or birth."

This dogma of ex nihilo creation, if it were true, would have major implications for man's eternal destiny. Though the most glorious of God's creations, man would be incapable of ever becoming like God because, according to traditional Christian teachings, man is a creature formed from nothing by a Creator distinctly different in nature and composition from his creation. This relationship between God and man is generally referred to as "creatureliness" and is described by one well-known theologian as:

> This absolute, incomprehensible reality [God] . . . is always infinitely different from the knowing subject [man]. It is also different from the individual, finite things known [creation] . . . Man is the finite existent, God is the absolute infinite. As the absolute and the infinite, God must be absolutely different. (Rahner, *Trinity*, pp. 77-8)

At the same time, man and all things in the universe exist solely because God, in his wisdom, sees fit to create them. "The world is radically dependent on God. It has nothing independent of Him." (*Ibid*) According to the ex nihilo dogma, it is the operation of His inscrutable will that brings man into existence, and each individual situation in this life is determined in the wisdom of God, for a purpose known only to God.

LATTER-DAY SAINTS: A PRE-MORTAL STATE

Latter-day Saints teach that man is a creation of God, organized from natural elements that have always existed. Matter is eternal. The amount of matter in all creation cannot be increased or destroyed, but it can be organized into different forms. (D&C 93:33)

Mortal birth or conception is not the beginning of man's existence. Rather, man's individual identity (referred to as "intelligence" in Latter-day Saint theology) is eternal, the same as all other natural elements. (D&C 93:29)

Each man, woman or child who has ever come or who will ever come to earth, was organized previously as a spirit. In this pre-mortal state, man's identity (intelligence) was united with spirit matter, through a procreative process, to become a spirit child of God. God is our Heavenly Father in a very literal sense. For this reason, Jesus Christ taught all mankind to address Almighty God as "Our Father which art in heaven." (Matt 6:9)

Before this earth rolled into existence, we lived as individual spirits, the literal offspring of God, each inheriting divine potential and qualities from the "Father of [our] spirits." (Heb 12:9) This divine potential provides each spirit child of our Heavenly Father with the opportunity to become like our exalted heavenly parent.

In that pre-mortal state, we lived with God and our eldest brother, Jesus Christ, the first born of our Father's spirit children. We knew our Father, and He knew us very intimately, as only a parent can know his or her own child. We loved our Father, and He loved us, both as a parent and as a divine being. We were instructed by Him and others, and each of us developed and matured as individual spirits in our own unique way. (Prov 8:22-31)

Because God knows each of us, individually, and understands our spiritual limitations, our talents and gifts, and the unique personal characteristics which we exhibited in our pre-mortal life, there is forethought and divine wisdom in the individual circumstances of our life.

We have all been given specific missions, in the wisdom of God, according to His knowledge of our individual needs and talents. Each spirit is sent to this earth with specific lessons to learn and individual contributions to make.

Our life's mission reflects who we were in that pre-mortal existence and assigns us certain roles and responsibilities, according to God's foreknowledge of each of His spirit children.

> [God] hath determined the times before appointed, and the bounds of [man's] habitation;
> That they [we] should seek the Lord, if haply they [we] might feel after him, and find him, though he be not far from every one of us:
> For in him we live, and move, and have our being . . . For we are also his offspring. (Acts 17:26-28)

WHICH TEACHINGS ARE NON-BIBLICAL?

Some Christians charge that these teachings of Latter-day Saints are not substantiated in the Bible. (MacArthur, Glory, pp. 21-2) An appropriate response to this charge will address at least three points.

First: every aspect of man's pre-mortal existence, as expounded by Latter-day Saints, is not detailed in the Bible. Latter-day Saints have the benefit of additional revelation from modern-day prophets. As will be discussed in chapter five, Latter-day Saints do not pretend that all their teachings are found in the Bible. Nevertheless, this particular doctrine of man's pre-mortal existence *is* clearly taught in the Bible, and specific teachings of Latter-day Saints concerning man's pre-mortal existence are completely consistent with related truths expounded in the Bible. In fact, these inspired doctrines provide answers to many questions raised but not fully explained within the pages of the Bible or in traditional Christian theology.

Second: there is again a great irony in this charge leveled by some Christians, because their dogma of ex nihilo creation is not found in the Bible. According to Dr. Gordon D. Kaufman, a Christian theologian, the earliest expressions of creatio ex nihilo appear about 170 - 190 AD in the writings of Theophilus of Antioch. (Kaufman, p. 289, also see Barker, p. 416)

> *Creatio Ex nihilo* is not a strictly scriptural formula . . . The formula itself is found nowhere in the Bible, and the opening chapters of Genesis even seem to deny it, suggesting that perhaps God worked with pre-existent primeval waters, though 'the earth was without form

and void . . . And the Spirit of God moved upon the face of the waters' 1:2 or with a pre-existent barren wilderness-earth 'when no plant of the field was yet on the earth' . . . (*Ibid.*, p. 288)

Attempting to assert Biblical support for ex nihilo creation, one Christian scholar points to Hebrews 11:3, "Through faith we understand that the worlds were framed by the word of God, so that things which are seen were not made of things which do appear." (Little, p. 62) However, this passage and all other references to creation in the Bible do not indicate God framed the worlds and made all things out of nothing, in one moment of spontaneous creativity.

The Bible is very clear that man's body was organized from pre-existing matter. "The Lord God formed man of the dust of the ground and breathed into his nostrils the breath of life; and man became a living soul." (Gen 2:7) What is to be understood from the metaphor of breathing life into the body of man is not explained in the Bible. However, it is an extrapolation completely without scriptural support that man sprang from nothing. (see Keeley, pp. 210 and 215)

Finally, there are many references in the Bible that clearly teach of a pre-mortal state in which the sons and daughters of God dwelt prior to coming to this earth which cannot be explained and, in fact, are at complete variance with the traditional doctrine of ex nihilo creation. Conversely, there are few facts as well-documented and as frequently attested to in the Bible as that of a pre-mortal state in which God's children were present and actively involved, before the foundation of the world.

A PRE-MORTAL STATE CLEARLY TAUGHT IN THE BIBLE

Most Christian denominations acknowledge that Jesus Christ existed in a pre-mortal state, before the foundations of the world. Many biblical passages attest to this truth:

In the beginning was the Word, and the Word was with God, and the Word was God.

All things were made by Him; and without him was not any thing made that was made.

And the Word was made flesh, and dwelt among us." (John 1:1, 3, 14)

Paul also identified Jesus as the creator of this world. "[God] Hath in these last days spoken unto us by his Son, whom he hath appointed heir of all things, by whom also he made the worlds." (Heb 1:2)

Obviously, since the worlds were created by Jesus Christ, He existed in a pre-mortal state with the Father.

The Apostle Peter testified that Christ "was foreordained before the foundation of the world" (1 Pet 1:20). This suggests that Christ understood his unique role in bringing about the salvation of man and was foreordained to fulfill that role prior to the creation of the earth.

The Savior referred to this pre-mortal state in his great intercessory prayer. "And now, O Father, glorify thou me with thine own self with the glory which I had with thee before the world was." (John 17:5)

Jesus Christ's pre-mortal existence would appear to establish the biblical basis for a pre-mortal state which most Christian denominations accept. So, differences of doctrine center not on whether the Bible teaches of a pre-mortal state, but on whether man's spirit dwelt with God and Jesus in that pre-mortal condition.

IDENTIFYING THOSE PRESENT
IN THE PRE-MORTAL STATE

Before addressing this point, it is appropriate to mention some other personalities that most Christian denominations agree were present in that pre-mortal state. Lucifer, son of the morning, was cast out of heaven and became Satan or the devil, prior to the creation. The prophet Isaiah speaks of these events:

> How art thou fallen from heaven, O Lucifer, son of the morning!
> For thou hast said in thine heart, I will ascend into heaven, I will exalt my throne above the stars of God.
> I will be like the most High. (Isa 14:12-14)

Not only was Lucifer present in this pre-mortal state but many angels were also present. John the Revelator writes of a war in heaven in which Lucifer led many others against Michael and the hosts of heaven, prior to the creation of Adam and Eve.

> And there was war in heaven: Michael and his angels fought against the dragon; and the dragon fought and his angels,
> and prevailed not; neither was their place found any more in heaven.
> And the great dragon was cast out, that old serpent, called the Devil, and Satan . . . he was cast out into the earth, and his angels were cast out with him. (Rev 12:7-9)

While the Revelator does not identify exactly when this war took place, it is evident these events preceded the creation of Adam and Eve and their posterity because the serpent (Satan) had been cast down from heaven and was present in the garden prior to Adam's fall. (Gen 3)

At this point, it should be apparent that those who dwelt in this pre-mortal state were numerous and diverse. Not only were God the Father and his son, Jesus, present, but also Lucifer and Michael and a host of angels on both sides. The Revelator records that those drawn to Lucifer were "the third part of the stars of heaven" (Rev 12:4), suggesting that two-thirds of those in heaven fought with Michael and Jesus at that time and remained with the Father following the war. Lucifer and his angels were cast out and "kept not their first estate." (Jude 1:6)

The Bible indicates that Jesus, Lucifer, Michael and these "stars of heaven," including all the host of "angels," are spirit children of our Heavenly Father. Christ was the first born of God's spirit children. Paul refers to the Savior as "the first born among many brethren" (Rom 8:29) and "the firstbegotten." (Heb 1:6) This also explains why Jesus addressed his prayers to "Our Father which art in heaven" (Matt 6:9) and taught us to do the same. (John 17:1) Elsewhere, the Savior introduced himself as "the Beginning of the creation of God" (Rev 3:14), and "the bright and morning star." (Rev 22:16) However, Christ was not the only "morning star," but rather the brightest of all morning stars.

The clearest reference to additional morning stars is recorded in questions put to Job by the Lord:

> Where wast thou when I laid the foundations of the earth? declare, if thou has understanding?
>
> when the *morning stars* sang together, and *all the sons of God* shouted for joy? (Job 38:4, 7; emphasis added)

Who are these other personages who rejoiced at the creation of this earth, before the foundation of the world? The key to their identity lies in the title, "sons of God."

This title is used in the Bible referring to both angels (Job 1:6, Job 2:1, Ps 89:6) and inhabitants of earth. (Ps 82:6, Hosea 1:10, Rom 8:16, Rom 8:14) Angels are the pre-mortal spirits placed in human bodies as part of the birth process. The union of body and spirit constitutes mortal life. Likewise, when one dies, the spirit separates from the body. "Then shall the dust [the body] return to the earth as it was: and the spirit shall *return unto God who gave it.*" (Eccles 12:7; emphasis added)

Just as Jesus Christ "was with God" (John 1:1) prior to the creation of this world, so the children of men dwelt with God as his spirit children, or "sons of God," from before the foundation of the world. The Lord reminded Job that he shouted for joy in a pre-mortal state as one of the morning stars or sons of God.

Amazingly, Isaiah identifies Satan as "a Son of the morning" "fallen from heaven" (Isa 14:12), and John the Revelator refers to those who fought on Lucifer's side during the war in heaven as "the third part of the stars of heaven." (Rev 12:4) All of these "stars" are sons and daughters of God, spirit children of our Father in Heaven, and were present when the foundations of the earth were laid.

ACCOUNTING FOR ANGELS

This explanation solves one of the great mysteries in traditional Christian teachings concerning the origins of a heavenly host referred to as "angels." Most traditional Christian scholars acknowledge the presence of angels with God prior to the creation. (MacArthur, Glory, pp. 154-8; Little, p. 102) However, these scholars fail to make a connection between angels and the pre-mortal spirits of those who eventually come to earth because of their dogma of ex nihilo creation.

Both in the Hebrew and Greek texts, the word used for angel means literally, "messenger." (Smith, W., p. 108; Little, p. 103) When appearing on earth, angels function as divine messengers from God or ministering spirits to the inhabitants of earth (Heb 1:13-14; Luke 1:11-38; Acts 10:1-8, 30-32; Gen 24:7; Matt 24:31; Dan 6:22; Rev 14:6). As such, the pre-mortal Jesus was referred to as an angel, the messenger of salvation. (Gen 48:15-16; also see Ex 3:2-6) Likewise, the disembodied Satan can appear as "an angel of light" (2 Cor 11:13-15) and is referred to by John as the "angel of the bottomless pit." (Rev 9:11) Two-thirds of the hosts of heaven who fought with Michael and kept their first estate are those spirits who have come or will come to earth and inhabit bodies created for man. The other one-third followed Lucifer and remain forever disembodied spirits, identified in the scriptures as Satan's angels. (Rev 12:9)

Only teachings of Latter-day Saints regarding pre-mortal existence of the spirits of man can account for the angels of heaven without resorting to an additional act of creation, not spoken of in the Bible, in which a separate species of beings comes into existence. (Little, p. 102; MacArthur, Glory, p. 154)

GOD'S FOREKNOWLEDGE OF HIS CHILDREN IN PRE-MORTALITY

This relationship between God and mortal man prior to life on this earth is attested to in other passages of scripture, as well. For example, the Lord told the prophet Jeremiah, "Before I formed thee in the belly I knew thee; and before thou camest forth out of the womb I sanctified thee, and I ordained thee a prophet unto the nations." (Jer 1:5) Jeremiah was chosen to be a prophet from the foundation of the world.

This is consistent with the teachings of the Apostle Paul when he writes, "For whom he [God] did foreknow, he also did predestinate to be conformed to the image of his Son." (Rom 8:29) In addition, Paul instructs the saints of Ephesus that God "hath chosen us in him before the foundation of the world." (Eph 1:4) Timothy is told that he and others are called "according to his [God's] own purpose and grace, which was given us in Christ Jesus before the world began." (2 Tim 1:9)

All of these scriptures attest to man's relationship with God in a pre-mortal state where each of us was chosen and foreordained to his mission on earth based on God's "foreknowledge" of our individual spirit.

Notions of a pre-mortal existence are not new with Latter-day Saints. Many references to this pre-mortal state can be found in writings of the Apostolic Fathers and early Christian teachers. (Kelly, pp. 344-5; Robinson, S., pp. 103-4) One non-LDS scholar observes,

> conceptions of pre-existence were very widespread in Judaism . . . These widespread conceptions of pre-existence which get fleshed out in Proverbs 8:22, a text continually cited in the Christian tradition, make it quite plain how easily heavenly, pre-existent beings were accepted by contemporary Judaism. (Studer, pp. 39-40)

GOD'S CHILDREN AND HIS ONLY BEGOTTEN SON

Other Christians have suggested that references to "all the sons of God," "offspring of God," etc., are figurative, and do not suggest anything about man's pre-mortal existence or his relationship to God. The "proof" advanced by some is the Biblical reference to Jesus Christ as "the Only Begotten Son" (John 1:14). Since Jesus is the only begotten of the Father, the spirits of man cannot be literal children of God, according to this line of thought. (*Presbyterians and Mormons*, p. 19)

However, the Bible teaches that Jesus Christ is the only begotten son of God *in the flesh*. His mortal mother was Mary, a pure virgin who knew not man. (Luke 1:34) His father in mortality was God, the Father. (Luke 1:35) The Bible refers to Jesus Christ as the "only begotten of the Father" or the "only begotten Son" in three passages, each authored by the Apostle John. (John 1:14, 18, 1 John 4:9) For example, "And the Word *was made flesh*, and dwelt among us, (and we beheld his glory, the glory as of the only begotten of the Father,) full of grace and truth." (John 1:14) The other two references to Jesus as the "only begotten Son" speak of him as "declaring the Father" (John 1:18), and as "manifest[ing] the love of God," key aspects of his mortal ministry. (1 John 4:9) Each passage describes Christ as the "only begotten Son" in the flesh.

Accordingly, the title of "only begotten of the Father" does not preclude a literal paternal relationship between all mankind and God prior to mortality, as is suggested in references to God as "the Father of spirits" (Heb 12:9) and mortal man as his children and offspring. It merely implies that Jesus is the only being born into mortality whose father, in the flesh, was God the Father.

As the only begotten in the flesh, Jesus' relationship with God is unique. However, this unique relationship does not diminish the significance of man's relationship to God. Clearly the Savior taught the relationship between God and man is one of Father to son (and daughter). (Matt 7:9-11; Luke 11:11-13; Mal 2:10; Matt 5:48; Luke 11:2; Eph 4:6) This explains why Jesus used phrasing differentiating his relationship with the Father while reiterating the literal fatherhood of God to all humankind. He spoke of "my Father and your Father; and . . . my God, and your God." (John 20:17) It is significant that Jesus did not refer to, "my Father and your God." Instead, he spoke in direct parallels affirming the reality of both relationships; my Father and your Father, my God and your God.

In numerous situations, he instructed his mortal followers to address their God as "Father," the most simple yet intimate of titles. (Matt 5:16 and 48, Matt 6:6 and 9, Matt 23:9, Luke 6:36). These are not mere figures of speech. Rather, they are an essential part of the revelation of God to man, confirmed by the Son. The relationship between ourselves and our God is literally one of son (and daughter) to Father.

As discussed in chapter one, the implications of who we are, as His children and offspring, are ennobling to mankind. Our divine origins provide a hope that is almost too good to be true. Through our Savior, we can become like our Father in Heaven by following the pattern set forth by our eldest brother, Jesus Christ.

WHERE WILL I GO AFTER I DIE?

For many, sensitivity to eternal things begins with the realization of one's mortality. This realization may be thrust upon them in tragedy when a loved one dies or when they, themselves, pass close to death's door. For others, the process of aging brings a dawning awareness in the soul, troubling the mind and pricking the psyche. The inescapable fact that mortality eventually ends for all of us takes on new relevance. Each soul grasps the simple truth that he or she will not live forever, at least not in this mortal sphere. So the second of the profound questions, "Where will I go after I die?" is often the first to penetrate our hearts and motivate our search for things of eternal worth.

CONTRASTING VIEWS OF THE AFTER-LIFE

Answers to this and related questions have many similarities and also some significant differences in the teachings of Protestants, Catholics and Latter-day Saints. Each body of doctrine is summarized below:

Table 3

Protestants	Catholics	LDS
Where does man's spirit go between death and the resurrection?		
The just go directly to heaven; the unjust go directly to hell to await judgment.	The just go directly to heaven; the unjust go directly to hell; the vast majority of Christian believers culpable of lesser (venial) sins go to purgatory.	All go to the Spirit World consisting of three realms: Paradise where the just dwell, the Spirit Prison where those who have not heard the gospel are taught, and Hell, where the wicked are purged for their sins.
What happens in the intermediate sphere?		
There is no intermediate sphere; the just go to heaven and the unjust begin a process of endless and eternal suffering which is briefly interrupted by the final judgment when they are consigned to the second death.	There is no intermediate period for the saintly (just) or worldly (unjust), but only for those consigned to purgatory where they suffer for a time and then are released into heaven.	All are given the opportunity to hear the gospel of Jesus Christ, to accept or reject it. Those who reject the atonement of Jesus Christ must suffer for their own sins.

Protestants	Catholics	LDS
What are the kingdoms to which men and women will be assigned in the final judgment?		
There are only two: heaven and hell.	There are only two: heaven and hell.	There are many but they can be grouped into four kingdoms: *heaven*, consisting of three kingdoms of glory: Celestial, Terrestrial and Telestial; and *hell*, a kingdom of no glory.
Will the majority of mankind be condemned to an eternity in hell at the final judgment?		
Yes	Yes	No, some will be consigned to Hell for all eternity, but most will be resurrected to a degree of glory. Many who inherit a kingdom of glory will not receive all that might have been theirs; in this they suffer a type of eternal damnation.

Of these bodies of doctrine, Protestant notions are the least-defined and evince the widest range of variation from one denomination to another. For example, in *The History of Christian Doctrines*, Dr. Louis Berkhof devotes only 12 pages out of 269 to what he calls the doctrine of last things, and *A History of Christian Theology* by Dr. William Placher makes no mention of heaven, hell or the final judgment. As Dr. Berkhof explains, "The doctrine of the last things never stood in the centre of attention, is one of the least developed doctrines, and therefore calls for no elaborate discussion." (Berkhof, HCD, p. 259)

A survey of Protestant writings, on balance, tends toward positions set forth in the table, although variations can be found on nearly every point. For instance, one author identifies one hell (Sheol or Hades) into which the righteous and wicked descend immediately following death, and a different hell into which the wicked are cast after the final judgment. (Connelly, pp. 64-5, 75-6) Others deny that hell is a physical location and define it in figurative terms. (Reid, ed., pp. 516-7; Keeley, p. 255) Universalism, a popular doctrine among a minority of Protestant groups, teaches that all mankind is eventually saved. (Reid, ed., p. 1205; Kaufman, p. 459) The majority of Protestant denominations, however, teach of one hell that is real where the wicked are consigned eternally, as noted above. (Chafer/Walvoord, p. 365; Graham, TC, pp. 71-8; Berkhof, HCD, pp. 267-8; MacArthur, Glory, pp. 69-71; Gibbs, pp. 57-70; Lutzer, OM, pp. 35-70)

With appropriate allowance for the diversity of Protestant teachings, all three bodies of doctrine: Catholic, Protestant and Latter-day

Saint, share several concepts in common. For instance, the prospect of a final judgment is present in all three, although in most Protestant teachings the final judgment applies only to those who refuse to accept Christ. Each body of doctrine speaks of a heaven and hell, though in the teachings of Latter-day Saints heaven is divided into three major kingdoms.

Perhaps the area of greatest divergence among these three bodies of doctrine centers on the concept of an intermediate period separating death and the final judgment. On this point, three significantly different positions emerge.

PROTESTANTS: NO INTERMEDIATE SPHERE

Protestant theology teaches that following death one passes through a personal judgment, being consigned immediately to heaven or hell. There is no intermediate period between death and judgment. For example, the Westminster Confession of Faith states:

> The bodies of men after death return to dust, and see corruption; but their souls, (which neither die nor sleep), having an immortal subsistence, immediately return to God who gave them. The souls of the righteous, being then made perfect in holiness, are received into the highest heavens, where they behold the face of God in light and glory, waiting for the full redemption of their bodies, and the souls of the wicked are cast into hell . . . Besides these two places for souls separated from their bodies, the Scriptures acknowledge none. (see also Connelly, p. 68; Ankerberg, p. 221; Keeley, p. 255; Graham, TC, pp.71-8; Lutzer, OM, p. 9; MacArthur, Glory, pp. 69-71; Gibbs, pp. 60-5)

For Protestants, the mention of an intermediate sphere conjures up negative images of Catholic teachings regarding purgatory. One practice of the Catholic Church universally decried by Protestants during the reformation was the selling of personal indulgences. This practice allowed individuals to pay a sum of money to representatives of the Church in exchange for promises of forgiveness for sins. Eventually, the selling of indulgences was extended to promise relief for departed loved ones suffering in purgatory. Dark and foreboding images of unrelenting pain and travail depicted in official teachings of the Catholic Church were among those doctrines condemned by Martin Luther in his 95 theses.

In our present day, much of the intense sentiment attached to this doctrine results from the conflict between Catholic notions regarding works of penance performed in purgatory and the Protestant doctrine of salvation by grace alone. Writing on this point, Dr. John Lawson, a Catholic scholar, has observed,

> Classic Protestantism reacted strongly against the Roman Catholic doctrine of purgatory, and has in general affirmed that at death all souls go immediately either to heaven or to hell (Luke 16:26; Hebrews 9:27). The basic theological reason for this is that the Roman Catholic doctrine of purgatory answers naturally to the conception of "salvation by grace and the merit of good works." The opposed Protestant principles of "salvation by grace alone," and "justification by faith alone" would appear to exclude the principle of meritorious remedial suffering, and therefore the notion of purgatory. (Lawson, p. 261)

For these reasons, the concept of an intermediate state is typically condemned in Protestant teachings.

CATHOLIC PURGATORY

In Catholic theology, the concept of purgatory is a well-developed doctrine. Roman Catholic teachings hold that those in a state of Christian grace cannot enter heaven prior to demonstrating complete repentance of sin, either through faithful behavior in this life or by suffering the punishments of a just God in purgatory. In the Catholic view, nonbelievers and wicked people of this world go immediately to hell, similar to Protestant teachings. A few souls comprising the most righteous saints go immediately to heaven. The majority of believers, however, are compelled to spend some time in purgatory before entering into heaven.

> Those who die in the mortal sins which separate the soul from God, such as pride and unbelief, are irrevocably lost. It is only those departed in a state of grace, and who are on the sure road to final salvation, who are admitted to purgatory to make amends for their lesser, or venial, sins . . . The general assumption of Roman Catholic teaching is that some period in purgatory is the destiny of the general body of believers. The great and illustrious saints, however, who have died full of the good works produced by grace, may go straight to heaven. (Lawson, pp. 260-1)

Catholics thus believe that the souls of believers who pass through purgatory are subjected for a time to the suffering of hell. However, in Catholic theology, there is a distinction between the temporary hell of purgatory, referred to in Biblical texts as Hades or Sheol, and the final or eternal hell, Gehenna, reserved for the wicked and non-believers. (*Ibid.*, p. 262) Purgatory is a state of suffering similar to the final hell of non-believers, but its duration is limited for purposes of completing the purification process in believers, allowing them to enter eventually into eternal bliss.

Purgatory is also the final resting place for infants that have not been baptized, according to Roman Catholic teachings. "Infants dying unbaptized cannot be admitted to heaven in the fullest sense, but exist in a state of relative happiness." (*Ibid.*, p. 261)

Many of the oppressive images of purgatory circulated in earlier times have been clarified and updated in teachings of the Catholic Church to appear less ominous and to emphasize the symbolic nature of the "fire" and "place" of purgatory and hell. (*Ibid.*) However, the concept of purgatory remains as basic and essential to Catholic theology as doctrines concerning heaven and hell. (see also, Smith, W., p. 156-159)

LATTER-DAY SAINTS: THE SPIRIT WORLD

Teachings of Latter-day Saints affirm an intermediate sphere between death and the final judgment, but this "spirit world," as it is called, is very different from Catholic purgatory. According to Latter-day Saint theology, all spirits go to this spirit world following the death of their mortal body. Individuals who have embraced the gospel of Jesus Christ, having lived faithful lives in mortality, are ushered into "Paradise," a state of relative bliss. Those who have not yet had the opportunity to hear and accept the gospel of Christ are consigned to a less favorable state, known as spirit prison, unless they have committed specific sins which require them to be cast into hell. In these two separate regions of the spirit world, the great work of salvation for all mankind continues. Those who have committed gross sins are committed to hell until the time of the second resurrection.

While many details related to the spirit world have not been revealed, there is a significant body of information about the great work taking place in the spirit world recorded by prophets in all periods of time. As will be shown, some of these specific activities are clearly described in the Bible.

Latter-day Saints teach that every man, woman and child who has ever lived on the earth or who will come here in the future will be given an opportunity to hear the gospel of Jesus Christ, allowing them to accept or reject it. For those who do not receive this opportunity while on earth, and that includes the vast majority of all people born into mortality, they will have the gospel preached to them in the spirit world. At that time, they will receive a full opportunity to accept or reject the gospel for themselves.

Those who accept the gospel of Jesus Christ and embrace the Savior as their personal Redeemer will receive ordinances of salvation, such as baptism, by proxy. Worthy men and women members of The Church of Jesus Christ of Latter-day Saints accomplish this sacred work of performing ordinances of salvation on behalf of others in sacred edifices called temples. This is the primary work to be performed during the one-thousand-year period known as the millennium, following the second coming of Jesus Christ. In the spirit world, each individual will be given an opportunity to accept or reject the gospel and receive ordinances of salvation performed by others on their behalf if they elect to receive them.

Those who reject the gospel of Jesus Christ, in this life or in the spirit world, will have to suffer for their own sins in hell. In addition, blasphemy against the Holy Ghost cannot be fully forgiven, either in this life or the next. (Matt 12:31; 1 John 5:16-17; 1 John 3:15) Those who commit this most grievous sin must suffer for their own transgressions in hell.

Those who cannot receive the atonement of Jesus Christ suffer the chastisement of hell until the scales of justice are balanced and the uttermost farthing is paid. This will take place before the second resurrection, which will occur at the end of Christ's millennial reign. (Rev 20:4-5, 12-13) After suffering for their own sins, almost all of the most wicked will be sufficiently humbled and refined "That at the name of Jesus every knee should bow" (Philip 2:10) and every tongue should confess the Savior and Redeemer of the world. This scene will precede the final judgment when all stand before the Lord to be judged.

COMPARING PURGATORY AND THE SPIRIT WORLD

Some Protestants claim that the spirit world as taught by Latter-day Saints is a type of Catholic purgatory. However, a comparison of the two bodies of doctrine clearly shows significant differences on major points:

- *Catholic:* purgatory is only for believers and unborn infants. *LDS:* the spirit world is for every soul who passes through mortality, the just and the unjust;
- *Catholic:* the major work of purgatory is suffering and penance. *LDS:* the major work in the spirit prison is missionary work allowing all to accept or reject the gospel of Jesus Christ;
- *Catholic:* purgatory is the permanent abode for infants who die without being baptized and are denied entrance into heaven. *LDS:* infants who die before reaching the age of accountability have had or will have the same opportunity as all others to accept or reject the gospel of Jesus Christ;
- *Catholic:* there is no clear counterpart in purgatory to Paradise where the just dwell in the spirit world, although some vague notions of Paradise can be found in select Catholic writings;
- *Catholic:* those in a state of Christian grace suffer and perform penance in purgatory. *LDS:* those who will not or cannot repent of their sins through the atonement of Jesus Christ suffer for their own sins in hell;
- *Catholic:* prayers and masses relieve the suffering and hasten the release of souls in purgatory. *LDS:* eventual suffering in hell can only be mitigated in the spirit prison through acceptance of Jesus Christ's atonement and ordinances of salvation performed by proxy;
- *Catholic:* no ordinances performed by proxy can be accepted by those in purgatory. *LDS:* accepting essential ordinances performed by proxy is a significant aspect of the work to be accomplished in the spirit prison.

At the same time, there are a few important similarities between Catholic purgatory and the spirit world as taught by Latter-day Saints. For instance, neither purgatory nor the spirit world guarantees "a second chance" to those who had an opportunity to accept the gospel of Jesus Christ in mortality but rejected it. Also, both teach that suffering during this intermediate period is for a limited duration. Though individuals suffer the chastisement of hell, this is not the permanent condition of those who pass through this intermediate state.

The most significant and fundamental similarity between the two bodies of doctrine is the affirmation of an intermediate sphere where additional work related to salvation is performed on behalf of men and women who have passed through mortality and await the resurrection.

This position is in direct contrast to the teachings of most Protestant denominations, giving rise to the charge by some that such teachings are non-biblical. This claim can be submitted to the light of scripture.

BIBLICAL EVIDENCE OF AN INTERMEDIATE SPHERE

All Christian denominations acknowledge an intermediate period of three days between the death of Jesus Christ and his resurrection on Easter morning. The Bible indicates that for at least some portion of this three-day period, Jesus was in "Paradise." (Luke 23:43)

As discussed in the preceding chapter, there is a difference of interpretation between Protestants and Latter-day Saints concerning the nature and location of Paradise. The word paradise is derived from the Persian language and means garden or park. Most Protestants teach that Paradise is heaven and that Christ went immediately to heaven following his death. However, the Bible records that the resurrected Savior appeared to Mary Magdalene in the garden, and he commanded her, "Touch me not; for I am not yet ascended to my Father . . ." (John 20:17) Since the Father resides in heaven (Heb 9:24) and Jesus had not yet ascended to his Father, it appears that Christ spent the three days between his death and his resurrection in paradise, a location separate from heaven.

This inference is supported by a larger body of biblical passages teaching of a world of spirits where all those who have passed through mortality hear the gospel, receive an opportunity to accept ordinances performed for the dead, and await the resurrection. In this sphere, some suffer for their own sins prior to the final judgment. These teachings are set forth clearly in the Bible.

THE DEAD HEAR THE GOSPEL

For example, the Apostle Peter indicates that Christ visited the dead and preached the gospel to them, following his death:

> For Christ also hath once suffered for sins, the just for the unjust, that he might bring us to God, being put to death in the flesh, but quickened by the Spirit:
>
> By which also he went and preached unto the spirits in prison; Which sometime were disobedient . . . in the days of Noah . . . (1 Pet 3:18-20)

These spirits who had died "in the days of Noah" were neither in heaven nor in hell. Peter records that they were in "prison," prior to their resurrection, apparently waiting for certain things to be accomplished, especially the visit of Jesus Christ, himself, to the spirit world.

Latter-day Saints teach that during the three days when Christ's body lay in the tomb, the Savior's spirit visited the spirit world and organized a great missionary work among the dead and preached to the souls dwelling there. The Apostle Peter wrote of this great work extended to all who pass through mortality: "For this cause was the gospel preached also to them that are dead, that they might be judged according to men in the flesh, but live according to God in the spirit." (1 Pet 4:6)

Two things are evident in this passage. *First:* the gospel of Jesus Christ is preached to the dead. The Apostle Peter states this in unambiguous language. "For this cause was the gospel preached also to them that are dead." (1 Pet 4:6) *Second:* this proselytizing among the deceased occurs prior to the final judgment, as evidenced by the second half of Peter's statement, "that they might be judged according to men in the flesh." (1 Pet 4:6) In essence, the Apostle Peter is saying: So that these men can be judged as others, it is necessary that they receive the gospel, even though they are dead "in the flesh."

Peter is not the only writer in the Bible to speak of this great work. The Savior himself prophesied that the dead would hear his teachings: "Verily, verily, I say unto you, the hour is coming, and now is, when the dead shall hear the voice of the Son of God: and they that hear shall live." (John 5:25)

Isaiah speaks of the "covenant people" of the gospel bringing a light to the unconverted in the spirit prison:

> I the Lord have called thee in righteousness, and will hold thine hand and will keep thee, and give thee for a covenant of the people, for a light of the Gentiles;
> To open the blind eyes, to bring out the prisoners from prison, and them that sit in darkness out of the prison house. (Isa 42:6-7)

Both Isaiah and Peter use the same term, prison, in referring to a location where the unconverted are gathered to receive this light of the gospel.

Isaiah describes this prison in detail:

> And it shall come to pass in that day, that the Lord shall punish the host of the high ones that are on high . . .

and they shall be gathered together, as prisoners are gathered in the pit, and shall be shut up in the prison, and after many days shall they be visited. (Isa 24:22)

In mortality, there is no such prison in which the Lord shall punish the host of the high ones that are on high and where prisoners are gathered in the pit. This prison is only found in the spirit world, where the unconverted had to abide for a time until they were visited by the Lord, Jesus Christ, following his death.

THE DEAD RECEIVE SAVING ORDINANCES

Not only does the Bible speak of the gospel being preached to the dead, but it also refers to sacred ordinances of salvation performed by the living on behalf of those who have passed out of this life. In his epistle to the Corinthians, the Apostle Paul offered supporting evidence for the literal resurrection of man. One argument advanced by Paul refers to the practice of baptizing for and on behalf of the dead. Paul asks, "Else what shall they do which are baptized for the dead, if the dead rise not at all? why are they then baptized for the dead?" (1 Cor 15:29)

This passage has been scrutinized by biblical scholars of all denominations because its precepts are not found in Protestant nor Catholic teachings. Harald Riesenfeld, a mainstream Christian theologian, concludes: "None of the attempts to escape the theory of a vicarious baptism in primitive Christianity seems to be wholly successful." (as quoted in Peterson and Ricks, p. 109) This conclusion is supported by a prominent Lutheran scholar of the New Testament, Krister Stendahl, who recently wrote referring to this passage: "The text seems to speak plainly enough about a practice within the Church of vicarious baptism for the dead. This is the view of most contemporary critical exegeses." (*Ibid.*, p. 109)

These assessments on the part of Protestant scholars acknowledge that saints of the New Testament were performing ordinances for the dead. (see also, Meeks, p. 162; Grosheide, pp. 372-4) If we are to make any sense of this activity, there must be an intermediate state where the dead are taught the gospel and await ordinances performed on their behalf by those in mortality. There would be no need to baptize for the dead if the dead were assigned to their eternal destination without passing through an intermediate state.

Elsewhere, the author of Hebrews refers to these ordinances performed by the living for righteous men and women who:

> having obtained a good report through faith, received not the promise:
>
> God having provided some better thing for us, that they without us should not be made perfect. (Heb 11:39-40)

For these righteous souls who "received not the promise" through ordinances of salvation in mortality, God provides a means of being made perfect through those who have been blessed to receive the better things of the gospel. Vicarious work performed by the living on behalf of the dead is absolutely essential to their salvation. For, "they [the dead] without us [the living] should not be made perfect" (Heb 11:40), lacking essential ordinances of salvation.

ONLY LDS TEACHINGS
QUIET SECULAR CRITICS OF CHRISTIANITY

Teachings of Latter-day Saints regarding additional work of salvation performed in the spirit world provide an answer to one of the most stinging criticisms leveled at the Christian world by philosophers and humanists. Skeptics have boldly challenged the attributes of a Christian God who consigns the majority of humanity to an eternal hell for not accepting the gospel of Jesus Christ, when the mass of people have never even heard the name of Jesus Christ, much less been taught the gospel sufficiently to accept or reject it. Catholic and Protestant teachings that non-believers go immediately to hell have the effect of condemning the majority of mankind to eternal misery without an opportunity to hear the gospel preached.

In response to these criticisms, some Christian denominations have begun to espouse a doctrine of recent origin that acceptance of Jesus Christ is not necessary to be saved for those denied exposure to the Savior's teachings. Concerning this doctrinal dilemma, a Catholic theologian, John Lawson, has observed:

> The assumption of some schools of evangelical teachings has been that all those who are not "soundly converted" are lost. This implies the damnation of the great majority of the human race (Matt 7:13-14). This in turn is a conclusion so fearsome that the mind of the average humane person refuses to take it altogether seriously. The reaction has been the spread of the prevalent, sentimental, and delusively comforting notion that all tolerably decent folk go straight to heaven, and quite

apart from any genuinely devout Christian discipleship. This is to short-circuit the whole Christian faith, and to produce that modern man who is not worrying about his sins. (Lawson, p. 262)

Mainstream Christians cannot have it both ways. Either, one must accept Christ as his personal Savior in order to be saved, in which case the vast majority of people are damned unjustly, according to their teachings; or else the requirement of accepting Jesus Christ must be waived for those who have not heard his name or been exposed to his teachings. As Dr. Lawson and evangelicals point out, this latter proposition is tantamount to denying the central concept of Christianity.

Another response to this dilemma among Catholics and Protestants has been to emphasize man's responsibility in choosing separation from the presence of God. (Reid, ed., pp. 516-7; Keeley, p. 255) For example, Dr. Douglas Connelly offers his personal reflections:

> What keeps my mind secure when I think about the awfulness of hell is the fact that those who spend eternity there have chosen separation from God in this life . . . When men and women make conscious decisions to reject God's offer of grace, God gives them what they want! (Connelly, p. 81)

In a similar vein, Drs. Lewis Chafer and John Walvoord have written, "No one is saved against his will, and no one disbelieves against his will. . . . No one will ever be able to stand before God and say, I wanted to be saved but was unable to do so because I was not elected." (Chafer/Walvoord, p. 234; see also, Bray, pp. 92-4; Little, pp. 117 and 135; Lutzer, OM, pp. 98-120)

However, these teachings do not address how the majority of humankind can be expected to exercise their moral agency when they have never heard the name of Jesus Christ. It is one thing to suggest man's culpability when he is exposed to light and refuses to embrace it. It is quite another issue when, according to traditional Christian teachings, billions of souls have been placed ex nihilo into circumstances which make it impossible for them to accept or reject Christ as their Savior. The explanation advanced by some is, "Those who never had an opportunity to hear the Gospel are condemned upon their rejection of the testimony of God in the natural world." (Chafer/Walvoord, p. 368; see also Connelly, pp. 85-7) This and similar responses do nothing to clarify how the majority of mankind will be given an opportunity to embrace salvation by accepting Jesus Christ as their personal Savior, as stipulated by the scriptures (1 Thes 5:9). It is this type of theology that has led many to reject God as unjust and Christianity as un-Christian. (see Marty, pp. 83-4)

These inconsistencies are resolved in the teachings of Latter-day Saints regarding an intermediate sphere in which all can hear the gospel and receive its saving ordinances by proxy. God's justice and mercy are extended to all mankind, and all receive the same opportunity. For those who will not accept their Savior after hearing his gospel, punishment is just. Teachings of Latter-day Saints regarding the spirit world uniquely reconcile requirements of salvation as taught in the scriptures (1 Thes 5:9) with the mercy and justice of a God worthy of man's total devotion. The existence of a spirit world between death and the final resurrection is an absolute prerequisite in preserving both propositions.

DIFFERENT CONCEPTS OF
HEAVEN, HELL AND FINAL JUDGMENT

Sometime following death, the spirits of those who have passed through mortality will stand before the Lord to be judged a final time. Catholic, Protestant and Latter-day Saint teachings are generally in agreement on a number of points related to this climactic scene. Specifically:

- In that moment, all who have dwelt upon the earth will have been resurrected.
- Those who have accepted Jesus Christ as their Savior and proven worthy of his grace are resurrected to eternal life and dwell forever in a sublime state, heaven.
- Those who fall short of the Lord's requirements are resurrected to eternal damnation.

On these broad outlines, Protestants, Catholics and Latter-day Saints generally agree.

Major differences in the teachings of Latter-day Saints and those of other Christians relative to the final destination of humankind lie in two areas: *first*, the range of conditions or degrees of glory in heaven and *second*, the number of souls consigned to an eternity in hell.

HEAVEN CONSISTS OF THREE KINGDOMS OF GLORY

In traditional Catholic and Protestant doctrine, heaven is a homogeneous state in which all who attain this glory enjoy a uniform degree of bliss and joy. The highest aspiration of faithful Protestants and Catholics is to be ushered into this blessed state.

According to teachings of Latter-day Saints, heaven is organized into different kingdoms of glory. At the resurrection, each individual will receive a degree of glory that varies one from another, commensurate with his or her faithfulness. Those resurrected to life will be assigned to one of three major kingdoms, namely, celestial, terrestrial or telestial. Each kingdom of glory is a blessed state more glorious than our finite minds can imagine. However, the celestial kingdom is more blessed and more glorious than the terrestrial kingdom, which in turn is superior to the telestial state. The glory and eternal blessings inherited by those dwelling in these three kingdoms varies as "one star differeth from another star in glory." (1 Cor 15:41)

The greatest desire of Latter-day Saints is to be resurrected with a celestial body and to dwell in celestial glory, forever, where God the Father dwells. Only those who attain this most blessed state will be privileged to inherit all the Father has and to be joint-heirs with Christ.

There are several passages in the Bible supporting the teachings of Latter-day Saints regarding multiple kingdoms and degrees of glory in heaven. The most direct references are found in writings of Paul to the Corinthians.

In chapter 15 of First Corinthians, Paul reaffirms the literal resurrection of man in the likeness of Christ's resurrection. In so doing, Paul anticipates the questions of many curious about this sublime doctrine. "But some man will say, How are the dead raised up? and with what body do they come?" (1 Cor 15:35) In other words, what are the qualities evident in a resurrected body? Paul then proceeds to answer these queries:

God giveth it [man] a body as it hath pleased him, and to every seed [man] his own body.
All flesh is not the same flesh. (1 Cor 15:38-9)

Resurrected bodies are not all alike. Each resurrected body varies as it hath pleased God.

Paul then instructs the saints that the glory of resurrected bodies can be divided into three broad groupings or kingdoms:

There are also celestial bodies, and bodies terrestrial: but the glory of the celestial is one, and the glory of the terrestrial is another.

There is one glory of the sun, and another glory of the moon, and another glory of the stars . . .

So also is the resurrection of the dead. (1 Cor 15:38-42)

This segmentation of heaven into three distinct kingdoms is consistent with other passages in the Bible. For instance, in the second epistle to the Corinthians, Paul refers to a man who beheld the third heaven in vision. "I knew a man in Christ . . . such an one caught up to the third heaven." (2 Cor 12:2) Logic suggests that where a third heaven exists, there must be a first and second heaven also; one kingdom each for those whose glory is likened to the sun, the moon and the stars.

In addition, Isaiah speaks of heaven as consisting of a multitude of stations in which all "lie in glory, every one in his own house." (Isa 14:18) Several parables spoken by Jesus refer to differences and gradations in rewards bestowed in heaven. For example, in the parable of the pounds, one faithful servant is given authority over ten cities, while another faithful servant presides over five. (Luke 19:16-19; see also Matt 25:21-24 and Matt 11:11) The Savior instructed his disciples, "In my Father's house are many mansions." (John 14:2) Heaven is not a single, uniform state.

THE PROPORTION OF SOULS CONSIGNED TO HELL

With regard to the proportion of those born into mortality who will be consigned to an eternity in hell, Catholic and Protestant doctrines are not always explicit. As one popular minister has wisely observed, "Terror never brought a man in yet." (Marsden, p. 35) However, implied in most of their teachings is a notion that the vast majority of mankind will suffer eternally with Satan and his angels in hell. (Bray, pp. 92-4; Chafer/Walvoord, p. 368; Connelly, pp. 85-7; Little, p. 117; Lutzer, OM, p. 120; Lawson, p. 262) As discussed above, scriptural requirements of accepting Jesus as one's personal Savior have the effect of consigning the majority of humankind to an eternity in hell in Protestant and Catholic theology.

At first blush, this proposition may appear to find support in the Bible. For example, the Savior taught his disciples, "Broad is the way, that leadeth to destruction, and many there be that go in thereat" (Matt 7:13); and "Then shall he say also unto them on the left hand, Depart from me, ye cursed, into everlasting fire, prepared for the devil and his angels." (Matt 25:41) "The wicked shall be turned into hell, and all the nations that forget God." (Ps 9:17)

According to Latter-day Saints, these passages refer to the chastisement of hell suffered during the intermediate period, prior to the final judgment. During that period between death and the final judgment, many will suffer the pains of hell. Those who would not accept their Savior will have to pay "the uttermost farthing." (Matt 10:29) On judgment day, even the most rebellious and hardened sinner will be sufficiently humbled to acknowledge his Savior. "At the name of Jesus every knee should bow" (Philip 2:10), confessing Jesus.

Then, all souls will be brought to stand before their Savior in a defined order. (1 Cor 15:22-24; Rev 20:4-6; Matt 27:52-53; 1 Thes 4:16; 2 Pet 2:9) First, the just will be judged, receiving the highest glory of heaven and being ordained joint-heirs with Christ. "He that overcometh shall inherit all things; and I will be his God, and he shall be my son." (Rev 21:7) Then those who have been less faithful will come forth, receiving lesser degrees of glory, each according to his degree of faithfulness in accepting and emulating Jesus Christ. This will be a mournful scene for many when they recognize their Savior and realize the blessings that might have been theirs.

According to the Bible, the vast majority of those born into mortality will be spared from an eternity in hell. Paul taught, "For as in Adam *all* die, even so in Christ shall *all* be made alive." (1 Cor 15:22; emphasis added) While this passage clearly refers to the resurrection of all mankind, it also speaks to the plan of God to save all his children. So the Savior instructed, "And this is the Father's will which hath sent me, that of all which he hath given me I should lose nothing, but should raise it up again at the last day." (John 6:39) Likewise Paul wrote:

> For this is good and acceptable in the sight of God our Savior;
> Who will have all men to be saved, and to come unto the knowledge of the truth. (1 Tim 2:4)

Of those who chose Christ during the war in heaven, being born into mortality, virtually none will be lost forever. However, despite avoiding an eternity in hell, those who fail to attain the highest degree of glory, the celestial kingdom, will experience a type of eternal damnation. In Latter-day Saint theology, the objective of man's existence is to dwell in the presence of the Father and to be like Him and the Lord, Jesus Christ. Those who fail to attain celestial glory will not dwell with the Father. Neither will they fulfill the highest purpose of their creation and receive all that the Father has offered them, as joint heirs with Christ. In this sense, there is an element of eternal disappointment for those consigned to a lower kingdom. Since they will be denied the presence of God the Father, they will have a continuing awareness of blessings that might have been theirs had they overcome all things.

SATAN AND HIS ANGELS: THOSE SPENDING ETERNITY IN HELL

The scriptures teach that Satan and his angels, those never allowed to enter mortality, comprise nearly all who will be cast into hell forever at the final judgment. The author of the epistle of Jude writes: "the angels which kept not their first estate, but left their own habitation, he [God] hath reserved in everlasting chains under darkness unto the judgment of the great day." (Jude 1:6) As discussed above, these spirits—one-third of the potential total population of this earth—followed Lucifer and rebelled against God in the pre-mortal state. They were cast out of heaven, their own habitation, and kept not their first estate. Peter refers to these rebellious spirits as "the angels that sinned, but (God) cast them down to hell, and delivered them into chains of darkness, to be reserved unto judgment." (2 Peter 2:4)

What will become of these lost souls? In the Revelator's vision of the final judgment, "the devil that deceived (mortal man) was cast into the lake of fire and brimstone . . . and shall be tormented day and night for ever and ever." (Rev 20:10) According to the Savior, hell with its "everlasting fire (is) prepared for the devil and his angels." (Matt 25:41)

Of this final scene, the Revelator writes, "whosoever was not found written in the book of life was cast into the lake of fire." (Rev 20:15) Of those who passed through mortality, all will eventually acknowledge their Savior at that future day when every knee shall bend to him. (Philip 2:10) The lost souls not found in the book of life at that point will consist almost exclusively of those denied the privilege of coming to earth as a consequence of their rebellion against the Father and his Son before the foundations of the earth.

Besides the devil and the one-third of the hosts of heaven who kept not their first estate, the Revelator identifies two mortals cast into the lake with Satan and his angels: "the beast . . . and . . . the false prophet."

(Rev 20:10; Rev 19:20) The beast appears to be the antichrist, and the false prophet is described as one who "wrought miracles before him [the antichrist], with which he [the antichrist] deceived them that had received the mark of the beast, and them that worshiped his image." (Rev 19:20)

The beast and the false prophet are mortals who will sojourn on earth. At death, their spirits will suffer for a time in hell along with all the wicked of the world. Then, John records that the beast and the false prophet "shall ascend out of the bottomless pit and go into perdition." (Rev 17:8) These two damned souls born into mortality "shall ascend out of the bottomless pit" (Rev 20:14) of hell when death and hell deliver up the dead. The beast and the false prophet will join the devil and his angels and go into perdition. At the final judgment, they will be "cast alive into a lake of fire burning with brimstone" (Rev 20:19) to spend eternity in hell.

The Savior spoke of these lost souls as sons of perdition who will not be forgiven, even after passing through hell:

> All manner of sin and blasphemy shall be forgiven unto men: but the blasphemy against the Holy Ghost shall not be forgiven unto men.
> Whosoever speaketh against the Holy Ghost, it shall not be forgiven him, neither in this world, neither in the world to come. (Matt 12:31-32; see also Mark 3:29)

Paul provides additional insight concerning those qualifying as sons of perdition. It becomes clear from his description that relatively few among those born into mortality will be so designated:

> For it is impossible for those who were once enlightened, and have tasted of the heavenly gift, and were made partakers of the Holy Ghost,
> And have tasted the good word of God, and the powers of the world to come,
> If they shall fall away, to renew them again unto repentance; seeing they crucify to themselves the Son of God afresh, and put him to an open shame. (Heb 6:4-6)

The number of souls born into mortality who fit the description put forth by Paul, specifically: to be enlightened, to have tasted of the heavenly gift, to be partakers of the Holy Ghost, to have tasted the good word of God, and then to have fallen away, is assuredly a small percentage of the total number of individuals who come to dwell on earth.

Wicked men and women of this world, including "the fearful, and unbelieving, and the abominable, and murderers, and whoremongers, and sorcerers, and idolaters and all liars, shall have *their part* in the lake which burneth with fire and brimstone: which is the second death." (Rev 21:8; emphasis added). Most other Christians will understand this passage as supporting traditional doctrines that consign the wicked to an eternity in hell with the devil and his angels. However, such an interpretation cannot be reconciled with promises cited above that "in Christ, shall all be made alive" (1 Cor 15:22); that Christ "should raise it [all] up again at the last day" (John 6:39); that "all manner of sin and blasphemy shall be forgiven unto men but the blasphemy against the Holy Ghost" (Matt 12:31); that mankind will be resurrected to one of three degrees of glory (1 Cor 15:38-42). As Paul taught, "we have borne the image of the earthy, we shall also bear the image of the heavenly" (1 Cor 15:49) and be "raised in glory . . . raised in power." (1 Cor 15:43)

These teachings are substantiated in the vision of Isaiah who also beheld the great and dreadful day of judgment. Isaiah testifies, "All the kings of the nations, even all of them, lie in glory, every one in his own house." (Isa 14:18) Everyone born into this life is of noble origin. As children of our Heavenly Father, all of us will receive glory, every one in his own house.

However, the Revelator's language indicates that the wicked of the earth "shall have their *part* in the lake which burneth with fire and brimstone." (Rev 21:8; emphasis added) Not having "sinned against the Holy Ghost" nor having "crucif[ied] to themselves the Son of God afresh," they will not be with those "sons of perdition" cast into the lake of fire "for ever and ever," but they "shall have their part" by suffering in the spirit-world hell prior to the second resurrection when the wicked will come forth and receive their resurrected bodies.

In addition, in the justice of God, those who chose wickedness will not dwell with the Father, the Son and the just who "inherit all things" in the highest kingdom of heaven. Rather, they will be assigned to one of the lesser kingdoms. In addition, "their part in the lake of fire" (Rev 21:8) may also involve an eternal awareness of the greater glory that might have been theirs had they been more faithful in the testimony of Jesus Christ.

THOU WILT NOT LEAVE MY SOUL IN HELL

Most other Christians insist that those consigned to hell prior to the final judgment can never be delivered. In support of this notion, some have cited the parable of Lazarus and the rich man. (Luke 16:19-31) In this parable, Lazarus, a beggar, and his mortal acquaintance, a rich man, die. Lazarus is carried to the bosom of Abraham; the rich man is consigned to suffer in hell. Being in torment, the rich man cries out for Abraham to send Lazarus to relieve his suffering. Abraham reminds the rich man of his circumstances in mortality and the appropriateness of his present discomfort. He then adds, "And beside all this, between us and you there is a great gulf fixed: so that they which would pass from hence to you cannot; neither can they pass to us, that would come from thence." (Luke 16:26) This passage is incorrectly interpreted by some as foreclosing any possibility of escaping from the chastisement of hell. (Connelly, pp. 68-9; Lutzer, OM, pp. 36-8)

When interpreting this passage, it is important to keep in mind that this parable describes conditions prior to the resurrection of Jesus Christ. The Savior broke the chains of death and hell, opening the way for the dead to "hear the voice of the Son of God: and they that hear shall live." (John 5:25) The atonement of Jesus Christ bridged the great gulf, allowing those with words of life to preach unto the spirits in prison (1 Pet 3:19), providing all with an opportunity to "hear" and to "live."

Other passages of scripture cited by some Christians to support a permanent condition of suffering refer to "everlasting punishment" (Matt 25:46), "everlasting fire" (Matt 18:8; 25:41), "everlasting destruction" (2 Thes 1:9) or the "eternal fire" (Jude 1:7) of hell. (see Connelly, pp. 80-1) A close look at these phrases reveals that adjectives, "everlasting" and "eternal," modify the nouns, "punishment," "fire" and "destruction." These phrases describe the nature of hell, but not the length of time all souls will spend there. The fires and destruction of hell are "everlasting" and "eternal," but the span of time spent by those subjected to these conditions is finite, prior to the final judgment. Only those condemned to the "second death" on the day of judgment are consigned to suffer forever. As David testified after committing tragic sins of adultery and murder, "thou wilt not leave my soul in hell." (Ps 16:10) He also wrote, "For great is thy mercy toward me: and thou hast delivered my soul from the lowest hell." (Ps 86:13)

CONTRASTING LDS TEACHINGS AND REINCARNATION

Before passing on to the last profound question confronting man in his search for purposeful existence, namely, why am I here on earth, it seems appropriate to address one of the more misleading charges thrown at Latter-day Saints by some Christians. Because Latter-day Saints teach of several stages in man's progression, some Christians have accused Latter-day Saints of teaching a type of reincarnation.

This is one more disappointing example of the lengths to which some are willing to go to distort and mislead, disparaging the beliefs of others and inciting prejudice among the uninformed. One might just as well contend that basketball and golf are essentially the same activity because both are athletic sports and use a round ball. The doctrines of Latter-day Saints regarding the process by which man progresses toward salvation share much in common with those of other Christian denominations, but have almost nothing in common with teachings of reincarnation.

The Hindu concept of reincarnation teaches that a soul returns to this earth numerous times in diverse forms and conditions in order to evolve and progress. This process supposedly recurs through many cycles over many centuries, until one reaches a state of perfection where the individual soul is merged into the essence of God. At this point, according to the Hindu concept, the individual soul ceases to be a separate entity. It is caught up into the eternal bliss of oneness with God. (H. Smith, pp. 100-1)

As discussed above, the plan of salvation taught by Latter-day Saints includes many of the traditional elements of other Christian doctrines, and there are only a few elements with any resemblance to reincarnation. Latter-day Saints and other Christians share in common such precepts as a single mortal life and death for each individual, man being resurrected as a separate and distinct entity, and a day of final judgment after the resurrection followed by an eternal assignment to heaven or hell. In Latter-day Saint teachings, there are no recurring cycles of mortal existence in diverse forms and no merging of the soul into God, as found in Hindu reincarnation.

A remote similarity between the plan of salvation as taught by Latter-day Saints and the doctrine of reincarnation is the element of multiple stages that man passes through in order to progress and become more like his Creator. Latter-day Saints believe in four stages in the development of individual spirits, including a pre-mortal existence,

mortality, an intermediate sphere known as spirit world, and a final resurrected state in heaven or hell. Catholic doctrine recognizes three
stages, mortality, purgatory and heaven or hell. Protestant teachings
acknowledge two stages, mortality followed by an eternity in heaven or
hell. In all three bodies of doctrine, the concept of progressing through
phases is present. Disparities lie in the number of stages. However, the
inclusion of one or two additional stages through which man progresses, as taught by Latter-day Saints, does not constitute a meaningful parallel with Hindu reincarnation.

Another aspect of reincarnation that finds a remote thread of similarity in Latter-day Saint theology is the concept of Karma: the law of
cause and effect. In Hindu and Buddhist teachings, the conditions into
which one is born are not coincidental nor haphazard; rather, they are
the result of previous lives and choices. (H. Smith, pp. 102-3, 171-3)
Likewise, in the teachings of Latter-day Saints, the conditions of mortality are influenced by the development of an individual's spirit in the
pre-mortal state.

Similar to the theology of other Christian denominations, choices
made in this life will directly affect the destiny of souls on the day of
judgment. Clearly the Bible teaches that "whatsoever a man soweth,
that shall he also reap." (Gal 6:7; see also 2 Cor 9:6) The concept of
cause and effect is evident in all of these bodies of doctrine and does
not link teachings of Latter-day Saints more closely than those of other
Christian denominations to the Hindu or Buddhist concept of Karma.

It should be emphasized that Latter-day Saints are not averse to
comparisons between their doctrines and those of Hindu reincarnation,
except to the extent that such a linkage is used to deny Latter-day
Saints their rightful place in the Christian community. The beliefs of
Hindus are sacred to those who embrace their faith and deserve to be
respected as honest attempts by man to arrive at ultimate truths. The
simple fact of the matter is that few similarities between these two bodies of doctrine support the assertion of meaningful parallels.

WHY AM I HERE ON EARTH?

Teachings of Latter-day Saints share several important points in
common with those of other Christians regarding the purpose of man's
mortal existence. In the final analysis, all Christian traditions recognize
that man is here on earth to gain experience, work out his salvation
with the Lord and glorify God. (Scott, p. 182; MacArthur, Glory, p. 68;

Howells, summary table; Gibbs, p. 20) The most profound differences among the various bodies of doctrine relate to how one lays hold of salvation. These differences were discussed in the preceding chapter.

GRAPPLING WITH HUMAN SUFFERING AND INEQUALITY

What remains to be explored now is the broader context within which man finds himself in this life and how he makes sense of an individual quest for salvation in the midst of massive challenges confronting his fellow human beings. One author has summarized the writings of philosophers and humanists by concluding, "The most staggering objection to belief in a personal God is the ugly, tragic, overwhelming fact of human inequality and suffering." (Madsen, p. 53; see also Tillich, EN, pp. 44-6) The gospel of Jesus Christ must answer the "why question" for the whole of creation, and not just for its individual Christian believers.

The charge of skeptics leveled against all religions, and Christianity specifically, goes something like this: If God is all-powerful and God created all things, then God is responsible, directly or indirectly, for everything that occurs in this life. Why would God create conditions and populate his creations with agents that produce senseless human suffering?

Many attempts have been made to put a human face on the cumulative mass of suffering. Such efforts are woefully inadequate to capture the sum of human tragedy. Man is left with many questions that beg sensitive and coherent answers.

What is the divine purpose in a devastating cancer that takes a young child's mother? Does the Creator escape all responsibility for the acts of a Hitler when he brings this creature into existence and allows him to work his designs of degradation and horror? Is the eternal plan advanced by the starving masses of Rwanda or the startling poverty of inner cities? What kind of justice or mercy brings one severely handicapped child into fetid squalor at the same moment that a gifted child is born to loving parents with all the advantages of civilization and culture? What is the divine wisdom that snuffs out the life of a promising young woman before she blossoms and bursts into full maturity? Is the God of such a creation worthy of adulation or condemnation? (Bray, pp. 89-91)

THE INADEQUACY OF
TRADITIONAL CHRISTIAN RESPONSES

Through the ages, Christian theologians have devised various and sundry responses to these profound and troubling questions. The answers put forth by traditional Christian denominations derive directly from doctrines discussed above regarding man's origins and his eternal destiny.

The official position of the Catholic Church denies that evil and its many manifestations, including suffering, exist in reality. Evil, they believe, is an illusion that appears to possess a poignant reality in this existence, but, with the perspective of eternity, it has no positive existence. It is merely an absence of goodness. As Saint Athanasius put it, "What is evil is not, but what is good is." (Marquarie, p. 255)

This twist of reason is necessary in Catholic theology in order to absolve God of responsibility for evil. In their concept of ex nihilo creation, where God creates all things from nothing, God is responsible for everything, the evil as well as the good. According to the Catholic Church, God only created the good, but He is not responsible for conditions that permit the absence of good. (*Ibid.*, pp. 254-9)

The problem with this reasoning is that the same God who created all things ex nihilo, from nothing, is also the author of conditions that allow for an absence of good. Even if God did not create evil in a positive sense, the all-powerful God of ex nihilo creation must be responsible for conditions that allow evil to exist in a negative sense, as an absence of good.

Many Protestants seem to ignore the question of who is responsible for evil and suffering. Protestant theology tends to focus on assurances that Christ's redemption will right all things. "Human suffering will be swallowed up in Christ." (Little, p. 60) However, this position creates its own kind of problem.

As discussed above, only a small percentage of God's children are born into circumstances that expose them to the gospel of Jesus Christ. At the same time, salvation comes only through accepting Jesus Christ in this life, according to most Protestants' theology. (Lutzer, OM, pp. 105-6) This creates one of those inequalities condemned most vociferously by the critics of religion. From the perspective of the skeptic, it is bad enough that God sends individuals into circumstances where the degree of suffering varies so widely in this life. But matters go from bad to worse when the majority of mankind is damned for an eternity by being born ex nihilo into conditions where they will never have an opportunity to accept the gospel of Jesus Christ. These poor lost souls which constitute the majority of mankind, would be better off never to issue forth from God only to go into eternal misery and suffering without a chance of salvation.

One response to this charge of injustice is to fall back on the absolute sovereignty of God. "God is not obligated to save any." (Chafer/Walvoord, p. 234; see also Bray, pp. 93-4)

Another response is to deny the legitimacy of human perspective. "If our concept of justice differs from God's . . . he will be unimpressed. No one is God's counselor." (Lutzer, OM, p. 120; see also Bray, pp. 93-4) This explanation creates distance between man and God, making it difficult, if not impossible, to exercise faith unto salvation in a divine being of perfect holiness, goodness, justice, mercy and love. If these attributes can only be discerned and comprehended by God, then man is left without a point of reference in exercising faith in the object of his adoration.

Other Protestant writers and theologians, including C. S. Lewis, explain the wrongs of the world as a perfect creation gone astray. (Lewis, p. 48; see also Murphee, p. 93; Chafer/Walvoord, pp. 232-4; Keeley, p. 255) God is responsible for the vehicle. Man, by responding to the promptings of God or Satan, is responsible for the direction and manner in which it is driven. God gave man and Satan moral agency:

> Because free will, though it makes evil possible, is also the only thing that makes possible any love or goodness or joy worth having . . . The happiness which God designs for His higher creatures is the happiness of being freely and voluntarily united to Him and to each other in an ecstasy of love and delight . . . (Lewis, p. 52)

The problem with this explanation is that it does not account for all inequalities and suffering of this world. For instance, is it man or Satan who is responsible for the child born without a spinal cord? Or in the example above, is it the fault of man or Satan that the majority of mankind is born into circumstances which will not allow them to accept the gospel of Jesus Christ in this life? Even in those situations where the shortcomings of man and the influences of Satan are evident, it is not reasonable to hold that an all-knowing, all-powerful God who creates all things ex nihilo bears no responsibility for sending a child into the home of alcoholic, abusive parents. The parents are not deserving of the blessing. The child has done nothing to warrant being placed in such deplorable conditions. Yet God, the creator of all things ex nihilo, wills that the sins of the parents be visited upon the heads of the children.

Faced with such contradictions and inconsistencies, traditional Christians retreat sooner or later to the shroud of mystery. "By faith we must assume that God chose the best possible plan, and that if a better plan could have been put into operation God would have chosen it." (Chafer/Walvoord, pp. 232-233) Alas, strange and inscrutable are the ways of the Lord. (Bray, pp. 92-3)

ALL THINGS SHALL BE FOR THY GOOD

Now, what if, as Latter-day Saints teach, God did not create all things, ex nihilo, from nothing, but rather organized this creation from eternal elements incorporating conditions and laws of the universe which are co-eternal with the elements? In that case, God is not the author of evil. Evil has always existed. It is a fact of existence that man must deal with and learn to overcome.

Under these circumstances, God is not responsible for the existence of evil. Of course, he is responsible for creating a world in which evil is present. This act of divine creation and organization must have been undertaken for a specific purpose in the wisdom of a loving God. So what is that specific purpose?

Latter-day Saints teach that it is impossible for man to progress and attain his full purpose without overcoming evil and its consequences. "It must needs be, that there is an opposition in all things. If not so . . . righteousness could not be brought to pass . . . neither holiness . . . neither good." (2 Ne 2:11) This is similar to the reasoning of C. S. Lewis, but with several important qualifiers uniquely revealed in teachings of Latter-day Saints.

First, a pre-mortal existence is necessary, as taught by Latter-day Saints, where individual spirits develop and progress in their own unique ways. Then the inequalities of this world will not be the result of chance or an inscrutable will. Rather, these inequalities will serve a benevolent purpose of completing the growth and development of God's children begun prior to mortality, so they can attain their noble destiny.

Second, there must be no other way to lay hold of this noble destiny except to pass through the conditions of this life. Under these circumstances, the inequalities and trials of this life are necessary stepping stones to a more blessed state.

Third, as taught by Latter-day Saints, each individual must have had full knowledge of the conditions and suffering of this life in that premortal state and some awareness of specific conditions and trials he or she would pass through in this world. With that knowledge and awareness, each individual must have willingly chosen to come to this earth believing that, despite difficulties, this course would ultimately bless him or her.

In pursuit of this higher goal, the rewards promised to each individual should more than compensate for the temporary discomfort experienced in this creation. This is not the "inscrutable will" of an all-powerful creator thrusting the spirits of man into conditions which they would have never chosen for themselves. These noble spirits chose with inspiring courage and foreknowledge to enter this world in the exact circumstances of their mortality. This was the understanding given to Job in his moment of trial. The Lord responded to his cries of discomfort with a question: "Where wast thou when I laid the foundations of the earth? . . . When the morning stars sang together, and all of the sons of God shouted for joy?" (Job 38:4,7) Job understood that he and the rest of us were there. The plan was presented to all. We shouted for joy at the opportunity to pass through the challenges of this life that we might grow and progress, with an opportunity of becoming like our Heavenly Father.

Fourth, the majority of mankind, who will never have an opportunity to embrace the gospel of Jesus Christ in this life, must be given an equal opportunity to hear its message and accept their Savior prior to the day of final judgment. This necessitates an intermediate sphere, as taught by Latter-day Saints, where the gospel is taught to all mankind and where the spirits of man can accept or reject the ordinances of salvation performed by proxy on their behalf, "that they might be judged according to men in the flesh, but live according to God in the spirit." (1 Pet 4:6)

Finally, when the suffering and challenges of this life are behind us, the Lord's plan must provide that those who courageously endured the contradictions and trials of mortality are granted a degree of glory in proportion to their valiancy, as taught by Latter-day Saints. If the plan is nothing more than a game of spiritual Russian-roulette where most are consigned to circumstances worse than those that characterized their beginnings, the proposition is unworthy of man's consideration and makes a mockery of God's omnipotence. The will of our all-loving Father is "that of all which he hath given me [the Son] I should lose nothing, but should raise it up again at the last day." (John 6:39) God's will shall be done.

When all of these conditions are provided, the plan of God is perfect in its justice, mercy and love toward all humankind. Each of us can look at our own circumstances and know "that all these things shall give [us] experience, and shall be for [our] good."(D&C 122:7)

We can view the lot of another with compassion born of understanding that we are here to serve and lighten the load of others as they struggle through their customized course of instruction and life. We need not wish for the circumstances of someone else nor wonder if the Lord has forsaken us in our trials. Those same trials are additional evidences of God's love for us, "For whom the Lord loveth he chasteneth, and scourgeth every son whom he receiveth." (Heb 12:6)

We can find comfort and direction in the knowledge that our life has purpose in the here and now. It is not by chance, but by deliberate design of a loving God who desires for us our ultimate happiness and honor. Whatever our circumstances, we may rest assured we are noble spirits possessing promises of eternal reward in Jesus Christ. This is the plan of salvation for all humankind. All glory be to God.

4

Priesthood Authority and Divine Organization

There are few issues in the Christian community where differences are more clearly evident and potentially divisive than the matter of priesthood authority and organization of Christ's church on the earth today. Positions of various denominations cover an entire spectrum and demonstrate the diversity or confusion within modern Christianity, depending on one's perspective. Even basic issues regarding what constitutes a church and when Christ's church was founded are in dispute.

Some Protestant denominations visualize the church primarily as a community of believers. According to this view, the church was formed on the day of Pentecost when the Spirit was poured out on believers, binding hearts and souls into a community of saints. Prominent scholar and theologian, Dietrich Bonhoeffer writes, "The church is a community of spirit and love. The relations of the members of the community are those of a community of spirit and not those of a society." (Bonhoeffer, p. 185)

According to those who espouse this view, the Holy Spirit is the central organizing force of the church, which explains why the church came into existence on the day of Pentecost, and not before. "The church as an empirical church could indeed be created only by the Holy Spirit . . . As a pioneer and model, Jesus is also the founder of a religious community, though not of the Christian church (for this came into existence only after the Pentecost)." (*Ibid.*, pp. 111-2)

As described by Bonhoeffer and others, the organizing principle of the church is the local unit or community. Indeed, the body of Christ consists of its members organized as a community of believers. "The church is 'Christ existing as the community.'" (*Ibid.*, p. 160; see also Godsey pp. 22 and 35-6; Tillich, ST, Vol. III., pp. 162-7 and 221-3)

Limited hierarchy and structure are necessary for order but do not define the church as an organization. "'The Protestant institution' is not set up by God over the congregation but is an act of the congregation itself." (*Ibid.*, p. 177, also see Howells, pp. 15-6 and summary table)

Roman Catholics, Eastern Orthodox Christians, a few Protestant denominations, and Latter-day Saints maintain that, during his mortal ministry, Jesus established a divine organization through which he would continue to administer the affairs of his kingdom after his ascension. There is general acknowledgment, even among Protestants, that Christ organized a church and gave authority to those he called to administer his kingdom. (Bonhoeffer, pp. 97-8) Where that authority is and how Christ's church is organized and administered today are matters of profound importance to those who would follow the Master and assist in establishing his kingdom.

CHRIST ORGANIZED HIS CHURCH

The Biblical record indicates that Christ organized his church and gave authority to those he chose to lead it. Clearly, this was more than an afterthought. From the beginning of his public ministry, Jesus Christ knew he would atone for the sins of the world and pass through the portal of death into immortality. Many of the choicest teachings of the Savior found in the gospels are directed to a small group of apostles chosen to lead the work of the kingdom after his resurrection and ascension.

Three of the four gospels mention the calling and ordination of twelve apostles and enumerate specific powers given to them:

> And when he had called unto him his twelve disciples, he gave them power against unclean spirits, to cast them out, and to heal all manner of sickness and all manner of disease . . .
>
> saying, The kingdom of heaven is at hand.
>
> Heal the sick, cleanse the lepers, raise the dead, cast out devils: freely ye have received, freely give. (Matt 10:1,7-8; see also Mark 3:13-15; Luke 6:12-13, 9:1-2)

Although the twelve apostles were most prominent, they were not alone in ministering to Christ's followers and spreading the good news of the gospel. Jesus called others from among his disciples to assist in the work. Luke records, "the Lord appointed other seventy also, and sent them two and two before his face." (Luke 10:1) Paul indicates that Christ organized his church with various offices and appointments. "And he [Christ] gave some, apostles; and some, prophets; and some, evangelists; and some, pastors and teachers." (Eph 4:11) The New Testament makes specific mention of other offices in the organization of the church including elders (Acts 14:23; Titus 1:5; James 5:14), bishops (Titus 1:7; Philip 1:1) and deacons (Philip 1:1; 1 Tim 3:8).

These different offices provided order and unity to Christ's church. Paul illustrates this point by likening the church to a human body with numerous parts or members functioning in unison:

> For the body is not one member, but many.
> But now hath God set the members every one of them in the body as it hath pleased him.
> But now are they many members, yet but one body.
> And God hath set some in the church, first apostles, secondarily prophets, thirdly teachers . . . (1 Cor 12:14, 18, 20, 28)

Throughout the New Testament, apostles and prophets were foremost among members in leading Christ's church under the direction of the Savior, who is "the head of the body, the church." (Col 1:18) So Paul writes:

> Now therefore ye are no more strangers and foreigners, but fellowcitizens with the saints, and of the household of God;
> And are built upon the foundation of the apostles and prophets, Jesus Christ himself being the chief corner stone." (Eph 2:19-20)

On this foundation and cornerstone was constructed an edifice of faithful saints organized into various offices and ministries comprising a holy priesthood. Addressing the "Elect according to the foreknowledge of God the Father" (1 Pet 1:2), Peter writes:

> Ye also, as lively stones, are built up a spiritual house, an holy priesthood.
> ye are a chosen generation, a royal priesthood, an holy nation, a peculiar people." (1 Pet 2:5, 9)

CHRIST DELEGATED PRIESTHOOD POWER

Those called to offices of the priesthood in Christ's church were granted great powers to administer the affairs of the Lord's kingdom. Some of these powers included authority to preach the gospel in Jesus' name (Matt 28:19; Mark 3:14; Luke 9:2), baptize (Matt 28:19), confer the Holy Ghost (Acts 8:6-17) and heal the sick (Matt 10:1; Luke 9:2), just to name a few.

With these powers, followers of Christ were expected to perform many good works in the name of the Lord. "Verily, verily, I say unto you, He that believeth on me, the works that I do shall he do also; and greater works than these shall he do; because I go unto my Father." (John 14:12)

Many Christian denominations maintain that, in addition to being the Son of God and a great teacher of mankind, Jesus was the organizer of a church which he established and directed, delegating power and authority through his chosen leaders. "Ye have not chosen me, but I have chosen you, and ordained you." (John 15:16)

CHRIST'S CHURCH CONTINUED AFTER HIS ASCENSION

The Bible provides substantial evidence of continuing operations of Christ's formal church following his resurrection and ascension. For example, the vacancy in the twelve apostles created by Judas' death was filled when other apostles and church leaders met to select Matthias. (Acts 1:21-26) At a later date, James, the half brother of Jesus was called as an apostle, presumably to fill another vacancy in the quorum of twelve. (Gal 1:19) Miracles continued such as John and Peter healing a lame man at the gate of the temple. (Acts 3:1-7) The Apostle Peter received a revelation from God and a visit from Cornelius, the centurion, opening the way for the gospel to go to the gentile nations. (Acts 10) Saul saw the resurrected Lord in vision and converted to Christianity. (Acts 9:4-19) He and Barnabas were ordained to preach the gospel. (Acts 13:1-4) New converts were baptized. (Acts 8:38; Acts 19:1-6; Acts 22:16) The Holy Ghost was conferred upon members. (Acts 2:1-4; Acts 8:6-17) Gifts of the spirit were manifest to edify and bless the saints. (1 Cor 12 and 14) Stephen, Timothy and others were ordained to offices in the priesthood. (Act 6:5-6; 1 Tim 4:14; 2 Tim 1:6; Acts 14:23; Titus 1:5) The work and ministry of Christ's church moved forward with power and extended its geographic reach throughout much of present-day southern Europe and western Asia.

As the church grew in numbers and public awareness, persecution intensified on many fronts. (Acts 7:59-8:1; Acts 14:1-6, 19) In 70 AD, Romans destroyed Jerusalem, the center of the church, and leveled the temple. One by one, the apostles died off or, more often, were killed. (Acts 12:2; Reid, ed., pp. 729,743,749) Congregations of saints in Asia and elsewhere fell under general condemnation. (Revelation, chapters 2 and 3) Around the end of the first century, the last writings of what is now the New Testament were completed, and God's revelations to man ceased. On these general outlines of church history, most Christian denominations agree.

THREE DIVERGENT EXPLANATIONS, TWO POINTS OF VARIANCE

At this point in the history of Christianity, three divergent positions emerge to explain subsequent events. Roman Catholics maintain the formal church of Christ continued under the direction of priesthood leaders and inspired church councils. Priesthood authority bestowed upon apostles passed to the bishop of Rome and in unbroken papal succession to the present-day Pope. Catholics claim to be the guardians of Christ's church today through apostolic succession.

Protestants contend the Christian church remained on earth and true believers in Christ have continued in force since the church was first organized (day of Pentecost for some; during Christ's ministry for others). Protestants recognize the councils of the Catholic Church as inspired and doctrinally correct through the eighth century, AD. After this time, Roman Catholicism fell into error and departed from teachings of the Bible, according to most Protestant denominations. (Ricks and Peterson, p. 43)

In addition, Protestants teach that the priesthood underwent fundamental change following the atonement. Specifically, the priesthood became available to all believers. Accordingly, when reformers broke from the Catholic Church and organized into diverse denominations, no formal line of authority passed down through church hierarchy was necessary. Present-day leadership structures and councils in many Protestant denominations serve to organize the work of the ministry and emphasize a pastoral role for priesthood leaders, although this varies significantly by denomination. (Hordern, p. 24; J. Z. Smith, p. 859; Chafer/Walvoord, pp.266-7; Ankerberg, pp. 74-5)

Latter-day Saints teach that the church organized by Christ fell into general apostasy and eventually ceased to function as his representative body, after the death of his apostles. This event was foretold by prophets and apostles of the Bible. According to Latter-day Saints, the Bible prophesies that God will stretch forth his hand in the last days, restoring the gospel of Jesus Christ in its purity, as it was in the days of the Savior and his chosen apostles and prophets. Latter-day Saints testify that, in 1820, Jesus Christ called a prophet and organized his church with apostles and prophets, similar to the one organized by Christ in the meridian of time. The first prophet called in this last dispensation before Jesus' second coming was Joseph Smith. Latter-day Saints believe the priesthood of God was restored to men by glorified, resurrected beings commissioned by Jesus Christ to confer this authority upon his chosen servants. With proper authority, the work of salvation is going forward to all nations under the direction of Jesus Christ as he administers his kingdom through chosen apostles and prophets. This "marvellous work and a wonder" (Isa 29:14) is the kingdom of God established in the last days as foretold by the prophet, Daniel, "which shall never be destroyed." (Dan 2:44)

Regarding priesthood and organization of Christ's church on earth today, major differences among Protestants, Catholics and Latter-day Saints can be distilled to two key points of differentiation. These are the following:

1. Catholics and Protestants maintain that the church established by Jesus Christ in the meridian of time has continued on the earth down to the present day, while Latter-day Saints teach that the original church of Christ fell into general apostasy and was restored in its fullness in the last days as prophesied in the Bible.

2. Catholics and Latter-day Saints insist that certain ordinances must be performed by one holding the priesthood, and that this priesthood must be exercised under the direction of the formal church and its chosen leaders (i.e., a person must be ordained by one having proper authority), while Protestants are divided on the importance of ordinances but teach that the priesthood is possessed by all believers of Christ (i.e., authority to minister to God's chosen can be claimed by the informal church of believers).

While this second point of differentiation is generally correct, there is one important exception. In Catholic teachings, baptism is a vital ordinance that can be performed by one not holding the priesthood, and yet it is recognized as valid by the church, provided the baptism is performed by invoking the three names of Deity: the Father, the Son and the Holy Ghost. (Barker p. 171; see also 763-4)

Notwithstanding this exception, these two points of differentiation go to the heart of matters regarding priesthood authority and organization of Christ's church as taught by Catholics, Protestants and Latter-day Saints. They deserve to be examined in light of Biblical teachings.

APOSTASY AND RESTORATION FORETOLD IN THE BIBLE

At issue on the first point of differentiation is whether the Bible foretells a falling away, or general apostasy, of the church organized by Christ in the meridian of time to be followed by a restoration (not merely a reformation) of his church in the last days. Numerous passages of scripture prophesy of these events to take place before the Savior's second coming.

A GENERAL APOSTASY PROPHESIED

For example, the prophet Amos prophesied of a time when the word of the Lord would be absent from the earth, likening the situation to a famine.

> Behold, the days come, saith the Lord God, that I will send a famine in the land, not a famine of bread, nor a thirst for water, but of hearing the words of the Lord:
>
> And they shall wander from sea to sea, and from the north even to the east, they shall run to and fro to seek the word of the Lord, and shall not find it.
>
> In that day shall the fair virgins and young men faint for thirst. (Amos 8:11-13)

Likewise, the Apostle Paul wrote to the saints of Thessalonia concerning a general falling away, or apostasy, of the church before the second coming of the Lord:

> Now we beseech you, brethren, by the coming of our Lord Jesus Christ, and by our gathering together unto him
>
> That ye be not soon shaken in mind, or be troubled, neither by spirit, nor by word, nor by letter as from us, as that the day of Christ is at hand.

> Let no man deceive you by any means: for that day shall not come,
> except there come a falling away first . . .
> Remember ye not, that, when I was yet with you, I told you these
> things? (2 Thes 2:1-3, 5)

Paul's understanding of an approaching apostasy of the church was
primarily the product of inspiration, but also of personal observation.
The early church was experiencing significant problems maintaining
correct doctrine and adhering to approved practices throughout the
period of Paul's ministry. At times, Paul seemed amazed by how rapid-
ly the apostasy of the church was advancing despite the energetic
efforts of inspired leaders in his day:

> I marvel that ye are so soon removed from him that called you into
> the grace of Christ unto another gospel:
> Which is not another; but there be some that trouble you and would
> pervert the gospel of Christ. (Gal 1:6-7)

Paul confided to local leaders in Ephesus that apostasy and dissension would soon enter into their congregation, some of it at the hands
of local church leaders:

> Take heed therefore unto yourselves, and to all the flock, over
> which the Holy Ghost hath made you overseers, to feed the church of
> God, which he hath purchased with his own blood.
> For I know this, that after my departing shall grievous wolves enter
> in among you, not sparing the flock.
> Also of your own selves shall men arise, speaking perverse things,
> to draw away disciples after them. (Acts 20:28-30)

The church in Ephesus was not the exception, but rather followed
the general pattern among far-flung congregations of believers in
Paul's day. For instance, Paul's first letter to the Corinthians was written in response to division and dissension prevailing among the saints
in that location. (1 Cor 1:10-13; 3:3-4; 15:12) Also, the saints throughout Asia appear to have rejected Paul, though he was the Lord's anointed. To Timothy, his dear friend in the gospel, Paul writes, "This thou
knowest, that all they which are in Asia be turned away from me." (2
Tim 1:15)

Paul's rejection foreshadowed a creeping apostasy among the seven
churches in Asia as noted by John the Revelator in the Book of
Revelation. Ephesus and Sardis were called to repentance. (Rev 2:5;

3:3) The works of Satan were in evidence at Smyrna, Pergamos and Philadelphia. (Rev 2:9, 13-14; 3:9) False teachers expounding seductive doctrines were leading many astray in Thyatira. (Rev 2:20-22) The church of the Laodiceans received the rebuke:

> I know thy works, that thou art neither cold nor hot:
> I would thou wert cold or hot.
> So then because thou art lukewarm, and neither cold nor hot, I will spue thee out of my mouth. (Rev 3:15-16)

Paul warned that these conditions and worse would envelop the church before the second coming of Christ.

> This know also, that in the last days perilous times shall come.
> For men shall be lovers of their own selves, covetous, boasters, proud, blasphemers, disobedient to parents, unthankful, unholy. *Having a form of godliness, but denying the power thereof . . .*
> Ever learning and never able to come to the knowledge of the truth. (2 Tim 3:1, 2, 5, 7; emphasis added)

> For the time will come when [members of Christ's church] will not endure sound doctrine; but after their own lusts shall they heap to themselves teachers.
> And they shall turn away their ears from the truth, and shall be turned unto fables. (2 Tim 4:3-4)

Old Testament prophets foresaw these times, too. For example, Isaiah spoke of a time when the world would be covered with the darkness of apostasy. "For, behold, the darkness shall cover the earth, and gross darkness the people." (Isa 60:2) The cause of this darkness would be the apostate conditions of the Lord's people who had deviated from his ways.

> The earth mourneth and fadeth away.
> The earth also is defiled under the inhabitants thereof; because they have transgressed the laws, changed the ordinance, broken the everlasting covenant.
> Therefore hath the curse devoured the earth, and they that dwell therein are desolate . . . (Isa 24:4-6)

Elsewhere, Isaiah describes the remnants of believers left during these times when darkness and apostasy cover the earth. "This people draw near me with their mouth, and with their lips do honour me, but have removed their heart far from me, and their fear toward me is taught by the precept of men." (Isa 29:13)

Other Christians generally maintain that these teachings about "a falling away" do not justify a conclusion that the whole church of Christ was taken from the earth. For example, Protestants believe the Catholic Church strayed from true teachings of Christ and introduced erroneous doctrines. However, Protestants also maintain that some remnant of true believers always remained on the earth and a return to Christ's true teachings was effected with aid of the Bible and inspiration of the Holy Spirit. (Barker, pp. 753-4, 764) Likewise, others insist the teachings of Amos and Isaiah are not a description of the conditions following the ministry of Christ. Rather, they associate these prophecies with conditions prevailing in Jewish worship prior to the first coming of the Lord.

These alternative interpretations might be more persuasive if not for an equal number of scriptural passages that speak of a restoration or restitution of the gospel in the last days. Webster defines "restore" as, "to bring back; establish again; bring back to a former condition." If the gospel is to be "restored," it must first be lost or removed. It makes no sense to restore something that was always here. In this light, the writings of Paul, Amos and Isaiah are transparent in predicting a general apostasy preceding a restoration of all things in the last days.

A RESTORATION OF ALL THINGS PROMISED

Perhaps the clearest reference to a restoration of the gospel prophesied for the last days is found in exhortations of Peter to potential converts following the ascension of the Savior:

> Repent ye therefore, and be converted, that your sins may be blotted out, when the times of refreshing shall come from the presence of the Lord;
>
> And he shall send Jesus Christ, which before was preached unto you:
>
> Whom the heaven must receive until the times of restitution of all things, which God hath spoken by the mouth of all his holy prophets since the world began. (Acts 3:19-21)

Peter was alluding to events in the future when all things would be restored, a "restitution of all things." Moreover, his inspired declaration indicates this time of restitution had been prophesied previously by prophets of God, "which God hath spoken by the mouth of all his holy prophets since the world began." (Acts 3:21) A number of these prophecies are recorded in the Bible.

For example, the prophet Daniel spoke of this restoration in interpreting the dream of King Nebuchadnezzar regarding events that would transpire in the latter days. Specifically, he referred to the last days when "the kingdom shall be partly strong, and partly broken" (Dan 2:42) when many nations will be established. In that day, a great work will come forth:

> And in the days of these kings shall the God of heaven set up a kingdom, which shall never be destroyed: and the kingdom shall not be left to other people, but it shall break in pieces and consume all these kingdoms, and it shall stand for ever.
>
> Forasmuch as thou sawest that the stone was cut out of the mountain without hands, and that it brake in pieces the iron, the brass, the clay, the silver, and the gold; the great God hath made known to the king what shall come to pass hereafter. (Dan 2:44-45)

The interpretation given by Daniel provides marvelous details regarding the timing of these events. By referring to great empires of gold (Nebuchadnezzar and Babylon), silver (the Medes and Persians), brass (Alexander the Great and Macedonia), and iron (the Roman empire), Daniel fixes the time of these important happenings as being after the meridian of time and after the fall of Rome. Only then, when many kingdoms or nations share power, would the God of heaven set up a kingdom which should never be destroyed.

Isaiah spoke of a great work to be preceded by an apostasy. "For the Lord hath poured out upon you the spirit of deep sleep, and hath closed your eyes: the prophets and your rulers, the seers hath he covered." (Isa 29:10) After a time, when prophets and seers cease to prophecy (first century AD) and after the people embrace "the precept of men" (Isa 29:13), then "behold, I [the Lord] will proceed to do a marvellous work among this people, even a marvellous work and a wonder." (Isa 29:14)

This great work of restoration will include temples, even the house of the Lord, as prophesied by Isaiah:

> And it shall come to pass in the last days, that the mountain of the Lord's house shall be established in the top of the mountains, and shall be exalted above the hills; and all nations shall flow unto it.

And many people shall go and say, Come ye, and let us go up to the mountain of the Lord, to the house of the God of Jacob; and he will teach us of his ways and we will walk in his paths. (Isa 2:2-3)

The prophet Joel also wrote of the last days and a great work that would precede the second coming of the Lord:

And it shall come to pass afterward, that I will pour out my spirit upon all flesh; and your sons and your daughters shall prophesy, your old men shall dream dreams, your young men shall see visions:

And also upon the servants and upon the handmaids in those days will I pour out my spirit. (Joel 2:28-29)

All of this was prophesied to occur in the last days, "before the great and the terrible day of the Lord." (Joel 2:31)

Other Old Testament prophets; including Jeremiah (Jer 31:31-40), Ezekiel (Ezek 37:26-28), Micah (Micah 4:2), Malachi (Mal 3:1-2 and 4:5-6) and Amos (Amos 3:7); spoke of marvelous latter-day events when prophets, visions, revelations and temples would abound. Truly, "God hath spoken [of the restitution of all things] by the mouth of all his holy prophets since the world began." (Acts 3:21)

These statements by prophets in all ages were well understood by the apostles and disciples of Christ. For example, just before the Savior's ascension, his disciples asked about the restoration of all things foretold by prophets.

When they therefore were come together, they asked of him, saying, Lord, wilt thou at this time restore again the kingdom to Israel?

And he said unto them, It is not for you to know the times or the seasons, which the Father hath put in his own power. (Acts 1:6-7)

The Savior then instructs his disciples on receiving the Holy Ghost and being a witness to his divine work. However, no indication is given of a restoration of all things in that day. (Acts 1:8)

This was not the first time the apostles had inquired of the Lord on this matter. During Christ's mortal ministry, the apostles queried the Lord about timing for the restoration of all things. After descending from the mount of transfiguration where the Savior and three apostles beheld Moses and Elias in vision, Jesus charged those with him to:

Tell the vision to no man, until the Son of man be risen again from the dead.

And his disciples asked him, saying, Why then say the scribes that Elias must first come?

And Jesus answered and said unto them, Elias truly shall first come, and restore all things. (Matt 17:9-11; Mark 9:12)

This restoration of all things was not fulfilled at that time, but was promised for a future day.

Paul, one of those who foretold the apostasy, wrote of this period in the future when all things would be gathered together in Christ. "In the dispensation of the fulness of times (God) might gather together in one all things in Christ, both which are in heaven and which are on earth; even in him." (Eph 1:10)

John the Revelator saw in vision an angel sent to the inhabitants of the earth, bringing the everlasting gospel prior to the second coming of the Lord:

And I saw another angel fly in the midst of heaven, having the everlasting gospel to preach unto them that dwell on earth, and to every nation, and kindred, and tongue, and people,

Saying with a loud voice, Fear God, and give glory to him; for the hour of his judgment is come. (Rev 14:6-7)

In light of so many biblical witnesses, it seems apparent Jesus and his disciples understood that the kingdom they were establishing in the meridian of time was not intended to remain on the earth forever. Theirs was not the kingdom spoken of by Daniel "which shall never be destroyed." (Dan 2:44) Rather, the kingdom of God established by Jesus Christ in a divine and inspired form provided a pattern for his restored kingdom of the latter days. This restoration would be preceded by a period of spiritual darkness and apostasy.

EVIDENCE OF APOSTASY
AND A NEED FOR RESTORATION

Without intending criticism of any denomination or body of beliefs, an objective study of the history of Christianity makes it evident the apostasy foretold by so many prophets did take place following the death of the apostles. Isaiah prophesied that one effect of the apostasy would be to substitute the precepts of men for truths of the gospel. As discussed in chapter one and acknowledged by most Christian theologians, influences of Greek philosophy are evident in the doctrine of Trinity as devised by fourth-century church councils. Human reasoning substituting for revelation has produced unique and innovative creeds not found in the Bible including adoration of images, the doctrine of original sin, celibacy and monasticism, transubstantiation, the sign of the cross, veneration of Mary and other saints, indulgences, ex nihilo creation, a closed canon of scripture, permanent cessation of revelation, an all-believers' priesthood, and salvation by grace without works, just to name a few. (see Morgan, p. 57)

Isaiah also foretold the changing of ordinances as a part of the apostasy. Many denominations have altered the original ordinance of baptism by immersion, substituting sprinkling and infant baptism or denying its necessity altogether. The pomp and splendor of a ritualistic mass is another example of innovative ordinances not practiced in the early church.

The organization of other Christian churches, without apostles and prophets, provides yet another example of changes introduced by man. Despite Paul's teachings that the foundation of the church was "the apostles and prophets, Jesus Christ himself being the chief cornerstone" (Eph 2:20), these inspired offices of priesthood leadership are nowhere to be found in traditional Christian denominations.

Many gifts of the spirit are denied by the majority of Christian denominations. For example, despite Paul's counsel to seek after the gift of prophecy (1 Cor 14:1,5), revelation is viewed with contempt and misapprehension in most Christian denominations, Pentecostals and charismatics being the exceptions. Even in these cases, prophetic utterances are rejected unless they conform to narrow interpretations of the Bible. (Dictionary of Christianity in America, pp. 948-9; Connelly, p. 33) In many congregations, gifts of the spirit, as delineated by Paul, including healing, the working of miracles, discerning of spirits, tongues and interpretation of tongues, (1 Cor 12) are strongly discouraged. In so doing, Christian denominations seem to fit Paul's description of apostate conditions, "having a form of godliness, but denying the power thereof." (2 Tim 3:5)

Some Christians will protest that such conclusions are harsh and uncharitable. However, if totally honest with themselves and others, it must be admitted that all of these changes in doctrines, ordinances and priesthood offices were introduced centuries after the death of Christ's apostles when, according to their own teachings, revelation had ceased. These precepts of men are the product of their human reasoning and logic as they have struggled to understand the workings of God. None of them can be wholly justified in the record of the Bible.

Without condemnation, Latter-day Saints offer a simple explanation. These are the fruits of the apostasy foretold by prophets and apostles of the Bible. They stand as a witness of the need for a restoration of all things in the latter days.

Latter-day Saints are not alone in this conclusion. Other sincere believers in Christ have come to a similar conclusion, praying for a day when the God of heaven would restore his church led by revelation. For instance, Roger Williams, the founder of Rhode Island and a leading religious reformer of the seventeenth century resigned his ministry, concluding there was "no regularly constituted church of Christ on earth, nor any person authorized to administer any church ordinances, nor can there be until new apostles are sent by the great head of the Church for whose coming I am seeking." (*Picturesque America*, p. 502, as quoted in Richards, p. 29)

PRIESTHOOD AUTHORITY IN CHRIST'S CHURCH

The other major difference regarding priesthood authority and church organization involves the process by which authority to act in God's name is conferred upon individuals. Catholics and Latter-day Saints teach that the priesthood of God can only be conveyed through formal church channels by one having authority to ordain others. Protestant denominations insist that priesthood authority is available to all believers of Christ in the spiritual or informal church.

PROTESTANT ALL-BELIEVERS' PRIESTHOOD

The primary scriptural reference cited by Protestants to support their position is found in Paul's epistle to the Hebrews, chapters seven through ten. (Richards and Martin, pp. 32-3; Dunnett, p. 13; Manson, pp. 48-62; Ankerberg, pp. 75-6; Scott, p. 215) This important passage of scripture makes frequent reference to "Melchisedec, king of Salem, priest of the most high God." (Heb 7:1) Melchisedec was singled out as a "great man" because "even the patriarch Abraham gave the tenth of the spoils" (Heb 7:4) to him. Melchisedec is described as: "Without father, without mother, without descent, having neither beginning of days, nor end of life; but made like unto the Son of God; abideth a priest continually." (Heb 7:3) Melchisedec, born well in advance of the time of Israel or Moses, did not hold the Levitical priesthood, a priesthood given to the tribe of Levi under the Mosaic law. The priesthood held by Melchisedec was of a higher order.

This higher priesthood was the same one held by Christ. Paul informs the Jewish saints of this fact. "For he testifieth, Thou art a priest for ever after the order of Melchisedec." (Heb 7:17) Jesus Christ did not descend through Levitical lineage, "for it is evident that our Lord sprang out of Juda; of which tribe Moses spake nothing concerning priesthood." (Heb 7:14) And yet, Christ was "a priest for ever after the order of Melchisedec." (Heb 7:17)

With the offering of Jesus Christ as the lamb of God, the law of Moses was fulfilled. No longer were priests required "to offer up sacrifices, first for his own sins, and then for the people's: for this [Christ] did once, when he offered up himself." (Heb 7:27) The Lord's atonement brought fulfillment to the law of Moses and an end to ordinances of the Levitical priesthood. "For the priesthood being changed, there is made of necessity a change also of the law." (Heb 7:12)

It also ushered in a new covenant between God and his elect. "And for this cause he is the mediator of the new testament, that . . . they which are called might receive the promise of eternal inheritance." (Heb 9:15; also see Richards and Martin, pp. 32-40) And what is this new testament? "For this is the covenant that I will make with the house of Israel after those days, saith the Lord; I will put my laws into their mind and write them in their hearts: and I will be to them a God, and they shall be to me a people." (Heb 8:10)

This change of priesthood and the introduction of a new covenant between God and His people are interpreted by Protestants as signaling a total break from priesthood hierarchies and the establishment of a new order in which the priesthood is available to all believers in Christ. (Richards and Martin, p. 20; Heppe, p. 458; Gibbs, p. 110; Little p. 98; Godsey, p. 50; Scott, p. 215) In this new order, Christ is the permanent high priest and each believer is his or her own priest. Lawrence O. Richards and Gib Martin write:

> Under the new covenant, every believer lives in the very presence of God, with full and immediate access to Him . . . Under the new covenant, Jesus Himself is 'revealed in our mortal bodies' . . . each

believer is now enabled to fulfill the changeless functions of the priesthood . . . The implications of these truths are staggering. Because each believer has personal and immediate access to and authority with God, there is no need for hierarchal structures as under the old covenant. (Richards and Martin, p. 40; see also Hordern, p. 24)

The rending of the veil in the temple following Christ's crucifixion is seen as symbolic of man being ushered into God's presence directly through Christ without need of priesthood ordinances and intermediaries.

According to many Protestant denominations, the role of priesthood leadership moves away from ritual and formal functions in the new covenant. Today, priesthood holders in most Protestant congregations are generally viewed as:

> Religious specialists who proclaim and teach the gospel and otherwise minister to the needs of congregants. Most Protestants—Anglicans and Episcopalians excepted—call their religious specialists 'ministers' or 'pastors' rather than priests, thus stressing pastoral rather than cultic functions. (J. Z. Smith, p. 859; see also Manson, p. 71; Richards and Gib, p. 38; Heppe, p. 612; Little, p. 94; Tillich, ST, Vol. III, p. 217)

This innovation of an all-believers' priesthood was expedient for Martin Luther and other Protestant reformers who broke with the Roman Catholic Church during the reformation. The Catholic Church asserted formal priesthood authority, claiming apostolic succession from the first apostle, Peter. When Protestant leaders denounced what they believed to be the errors of the church of Rome, those in authority within the Catholic Church excommunicated the reformers and allied political leaders. This meant Protestant leaders and their supporters, including supporters in positions of secular authority, were cut off from the saving sacraments and priesthood authority of the formal church.

Faced with such prospects, Luther and later Protestant theologians asserted that the writings of Paul describe a new order of priesthood authority available to the informal church of believers, not needing to be transmitted through formal processes of an established church. (Marty, pp. 143-8; Barker, pp. 708,737,748-9) Drs. Richards and Martin assert that the reformers of the sixteenth century "stressed 'a priesthood of all believers' to affirm the significance of each Christian, against a system that viewed the clergy as the church." (Richards and Martin, p. 38)

PROBLEMS WITH THE PROTESTANT POSITION

But there are major problems with this interpretation by Protestant faithful. The most obvious one is that nothing in these chapters of Hebrews, or any other passage in the Bible, states directly or indirectly that the priesthood is available to all believers independent of the formal church. This assertion is an extrapolation of monumental significance with little to support it.

Attempting to demonstrate a Biblical basis for this novel doctrine, some Protestant scholars cite the Apostle Peter's letter to the saints (Little, p. 98; Manson, p. 49; Dunnett, p. 13; Scott, p. 216):

> Ye also, as lively stones, are built up a spiritual house, an holy priesthood to offer up spiritual sacrifices, acceptable to God by Jesus Christ.
> Ye are a chosen generation, a royal priesthood, an holy nation, a peculiar people. (1 Pet 2:5,9)

However, this seems shaky ground on which to base such a major doctrinal development, since Peter was apparently writing to those who held priesthood authority. And Moses spoke similar words to the nation of Israel, while clearly not asserting that every believer would hold priesthood authority:

> Ye shall be a peculiar treasure unto me above all people: for the earth is mine:
> And ye shall be unto me a kingdom of priests, and an holy nation. (Ex 19:5-6)

Moses was not declaring an all-believers priesthood, and neither was Peter.

A second problem is the continuing practice in Protestant denominations of ordaining ministers. Though not categorized as a sacerdotal ordinance within most Protestant denominations, this rite has been acknowledged by some Protestant authorities as "confusing," since all believers are said to hold the priesthood. (Marty, p. 151; see also Tillich, ST, Vol. III, p. 217) At the same time, controversies continue to swirl within Protestant congregations regarding who can hold the priesthood. This seems inconsistent with a position maintaining all believers have equal access to priesthood authority.

Finally, Paul's Epistle to the Hebrews indicates priesthood authority was conveyed to Jesus Christ through a formal process and Christ conferred this power on chosen leaders in like manner, using an orderly and formal process. The epistle is clear that Jesus did not assume this higher authority on his own. An oath was administered to him by his Father. The epistle's author writes:

> Not without an oath he [Christ] was made priest.
> The Lord sware and will not repent, Thou art a priest for ever after the order of Melchisedec. (Heb 7:20-21; see also Heb 5:5-6)

A formal process is equally necessary for others who receive the priesthood of God.

Many references throughout scripture demonstrate the absolute necessity for priesthood to be conferred by one having proper authority. God's house is a house of order, especially as it relates to those who act in his name and perform his sacred ordinances among mankind.

THE BIBLICAL PATTERN FOR CONFERRING PRIESTHOOD

This same epistle declares,

> For every high priest taken from among men is ordained for men in things pertaining to God.
> And no man taketh this honour unto himself, but he that is called of God as was Aaron. (Heb 5:1,4)

According to the instructor, the pattern approved by God is the process used to call Aaron. The manner in which Aaron received his calling is recorded by the author of Exodus. God spoke to his prophet, Moses, and gave directions:

> And take thou unto thee Aaron, thy brother, and his sons with him, from among the children of Israel, that he may minister unto me in the priest's office . . .
> consecrate him that he may minister unto me in the priest's office. (Ex 28:1,3)

Later, the Lord gave Moses additional instructions: "And thou shalt anoint Aaron and his sons, and consecrate them, that they may minister unto me in the priest's office." (Ex 30:30)

Following the pattern recommended by Paul, a priesthood holder should be called under the inspiration of established leaders in Christ's church. This calling should be formalized by the laying on of hands, conferring authority to the one ordained.

Again, the epistle to the Hebrews points to the great exemplar, Jesus Christ, emphasizing he was chosen and given an oath by his Father:

> So also Christ glorified not himself to be made an high priest; but he that said unto him, Thou art my Son, to day have I begotten thee.
>
> As he saith also in another place, Thou art a priest for ever after the order of Melchisedec. (Heb 5:5-6)

The Savior bore the same witness that authority was given to him by his Father, and without that authority, he could do nothing:

> For as the Father hath life in himself; so hath he given to the Son to have life in himself;
>
> And hath given him authority to execute judgment also . . .
>
> I can of mine own self do nothing. (John 5:26-27,30)

Jesus Christ organized his church using the same principles. As divine head of the church, Jesus selected those called to offices in the priesthood, and he ordained the same. "Ye have not chosen me, but I have chosen you, and ordained you." (John 15:16) "Then he called his twelve disciples together, and gave them power and authority . . ." (Luke 9:1)

The Savior taught the pattern by which authority was delegated to others in his parables. "For the Son of man is as a man taking a far journey, who left his house, and gave authority to his servants, and to every man his work." (Mark 13:34) In each instance, the Lord was meticulous to describe a process in which authority was "given" by one with higher authority; in this case, by the master of the house.

This same pattern was adhered to by his disciples following the Savior's ascension. For example, Saul and Barnabas were ordained to preach the gospel by recognized leaders of the church who received inspiration in extending these callings:

> Now there were in the church that was at Antioch certain prophets and teachers . . .
>
> As they ministered to the Lord, and fasted, the Holy Ghost said, Separate me Barnabas and Saul for the work where unto I have called them.
>
> And when they had fasted and prayed, and laid their hands on them, they sent them away. (Acts 13:1-3)

This pattern appears repeatedly throughout the Bible. For example, Paul was later ordained an apostle. (1 Tim 2:7) By the laying on of hands, Timothy was set apart to be a bishop. (1 Tim 4:14; 2 Tim 1:6) Stephen received his office after the apostles prayed and received inspiration. Then the apostles laid their hands upon him. (Acts 6:1-6) Paul ordained "elders in every church" after "praying with fasting" to receive the Lord's inspiration. (Acts 14:23) In the Bible, laying on of hands is mentioned more than 24 times in conjunction with bestowing authority on others and performing priesthood ordinances.

One of the more instructive events related to priesthood authority is recorded in the book of Acts where Philip entered into the city of Samaria and preached the gospel. Many accepted the teachings of Philip and were baptized.

> Now when the apostles which were at Jerusalem heard that Samaria had received the word of God, they sent unto them Peter and John:
>
> Who, when they were come down, prayed for them that they might receive the Holy Ghost:
>
> Then laid they their hands on them and they received the Holy Ghost. (Acts 8:14-15,17)

This episode is particularly significant because it describes the priesthood functioning under the direction of the apostles, the established leaders of Christ's church. Though Philip held the priesthood, he was not permitted to exercise it beyond bounds prescribed by the apostles. The priesthood conferred by the apostles was not available to all believers. In fact, having the priesthood was not sufficient in and of itself. The Bible describes an established order and respect for priesthood hierarchy.

UNAUTHORIZED EXERCISE OF PRIESTHOOD IN THE BIBLE

Throughout the Bible, examples abound of those severely chastened for attempting to perform priesthood functions without having received authority through formal channels. King Saul was stripped of his kingdom after performing sacrifices to the Lord without proper authority. (1 Sam 13:8-15) King Uzziah was stricken with leprosy when he entered the Lord's house and burnt incense upon the altar, a priesthood function. (2 Chron 26:16-20) The Sons of Sceva were wounded by one having an unclean spirit while attempting to cast out this evil spirit without proper authority. (Acts 19:13-16) Simon, a convert, tried to acquire power to confer the Holy Ghost without being called under the inspiration of the Lord's anointed leaders. For this offense, Simon was severely rebuked by Peter. (Acts 8:18-23)

In the Old Testament, Korah and 250 "princes of the assembly" accused Moses and Aaron of inappropriately restricting the exercise of priesthood authority. (Num 16) Korah's words are most illuminating, echoing those who contend for an all-believers' priesthood in our day. "Ye take too much upon you, *seeing all the congregation are holy, every one of them . . .*" (Num 16:3; emphasis added) The Lord was uncompromising in destroying those who sought to usurp priesthood authority in not submitting to properly called and ordained leaders.

In another situation, Paul re-baptized "certain disciples" who had been baptized previously when questions arose about the authority of those who had performed the ordinances. (Acts 19:1-6) Receiving baptism at the hands of unauthorized believers was not sufficient. To be valid in the eyes of the Lord and his church, ordinances had to be performed by one having proper authority.

Many more examples from the Bible could be cited in support of an established process by which God provides for an orderly delegation of priesthood power through chosen, ordained leaders. The foregoing will suffice to demonstrate the need for designated leaders with proper authority receiving inspiration of the Lord and acting in the office of their priesthood within the framework of the formal church.

ECUMENICAL RECOGNITION OF PRIESTHOOD NOT SUFFICIENT

Recent efforts within the ecumenical movement have been successful in persuading many Protestant and Catholic congregations to recognize the efficacy of ordinances performed in other denominations. Such concessions are sought in the name of unifying the larger, fragmented Christian community. There is a certain spirit of tolerance and liberal-mindedness that seems to recommend these efforts.

However, in light of the foregoing, it seems clear that priesthood authority cannot be determined by vote of a democratic body. The matter is not one that belongs in the domain of diplomacy and negotiations.

The relevant question is whether God honors such acts performed in his name.

According to the Bible, not everything done with sincerity and good intent in the Savior's name will be acceptable to him:

> Many will say in that day, Lord, Lord, have we not prophesied in thy name? and in thy name have cast out devils? and in thy name done many wonderful works?
>
> And then will I profess unto them, I never knew you: depart from me, ye that work iniquity." (Matt 7:22-23)

Only when priesthood leaders with proper authority perform sacred ordinances in the prescribed manner can one receive promises of eternal worth. This begs two questions: Which structure or organization is recognized by the Lord? And which leaders are authorized to perform acts in the name of God?

THE BODY OF CHRIST

When confronted with such questions, many Christians contend the formal organization of the church is unimportant. According to this school of thought, the thing that matters most is spiritual similarities shared by all Christian denominations, what is often referred to as the "invisible structure." (Tillich, ST, Vol. III, pp. 162-7) They believe that overemphasis of formal structure and organization can intensify division, detracting from the Spirit shared within a community of believers. "The church, as the body of Christ, includes every Christian joined to Christ as the head of the body by the baptism of the Spirit." (Chafer/Walvoord, p. 266, also see Berkhof, HCD, pp. 234-9)

This reasoning seems benevolent enough, but it rings hollow in practice. As one mainstream Christian author observes,

> It stretches credulity to believe that a situation in which churches of twenty different rival denominations compete for members within the same locality is really what the New Testament meant by unity, however friendly and co-operative the relations between the different churches. (Beaver, et. al., editors, p. 356)

The Savior and his apostles consistently condemned division, fragmentation and disputations of doctrine. Paul spoke of "one Lord, one faith, one baptism." (Eph 4:5) Peter admonished the saints, "be ye all of one mind." (1 Pet 3:8) The Savior taught his disciples, "there shall be one fold and one shepherd." (John 10:16) In his great intercessory prayer, the Son prayed to the Father that his disciples in all ages might be one:

> Holy Father, keep through thine own name these whom thou hast given me, that they may be one, as we are.
>
> Neither pray I for these alone, but for them also which shall believe on me through their word;
>
> That they all may be one; as thou, Father, art in me, and I in thee, that they also may be one in us. (John 17:11, 20-21)

It is difficult to imagine how the current state of Christianity has any resemblance, spiritual or otherwise, to the unity referred to by the Savior and his apostles. The loss of such unity is one more evidence of a great apostasy from the church organized by Christ.

UNITY THROUGH DIVINE ORGANIZATION OF CHRIST'S CHURCH

Paul indicates the Savior made provision for perpetuating unity in his church. The vital method for retaining this unity was the formal structure of the church as Christ organized it:

> And he (Christ) gave some, apostles; and some, prophets; and some, evangelists; and some, pastors and teachers;
>
> For the perfecting of the saints, for the work of the ministry, for the edifying of the body of Christ:
>
> Till we all come in the unity of the faith, and of the knowledge of the Son of God, unto a perfect man, unto the measure of the stature of the fulness of Christ: That we henceforth be no more children, tossed to and fro, and carried about with every wind of doctrine . . . (Eph 4:11-14)

According to Paul, Christ's church is organized in pursuit of common objectives, "For the perfecting of the saints, for the work of the ministry, for the edifying of the body of Christ." The church is characterized by a unity of doctrine: "That we henceforth be no more children, tossed to and fro, and carried about with every wind of doctrine." In large part, this unity is achieved through inspired leaders organized into priesthood offices within the formal church. For this reason, Christ "gave some, apostles; and some, prophets; etc."

Paul is equally clear this divinely inspired organization was not established as a fleeting form intended to transition over time to different offices such as popes, cardinals, councils of elders, etc.. This was the Church of Jesus Christ, established by the master himself. The pattern and structure were to endure through the ages, "Till we all come in the unity of the faith, and of the knowledge of the Son of God, unto a perfect man, unto the measure of the stature of the fulness of Christ." (Eph 4:14)

Division and fragmentation within the Christian community are evidence that followers of Christ have not achieved "a unity of the faith." The observations of one Protestant theologian can be appropriately applied to the entire the Christian community:

> [Christianity] has been split into churches, sects, denominations, parties, factions, emphasis groups, and national entities—and at times such a premium was placed on 'the right of private judgment' that the meaning of [Christianity] was reduced to autonomous and private forms of individualism. (Marty, p. 51, Christianity substituted for Protestantism; see also Little, pp. 87-92; Tillich, ST, Vol. III, pp. 168-170)

A corresponding multiplication of ecclesiastical offices and hierarchies demonstrates unwarranted migration away from the inspired organization established by Christ to maintain unity in his kingdom.

At the same time, a need to unify the faith and perfect the saints remains. Conditions of the world, at large, and of congregations throughout the Christian community, make it apparent that Christ's people have not come "unto a perfect man, unto the measure of the stature of the fulness of Christ." (Eph 4:13)

Jesus came to minister to the sinner. "They that be whole need not a physician." (Matt 9:12) Paul taught that the church as established by Jesus Christ is necessary and essential until we as a body reach a point where we no longer need the physician. Until that day, "the household of God [is to be] built upon the foundation of the apostles and prophets, Jesus Christ himself being the chief cornerstone." (Eph 2:20; see also Eph 2:19)

LIVING APOSTLES INTENDED TO BE PERMANENT

Some Christians maintain apostles were never intended to be a permanent, physical presence in the church. According to this position, the writings of apostles and prophets as contained in the Bible are the foundation upon which the church was built.

However, this is not the testimony of Paul. His comments refer directly to the organization of the church and its inspired offices. The Savior established this divine organization to administer the affairs of his kingdom on earth until his second coming.

The New Testament gives every indication that God intended apostles and prophets to be perpetuated. The first official act of the eleven apostles recorded in the Bible was to call Matthias to complete the quorum of twelve apostles following the demise of Judas Iscariot. (Acts 1:13-26) The scriptures provide evidence of additional apostles, including James, the half brother of Jesus, (Gal 1:19) and Paul. (Acts 14:14) Paul's calling and ordination was accomplished through a formal process, according to the pattern for conferring priesthood power. Paul testified, "Whereunto I am ordained a preacher, and an apostle . . ." (1 Tim 2:7; see also 2 Tim 1:11)

Apostles were called as special witnesses of the resurrected Lord. (Acts 4:33; see also 1:22) Paul's calling to the apostleship demonstrates that special witnesses of Christ are not limited to those who were present with the Savior during his mortal ministry. Paul received his special witness in vision. (Acts 9:1-6) All subsequent apostles called to this holy office qualify as special witnesses of the Lord in like manner.

The record of the Bible does not support the assertion that the office of apostle was intended to pass out of existence. In all generations of time, prophetic and apostolic powers are needed to administer the affairs of the kingdom, and living witnesses of Jesus Christ are required to testify of the Savior from personal knowledge of him.

CONTINUING REVELATION
NECESSARY IN CHRIST'S CHURCH

In light of emphasis placed on the office of apostles and prophets, first by the Savior himself and subsequently by Paul, it seems reasonable to inquire: Why are apostles and prophets so important in Christ's church? The relationship between the foundation of the church, apostles and prophets, and the chief cornerstone, Jesus Christ, is a critical one to understand, since it forms the underpinnings of the Savior's church.

During his mortal ministry, the Savior spoke of the foundation upon which he would build his church. In teaching his apostles, the Lord queried them: "But whom say ye that I am?" Simon Peter, speaking under the influence of the Holy Spirit and testifying of knowledge given him by revelation, replied: "Thou art the Christ, the Son of the living God. And Jesus answered and said unto him, Blessed art thou, Simon Bar-jona: for flesh and blood hath not revealed it unto thee, but my Father which is in heaven." (Matt 16:15-17)

Continuing to address Peter, Jesus proclaimed: "And I say also unto thee, That thou art Peter, and upon this rock I will build my church; and the gates of hell shall not prevail against it." (Matt 16:18)

Catholics have emphasized the importance of this passage because they believe it supports their position that Christ's church was founded upon Peter, the first apostle. Roman Catholics then claim to be Christ's church through apostolic succession from Peter.

At one level, this interpretation does not conflict with Paul's image of living apostles and prophets as the foundation of the church. Peter was an apostle himself and would be the chief apostle after the ascension of Christ. However, Paul does not say Peter is the chief cornerstone in Christ's church. That position is reserved for "Jesus Christ himself."

An alternative interpretation suggests "the rock" upon which the church was built refers to the Savior's preceding remarks, "flesh and blood hath not revealed it unto thee, but my Father which is in heaven." (Matt 16:17) According to this interpretation, "the rock" of Christ's church is revelation from God. Divine revelation is the link between chosen leaders of the church and the chief cornerstone, Jesus Christ. The same inspiration that allowed Peter to respond with sure knowledge, "Thou art the Christ, the Son of the living God" (Matt 16:16) is the rock upon which Christ intended to build his church.

Because he was human, the gates of hell could prevail to some degree against Peter, the man, but they could never prevail against revelation from God to his chosen servants. Through this link of revelation, Christ continued as the head of his church, "being the chief corner stone," (Eph 2:20) even after his ascension into heaven.

This interpretation is consistent with the manner in which God has always dealt with his children on earth throughout recorded scripture. He has called prophets and apostles through whom he reveals his will in discharging the affairs of his kingdom on earth. As the prophet Amos taught, "Surely the Lord God will do nothing, but he revealeth his secret unto his servants the prophets." (Amos 3:7)

PERSONAL REVELATION INSUFFICIENT TO LEAD CHRIST'S CHURCH

Many Christians contend the Lord's inspiration is directly available to individuals without the intermediary of apostles and prophets. Latter-day Saints enthusiastically embrace the concept of personal revelation between God and each of his children. This is the basis for personal spiritual knowledge and conviction which only come through revelation of the Holy Spirit communing with the spirit of man. These sacred impressions and promptings are a source of divine guidance and comfort in the lives of those open to God's direction.

However, in the record of the Bible, God has always provided order and direction to lead his kingdom through established priesthood leaders, called and ordained as apostles and prophets. Personal revelation cannot substitute for direction and guidance provided to the church as a whole through Christ's chosen channel. As the Savior taught, "He that receiveth a prophet in the name of a prophet shall receive a prophet's reward." (Matt 10:41)

THE KEYS OF THE KINGDOM HELD BY APOSTLES

In addition to receiving revelation from God, apostles and prophets of Jesus Christ were given special power and authority essential to administering the affairs of his church. Throughout the Bible, such special powers were crucial to the functioning of Christ's kingdom on earth, allowing it to fulfill its divine mission.

For example, Jesus gave the apostles certain keys of priesthood authority. "I will give unto thee the keys of the kingdom of heaven: and whatsoever thou shalt bind on earth shall be bound in heaven: and whatsoever thou shalt loose on earth shall be loosed in heaven." (Matt 16:19; see also Matt 18:18) This binding power is the essence of priesthood authority. Without it, ordinances performed on earth are not recognized in heaven. Baptisms, marriages and conferral of priesthood will be performed by those claiming priesthood authority in this life, but these ordinances will not be recognized in heaven unless administered by one having the binding power given to Christ's apostles and delegated through proper lines of authority. As previously cited:

> Many will say to me [Christ] in that day, Lord, Lord, have we not . . . in thy name done many wonderful works?
> And then will I profess unto them, I never knew you: depart from me." (Matt 7:22-23)

Another dimension of these keys includes the power to remit sins. "Whose soever sins ye remit, they are remitted unto them; and whose soever sins ye retain, they are retained." (John 20:23) Without this power, baptism for the remission of sins is a sincere act of belief, lacking authority to remit sins and usher one into Christ's kingdom.

A third aspect of apostolic powers is the authority to be a judge among God's people.

> And I appoint unto you a kingdom, as my Father hath appointed unto me;
> That ye may eat and drink at my table in my kingdom, and sit on thrones judging the twelve tribes of Israel. (Luke 22:29-30; see also Matt 19:28)

As noted above, the Bible informs us that apostles are special witnesses of the resurrected Lord. (Acts 4:33; Acts 1:22) In all generations of time, the testimony of Jesus proclaimed by his living apostles and prophets from personal experience is accompanied by a great outpouring of the spirit, converting honest seekers of truth.

These unique apostolic powers comprise "the keys of the kingdom of heaven." (Matt 16:19) There is nothing in the Bible indicating these keys were entrusted to and administered by anyone other than apostles and prophets of the Lord, Jesus Christ. Powers of this holy priesthood were reserved for those formally ordained, delegating specific authority to act in the office of their calling.

THE FOUNDATION: LIVING APOSTLES AND PROPHETS

As long as apostles and prophets were on earth, Christ directed his church through his chosen servants, and they, in turn, administered his kingdom with the binding power of priesthood authority. Likewise, while apostles and prophets continued, the foundation of the church and the edifice it supported was sound, with Jesus Christ being the chief cornerstone as he led and sustained his followers through appointed channels.

In our day, the need for apostles and prophets is evident to achieve unity of doctrine, perfect the saints, perform ordinances binding in heaven, witness of the resurrected Lord, and administer Christ's kingdom. Since provision was made for the perpetuation of apostles and prophets as the foundation of Christ's church and the revelatory link to the divine head, it seems reasonable to ask: Where are apostles and prophets to administer Christ's church today?

Contemporary mainstream Christian denominations are structured using one of three broad concepts of church organization. These include:

- *Episcopalian form*—organized under a bishop or formal head of the church, e.g., Pope, Patriarch, Archbishop, etc., with power to direct local churches through a central hierarchy; Roman Catholics, Eastern Orthodox, Anglican, Episcopalian and Methodist Episcopalians are examples.
- *Representative form*—local units typically grouped geographically with local leaders, e.g., elder, coming under the supervision and direction of a larger body or synod; in turn, synods are organized under a larger body or general assembly; Examples include Reformed and Presbyterian churches.
- *Congregational form*—seat of authority resides at the local level, with minimal accountability back to a higher body and major decisions including election and ordination of ministers and use of treasury determined at the local unit; Congregational churches or United Church of Christ, the Disciples churches and Baptist churches are examples. (Chafer/Walvoord, pp. 266-7; see also Little, pp. 95-7; Howells, pp. 17-9)

Among mainstream Christian denominations, apostles and prophets are not to be found. It is generally agreed, "the early churches recognized the apostles as having primary authority. This seems to have passed, however, with the first generation of Christians." (*Ibid*, p. 267) Why the apostles were not perpetuated is unclear in both Catholic and Protestant thought. However, most, if not all, mainstream denominations maintain apostles and prophets are strictly a thing of the past. (Barker, p. 765)

When the foundation of a building is compromised, the edifice falls into decay and ruin. Likewise, when the foundation of Christ's church was removed, the edifice fell into apostasy and error, as prophesied by inspired writers of the Bible. This conclusion seems especially compelling since, according to teachings of most traditional Christian denominations, revelation ceased near the end of the first century. Yet all historians of Christianity affirm that changes in doctrine, ordinances, offices of the priesthood and church organization present in mainstream Christian churches today occurred centuries after revelation from God had ended.

Who could have authorized changes to the inspired organization of the church set up by our Savior? Lacking the revelatory link between the church and the Lord, Jesus Christ, these changes are one more evidence of the precepts of men. From such organizations, though perhaps often administered by sincere and well-meaning men and women, have sprung division, diverse interpretations of doctrine, contradictory claims of priesthood authority, and unauthorized changes in ordinances and covenants between God and his people. All of these things and their consequences were foretold by Isaiah:

> The earth also is defiled under the inhabitants thereof; because they have transgressed the laws, changed the ordinance, broken the everlasting covenant.
>
> Therefore hath the curse devoured the earth, and they that dwell therein are desolate. (Isa 24:5-6)

An appropriate conclusion to draw from the record of the Bible is that all churches lacking living apostles and prophets are not the Lord's authorized church. These churches do not possess the "keys of the kingdom" and the "rock" of revelation provided through "apostles and prophets, Jesus Christ himself being the chief corner stone." (Eph 2:20)

ONE LORD, ONE FAITH, ONE BAPTISM

Some Christians may view teachings regarding the apostasy as exclusionary, and even attempt to label them as arrogant and hostile toward other religions. A position maintaining that other religious bodies lie in various degrees of error can seem narrow and intemperate, and some will be turned off by what they see as elitism and effrontery. (Ankerberg, p. 74)

To be clear, Latter-day Saints are not suggesting traditional Christian churches are wicked and evil. Quite the opposite, God's work is evident in all religions when an appeal is made for the spirit of man to triumph over baser instincts and act in true charity and love. However, traditional Christianity and all other groups lie in apostasy insofar as they are cut off from the revelatory link that enthrones "Jesus Christ himself [as] the chief corner stone" (Eph 2:20) of his church. Without this link, it should not be surprising that unwarranted changes and error have crept in over time, though some enduring truths of the gospel of Jesus Christ have been preserved in all Christian organizations.

Lacking the revelatory link that places Christ at the head of his church, other churches do not possess true priesthood authority to bind in heaven and on earth. Again, this will seem intemperate to many, especially, because in the teachings of Catholics and Protestants, such a position is tantamount to condemning the rest of the Christian community to eternal damnation. As discussed in the preceding chapter, Latter-day Saint teachings provide a full opportunity for all mankind to accept or reject the gospel of Jesus Christ and receive saving ordinances of salvation before the final judgment. In this sense, teachings of Latter-day Saints regarding one true church and one proper line of priesthood authority are at the same time tolerant and just toward all, not condemning those who have been denied an opportunity to receive the fullness of Christ's gospel.

As much as our democratic natures may prefer to draw a wide circle that includes all faiths and their designated leaders, the scriptures affirm one body of Christ, one Lord, one faith, one baptism. (Eph 4:4-5) Finding Christ's one true church becomes more vital to personal salvation when we accept that truth does not stretch to accommodate all opinions and preferences.

THE RESTORATION OF ALL THINGS ROLLING FORTH

The Church of Jesus Christ of Latter-day Saints is unique among Christian faiths in teaching of a restoration of all things in these last days. This restoration foretold by ancient prophets and apostles is the establishment of Christ's "kingdom which shall never be destroyed." (Dan 2:44) It rests on the same foundation as Christ's original church: revelation through living apostles and prophets. Under the direction of Jesus Christ, God's priesthood power has been restored and Christ's church organized in a manner identical to the church established by Jesus in the meridian of time.

This great latter-day restoration was ushered in when God raised up a prophet, Joseph Smith, in 1820. His testimony is published to all the world. For this testimony, Joseph Smith eventually gave his life, sealing this witness with his blood. Joseph recorded:

> I was at this time in my fifteenth year. My father's family was proselyted to the Presbyterian faith, and four of them joined that church . . .

> During this time of great excitement my mind was called up to serious reflection and great uneasiness; but though my feelings were deep and often poignant, still I kept myself aloof from all these parties, though I attended their several meetings as often as occasion would permit . . .

> My mind at times was greatly excited, the cry and tumult were so great and incessant. The Presbyterians were most decided against the Baptists and Methodists . . . On the other hand, the Baptists and Methodists in their turn were equally zealous in endeavoring to establish their own tenets and disprove all others.

> In the midst of this war of words and tumult of opinions, I often said to myself: What is to be done? Who of all these parties are right; or are they all wrong together? If any one of them be right, which is it, and how shall I know it?

> While I was laboring under the extreme difficulties caused by the contests of these parties of religionists, I was one day reading the Epistle of James, first chapter and fifth verse, which reads: *If any of you lack wisdom, let him ask of God, that giveth to all men liberally, and upbraideth not; and it shall be given him.*

> Never did any passage of scripture come with more power to the heart of man than this did at this time to mine. It seemed to enter with great force into every feeling of my heart. I reflected on it again and

again, knowing that if any person needed wisdom from God, I did; for how to act I did not know, and unless I could get more wisdom than I then had, I would never know; for the teachers of religion of the different sects understood the same passages of scripture so differently as to destroy all confidence in settling the question by an appeal to the Bible.

At length I came to the conclusion that I must either remain in darkness and confusion or else I must do as James directs, that is, ask of God . . .

So in accordance with this, my determination to ask of God, I retired to the woods to make the attempt.

It was on the morning of a beautiful, clear day, early in the spring of eighteen hundred and twenty.

After I had retired to the place where I had previously designed to go, having looked around me, and finding myself alone, I kneeled down and began to offer up the desires of my heart to God.

What occurred next is arguably the most important event in the world since the resurrection of the Lord, Jesus Christ. In the words of Joseph Smith:

I saw a pillar of light exactly over my head, above the brightness of the sun, which descended gradually until it fell upon me . . .

When the light rested upon me I saw two Personages, whose brightness and glory defy all description, standing above me in the air. One of them spake unto me, calling me by name and said, pointing to the other—*This is My Beloved Son. Hear Him!* (JS-H 1:7-17)

The heavens were open once again to man, as they have always been when the Lord's anointed are on earth. Under the direction of Jesus Christ, Joseph Smith and his fellow servant, Oliver Cowdery, received the priesthood of God by ordination from resurrected beings, John the Baptist and three of the original apostles, Peter, James and John. In 1830, Joseph Smith organized the Church of Jesus Christ, as directed by the Savior, and in 1835, twelve apostles were ordained to be special witnesses of Jesus Christ, forming the foundation of Christ's restored church in these latter days.

As prophesied by Daniel, this "stone was cut out of the mountain without hands." (Dan 2:34) In other words, this is not the work of man. Rather, it is a work issuing from the hand of God. It is the latter day "kingdom, which shall never be destroyed . . . and it shall stand forever." (Dan 2:44-5)

5

The Bible and Other Revelation

During his life, the prophet Joseph Smith was asked many times to identify teachings which distinguish Latter-day Saints from more traditional Christian denominations. Depending on the occasion and points to be highlighted, Joseph Smith provided various answers to this question. On more than one such occasion, he responded that Latter-day Saints are different because they believe the Bible and its teachings. The young prophet understood and relished the irony of his response.

STATURE OF THE BIBLE

From the beginning of the restored church, Latter-day Saints have been accused of rejecting the Bible or, at a minimum, of relegating it to a second-class status far beneath the significance attached to other canons of scripture revealed through modern-day prophets. (Ankerberg, p. 88; Scott, pp. 95-7) In terms of both doctrine and practice, this is an incorrect perception. For example, the teaching manuals provided to the worldwide church as course material in all sanctioned programs of study spend an equal amount of time on the Bible as on all other canons of scripture combined. Currently a four-year cycle of study consists of one year each on Old Testament, New Testament, Book of Mormon, and Doctrine and Covenants/Church History.

It should be apparent from foregoing chapters that Latter-day Saints cherish the Bible and rejoice in reading this important record of God's dealings with man. An honest-minded reader may disagree with specific interpretations of Biblical passages presented in this book, just as the interpretation of one Christian denomination varies from another. However, it is totally misleading to suggest Latter-day Saints do not look to the Bible as one of the great revelations of God.

An authoritative statement by one prominent LDS leader affirms, "The Church of Jesus Christ of Latter-day Saints accepts the Holy Bible as the foremost of her standard works." (Talmage, p. 236)

The pre-eminent position of the Bible in LDS teachings is viewed as insufficient by many in the Christian community. For these, the Bible is considered the definitive and sole authoritative source of true doctrine. This position, which they often refer to as "sola scriptura," is defended most vigorously within evangelical Protestantism, although most traditional denominations would feel comfortable with the statement of one mainstream Christian theologian, "any recognizably Christian faith must be based on the Bible." (Beaver, *et. al.*, editor, p. 372)

Within the traditional Christian community, this position is adhered to more in theory than in practice. Significant differences exist among Protestant denominations, as noted by this same Christian author.

> In theory, therefore, all Christians accept the Bible as authoritative, both in guiding their actions and in forming their beliefs.
>
> In practice, however, Christians have differed on this. The Protestant Reformation aimed to restore the Bible to a place of authority above the pronouncements of the leaders of the church and the traditions which had grown up. Within Protestant Christianity, the Enlightenment of the eighteenth century led to a new confidence in human reason as the ultimate guide to truth and the Bible was treated only as a record of human religious development, not as a divine revelation.
>
> Today, while evangelical Christianity accepts the Bible as its supreme authority more liberal Protestantism increasingly questions its importance. (*Ibid.*, p. 372)

Ironically, even evangelical Protestants do not base their teachings exclusively on the Bible, accepting official pronouncements of the Roman church through the eighth century and granting equal authority to confessional statements and catechisms such as the Augsburg Confession, the Book of Concord, the Heidelberg Catechism, the Book of Common Prayer, the Westminster Confession of Faith and the Book of Confessions. (Ricks and Peterson, p. 43; also Barker, p. 411; Marty, pp. 41-2; Toon in OGT, p. 27) Teachings from these non-biblical sources, related to such beliefs as the Trinity, original sin and ex nihilo creation, are defended vigorously by many though they still assert the Bible to be the sole and definitive source of revelation.

Our Catholic friends have always been more ambivalent about the importance of the Bible, emphasizing tradition, official statements emanating from church councils and current positions advocated by the Pope. Since Vatican II, an increased interest in Bible study and dialogue has been encouraged by the church and is in evidence within many Catholic congregations. However, this recent emphasis on the written Word of God in no way diminishes the significance attached to traditions of the church and official statements of its leaders.

REASONS FOR CRITICIZING THE LDS POSITION

With such diversity among traditional Christian denominations, one might expect a moderate degree of tolerance toward Latter-day Saints and their beliefs regarding the Bible. Unfortunately, this is not always the case, especially among evangelicals. Despite diverse positions within the Christian community, some seem determined to label Latter-day Saints as non-Christian for not embracing the Bible as the sole, inerrant Word of God. (Chafer/Walvoord, pp. 17-20; see also Peterson and Ricks, p. 117; Ankerberg, pp. 345, 375-82)

Using this standard of Biblical inerrancy and exclusivity, Latter-day Saints are singled out for criticism on three points. These include:

1. An official statement by Latter-day Saints states, "We believe the Bible to be the word of God as far as it is translated correctly" (Article of Faith, no. 8); some Christians take exception to any qualifier suggesting the Bible to be less than perfect and complete;

2. Latter-day Saints recognize other written volumes as scripture, attributing canonical status to the Bible, Book of Mormon, Doctrine and Covenants and Pearl of Great Price; this position is at variance with those who insist the Bible is the end of all revelation;

3. Pronouncements of modern prophets and apostles are accepted by Latter-day Saints as the word of God to direct the kingdom of God on earth today; according to other Christians, additional prophets and apostles are not possible because this would permit adding to the complete word of God as contained in the Bible.

Latter-day Saints rejoice in the Bible as much or more than the members of any other Christian denomination, but they do not accept a position that the Bible is perfect and complete. The Bible does not claim these attributes of inerrancy and completeness for itself. (Evans and Berent, pp. 77-95, especially 77 and 83) On the contrary, the Bible prophesies of additional writings and revelations to come forth in the last days complementing this sacred record of the Jewish people and bringing forth additional light to correct errors of doctrine.

INERRANCY AND
DIFFERENT TRANSLATIONS OF THE BIBLE

When some Christians insist the Bible is perfect and free of errors, the first challenge is to identify the version or translation of the Bible having attained such a state of perfection. Christian author, F. F. Bruce, in *History of the Bible in English,* lists at least 34 complete English translations of the Bible ranging from early efforts of Tyndale and Coverdale, The Great Bible, and the Geneva Bible to the most widely quoted King James or Authorized Version, to more modern translations such as the Revised Standard Version, The New American Bible, and The New International Bible. All of these are more or less mainstream translations. Many more Bible translations can be added to this number with the so-called "inclusive" versions which minimize reference to gender, patriarchy and hierarchy. Each translation or version has differences of content and nuance.

One reason for some of these differences is the fact that major translations derive from different source materials. The New Testament portion of the King James Version is a translation taken from several thousand fragments of ancient manuscripts referred to collectively as the Byzantine Greek texts. New Testament passages found in The Revised Version, The American Standard Version, and the Revised Standard Version are translated from manuscripts discovered after the King James Version had been completed. These manuscripts, unearthed in northern Egypt, are known as the Alexandrian Greek texts. A third major collection of Biblical translations, including The Luther Version, The New American Bible, The Jerusalem Bible and most Catholic Bibles, are derived from the Vulgate and other early Latin manuscripts.

Differences among these translations are significant. For example, the Alexandrian text in its original Greek contains 5,337 changes not found in the Byzantine texts. Translation styles and techniques compound these variances, producing more than 30,000 text changes in English renditions, an average of more than four changes for each verse of scripture. Many of the changes in the Alexandrian text seem to reflect an Aryan influence, deleting references to the divinity of Jesus Christ and minimizing the operation of miracles and spiritual gifts. (NT Student Manual, p. 354)

Additional variances in Bible translations have been introduced as a result of human errors in copying and transcribing sacred texts. The same non-LDS Biblical scholar, Dr. Bruce, has written, "Throughout centuries of copying and recopying even the Byzantine text-type was no longer represented in its purity by the later manuscripts which were so largely drawn upon by the editors of the earliest printed texts." (Bruce, p. 127; see also Little, p. 14)

> Scriptures deserve to have intelligent readers, and intelligent read-
> ers will not have their faith shaken by being reminded that the men
> who copied the sacred text throughout the early Christian centuries
> could occasionally fail to copy exactly what lay before them in the
> master-copy. (*Ibid.*, p. 140)

In addition to innocent transcription errors, some differences in translation have been introduced by scribes and translators changing specific content in ancient texts to render passages of scripture consistent with their preconceived biases. As discussed in chapter One, the Hebrew texts of Psalms records David's introspection:

> What is man that thou art mindful of him? . . .
> For thou hast made him a little lower than the Gods. (Ps 8:4-5)

The translator has changed the word "Gods" to "angels" so as to read: "For thou hast made him a little lower than the angels." Likewise, the Hebrew texts of Ecclesiastes clearly speak of plural "Creators," but the translator has changed the English translation to refer to a single "Creator." (Eccl 12:1)

Another striking example can be found in the translation of Paul's instructions to the Philippians. In the King James Version, Paul's counsel is rendered, "Wherefore, my beloved . . . work out your own salvation with fear and trembling." (Philip 2:12) Translators of The Living Bible have modified these phrases to be more sympathetic to the doctrine of salvation by grace alone. The translation reads, "Dearest friends, . . . you must be even more careful to do the good things that

166   SHARED BELIEFS, HONEST DIFFERENCES

result from being saved." Clearly, these two translations are fundamentally at variance with each other.

Another well-documented example is found in 1 John 5:7, one of the so-called proof-texts for the Trinity. "And there are three that bear record in heaven, the Father, the Word, and the Holy Ghost: and these three are one." According to Protestant theologian Millard J. Erickson, "both conservative and liberal scholars concluded that the crucial portion of the First John proof text was not part of the original reading of the biblical text, since no Greek manuscript earlier than the sixteenth century contains it." (Erickson, p. 97)

Different source manuscripts, human errors in transcription and copying, and alterations in translation raise important questions for those who maintain Biblical inerrancy. Which Biblical rendition is perfect; one of those taken from Byzantine Greek texts emphasizing the Godhood of Jesus Christ, or one from the Alexandrian texts deleting many of these references? One recorded in Hebrew positioning man a little lower than the Gods and referring to multiple Creators or one rendered by English translators making man a little lower than the angels and asserting a single Creator? One supporting salvation by grace alone or one suggesting man must work out his salvation with fear and trembling?

These are matters of greatest importance to our understanding of divine truths which can be directly influenced by differences in translation. As other mainstream Christians have pointed out, "Different versions (of the Bible) often do significantly alter the wording, depending on the particular interpretation that the translator or editor wants to place on the verse." (Evans and Berent, p. 89)

Those involved in the work of Bible translation are not so presumptuous as to assert that a perfect product has emerged from this human process, and those with less awareness of limitations inherent in translating from ancient texts should be cautious to attribute such perfection to any version of the Bible. Dr. Bruce has written with appropriate modesty,

> An honest translator is bound to confess that something is lost, something is changed in the course of translation . . . No doubt the Bible suffers less in translation than many other books, but no Bible translator who knows his business counts himself to have attained perfection. (Bruce, p. ix)

Latter-day Saints believe the writings of the Bible are inspired and represent the word of God as they issued forth from the hand of original writers of Biblical texts. Unfortunately, "no original manuscript of any book of the Bible is known to exist." (Evans and Berent, p. 94) Interpretations and changes introduced by scribes and translators are not allowed the same authority.

The qualified statement of Latter-day Saints, "We believe the Bible to be the word of God as far as it is translated correctly" merely recognizes an historical fact. Texts of the Bible have been transcribed through the ages and are rendered in modern languages through a process of translation. Each human interaction, regardless of how careful and well-intentioned, opens the possibility for error. Any shadow of variance from the intended message of those who authored God's word can introduce mistakes and obscure truth. The Bible, in our day, has passed through this precarious process.

Latter-day Saints do not recognize any translation to be perfect or free of defects. For a variety of reasons, church leaders have recommended the King James Version for general use among its members. Despite limitations, the Bible is a marvelous record of God's dealings with his children that has been watched over and preserved by the hand of God. (Darrick, p. 145) It is truly the word of God to the extent it remains free of human interpolations and mistakes. As one LDS authority has observed regarding the Bible, "An impartial investigator has more to wonder at the paucity of error than that mistakes are to be found at all." (Talmage, p. 237)

IRRECONCILABLE INCONSISTENCIES IN THE BIBLE

Those who insist on Biblical inerrancy face an additional challenge in justifying their position. Within the pages of the Bible are seeming contradictions that scholars and theologians have been unable to reconcile. A partial listing of discrepancies found within the writings of the Bible include:

- The genealogy of Jesus as put forth by Matthew differs markedly from that recorded in Luke, despite the fact both purport to trace the lineage of Joseph, the husband of Mary (Matt 1; Luke 3);

- Accounts of Paul's meeting with the apostles clarifying requirements for gentile converts to conform to the Mosaic law differ in
specifics and tone (Acts 15; Gal 2);
- Matthew refers to a prophecy regarding thirty pieces of silver,
the price paid to Judas Iscariot for betraying the Savior, and
attributes it to the prophet Jeremiah. In the Old Testament, this
prophecy is recorded in Zechariah but not found in the writings
of Jeremiah (Matt 27:9; Zech 11:2);
- Three accounts of Saul's vision on the road to Damascus seem
to contradict each other, recording in the first account, "And the
men which journeyed with him *stood* speechless, *hearing a
voice, but seeing no man.*" (Acts 9:7; emphasis added) In a later
chapter, it is recorded "they that were with me saw indeed the
light, and were afraid; but *they heard not the voice of him that
spake to me.*" (Acts 22:7-9; emphasis added) In the final
account, the author writes, "And when *we were all fallen to the
earth,* I heard a voice speaking unto me." (Acts 26:14; emphasis added)
- As discussed in chapter two, John is often quoted, "No man has
seen God at any time." In other passages, the beloved apostle
indicates that holy men have seen God and Moses records the
appearance of God to more than seventy men who "saw the God
of Israel." (John 1:18; John 6:46; Ex 24:10-11)

Suffice it to say other inconsistencies can be cited from both the Old
Testament and New Testament. (Compare Matt 27:5 and Acts 1:18;
Matt 20:20-21 and Mark 10:35-37; Luke 24:33 and John 20:19,24;
Matt 23:35 and 2 Chron 24:20-22 and Lev 11:6; 1 Chron 21:5 and 2
Sam 24:9; 2 Sam 10:8 and 1 Chron 19:18; 2 Kings 24:8 and 2 Chron
36:9; 2 Chron 22:2 and 2 Kings 8:26; Ezra 2 and Nehemiah 7) These
discrepancies do not diminish the value of sacred writings contained in
the Bible. Biblical scripture has received the approbation of the Savior
and his prophets. These inspired words are accompanied by light and
power flowing from the spirit of God. However, it is simply naive and
misleading to suggest the Bible, as we have it today, is free of all error.

PROMINENT REFORMERS:
RESERVATIONS ABOUT THE BIBLE

Latter-day Saints are not alone in expressing reservations about the inerrancy of the Bible. Some very prominent figures in traditional Christianity have been vocal about concerns regarding accuracy and value of portions of the Bible.

For example, Martin Luther was very selective in his assessment of which books of the Bible qualify as canonized scripture. Otto Scheel, a noted professor of religious studies, writes, "That Luther was critical of the scriptures is too well known for me to have to emphasize it." (as quoted in Peterson and Ricks, p. 125) Martin Luther took a dim view of any book in the Bible not supporting his theological idea of salvation by grace alone. (Marty, pp. 105 and 122) His favorite target was the Epistle of James. Luther wrote,

> I hold that some Jew wrote it who probably had heard about Christians but had never run into any. Since he had heard that Christians put so much emphasis on faith in Christ, he thought [to himself]: "Wait a minute! I'll oppose them and emphasize works." And that's what he did. (as quoted in Peterson and Ricks, pp. 125-6)

In addition to the epistle of James, Luther had reservations about the Book of Revelation, Esther, and the epistles of Jude, Hebrews, and Second Peter. Those who followed his teachings later published editions of the Bible segregating most of these books from the rest of the Bible and identifying them as "noncanonical." (Robinson, S., p. 53)

Luther preferred the gospel of John to the synoptic gospels and went so far as to refer to the Sermon on the Mount as "the devil's masterpiece." He also argued that First Maccabees deserved to be canonized. (Ricks and Peterson, pp. 125-7)

Likewise, other great reformers, including Huldreich Zwingli of Switzerland and John Oeclampadius of Basle, expressed doubts about the Book of Revelation. John Calvin had his own ideas about which books of the Bible were to be trusted and which were of dubious origin. Lloyd Averill, a Protestant writer, has written,

> Calvin cannot be identified with the scriptural literalism affirmed by present-day fundamentalists. Nor, indeed, can any other major figure in the history of Christian thought prior to 1800. Contrary to fundamentalist claims, the doctrine of biblical inerrancy as they have

formulated it is not a return to primitive Christianity or to Christian orthodoxy. Rather, it was an innovation fashioned scarcely more than a hundred years ago . . . (as quoted in Peterson and Ricks, p. 127)

Faced with this record of questioning and skepticism among such prominent Protestants, it is difficult to defend the passion of those taking umbrage at the position of Latter-day Saints regarding the Bible. The doubts expressed by esteemed reformers go far beyond any reservations of Latter-day Saints.

LACK OF AGREEMENT ON BIBLICAL INERRANCY

As noted above, the Protestant community is far from unified on the matter of Biblical inerrancy. Among those who ascribe inerrancy, some fundamentalist groups insist the Bible is free from error of any sort, while other denominations have evolved a more moderate position asserting a kind of spiritual inerrancy in which "freedom from error is limited to matters of faith and practice." (J. Z. Smith, p. 489) According to this notion of inerrancy, the truth of the Bible can be accessed unerringly through the spirit by the community of believers. (Marty, p. 117)

However, practical experience demonstrates that relying solely on the inspiration of sincere men and women searching the scriptures does not produce unity of doctrine. If the truths of the Bible could be accessed unerringly through the spirit poured out on sincere believers, fragmentation and diversity of teachings within the Christian community would not exist. (Tillich, ST, Vol. III, pp. 162-170) Recognizing the limitations of relying on scripture alone, one mainstream theologian has acknowledged, "Before one confronts the sola scriptura he has normally already encountered or been shaped by a culture and a church." (Marty, p. 78) Frustrated by division and fragmentation produced by believers from different cultures and religious traditions interpreting scripture, the Bible scholar, Erasmus, chided early reformers, "All of you appeal to the true word of God, and you believe you are true interpreters of it. Agree then, among yourselves . . ." (as quoted in Barker, p. 765)

A CLOSED CANON OF SCRIPTURE
NOT SUPPORTED IN THE BIBLE

In addition to Biblical inerrancy, many Christians insist the Bible is the definitive and complete canon of scripture. Again, the Bible makes no such claim for itself. The passage most frequently quoted by other Christians to support their position is found near the end of The Book of Revelation, the last book of the Bible.

If any man shall add unto these things, God shall add unto him the plagues that are written in this book:

And if any man shall take away from the words of the book of this prophecy, God shall take away his part out of the book of life . . . (Rev 22:18-19)

According to some Christians, the Revelator was inspired to end the Bible with this admonition against adding to or deleting from the Bible, making it a closed canon of scripture. Any additional writings claiming to be scripture would violate John's admonition by adding to it.

There are several problems with this interpretation. *First*, the writer of Deuteronomy issues a similar warning in two separate passages. (Deut 4:2 and Deut 12:32) Likewise, the writer of Proverbs records similar counsel near the close of his collection of aphorisms. (Prov 30:6) If we are to apply the same logic to these verses, all subsequent writings including the entire New Testament would constitute unauthorized additions to the word of God.

Second, most Biblical scholars agree the Book of Revelation was not the last book of the Bible to be penned by its author. Specifically, John the Revelator is believed to have recorded the Book of Revelation while confined to the Isle of Patmos. Years later when he had rejoined the saints in Asia, it is generally thought that he wrote the Gospel of John and sent forth the three epistles bearing his name. (Barker, pp. 8-9) This would suggest John violated his own injunction against additional scriptures, according to the interpretation of some Christians.

Finally, the phrase used by the Revelator prohibiting adding or subtracting seems to refer specifically to The Book of Revelation and not to the Bible as a whole. John's phrase, "the words of the book of this prophecy," (Rev 22:19) seems an apt description of the Book of Revelation, an open vision of the end of the world. By contrast, the Bible is not a book, but rather a compilation of many books, each written by individual authors at different times. The name, Bible, is taken from the Greek word, *biblia*, meaning books (Beaver, et. al., editor, p. 371) or a "collection of books." (Morgan, p.87) Not all of these writings consist of prophecy; some are history, others expound the law, some record inspired verse. These varied and disparate books were assembled together several centuries after John recorded his warning. (Beaver, et. al., editor, p. 371) It may surprise some Christians that the early church conducted itself without a Bible for more than 300 years. (Bernstein, pp. 4-7; Payne, p. 1005) It is pure speculation to assert John was speaking of a future compilation of books, the Bible, rather than of his book of prophecy, the Book of Revelation.

Additional evidence that John's admonition is limited to his Book of Revelation is found in the Bible itself. The Bible does not limit sacred scripture to those writings contained within its own pages. This is a fact acknowledged by other Christian scholars. (Evans and Berent, p. 95) For instance, Matthew refers to a prophecy not recorded elsewhere in the Bible. "And he [Jesus] came and dwelt in a city called Nazareth: that it might be fulfilled which was spoken by the prophets, He shall be called a Nazarene." (Matt 2:23) Paul quotes the words of Christ, not found in the written accounts of his ministry. "It is more blessed to give than to receive." (Acts 20:35) Clearly, Matthew and Paul ascribed authoritative status to these statements though not found in any other book of the Bible.

The Epistle of Jude draws heavily from the first book of Enoch and the Assumption of Moses, neither found in the Bible.

> And Enoch . . . prophesied of these, saying, the Lord cometh with ten thousands of his saints,
> To execute judgment upon all and to convince all that are ungodly . . ." (Jude 1:14-15)

So extensive are these references to a non-canonized source that Martin Luther questioned the status of this epistle. (Peterson and Ricks, p. 121)

In addition, it is generally acknowledged by other Christian scholars that the Bible refers to at least fifteen books, epistles and records not found in our Bible but having equal authority and value. (Evans and Berent, p. 95; see also Hopkins, pp. 249-52) These include the Book of the Covenant (Ex 24:7), the Book of Jasher (Josh 10:13; 2 Sam 1:18), The book of Nathan the Prophet (1 Chron 29:29; 2 Chron 9:29), the book of Gad the Seer (1 Chron 29:29), the prophecy of Ahijah, the Shilonite, and the visions of Iddo, the Seer (2 Chron 9:29), the book of Enoch (Jude 1:14), a third epistle to the Corinthians (1 Cor 5:9), an epistle from Laodicea (Col 4:16) and a written record of the "sayings of the seers" (2 Chron 33:19), to name just a few. (See detailed list in Hopkins, pp. 249-52)

The writers of the Bible accepted and drew upon a larger canon of scripture than that contained in our Bible today. An assertion that the Bible is a complete and closed canon of scripture is contradicted by the Bible itself.

DIFFERENT BIBLES, WHICH ONE IS COMPLETE?

An even bigger problem for those claiming the Bible to be a closed canon of scripture is the fact that Christians cannot agree on which writings belong in this canon. The Protestant Bible consists of 66 books, 39 in the Old Testament and 27 in the New Testament. The Bible of Roman Catholics includes all 66 books in Protestant Bibles and adds the 12 books of the Apocrypha comprising about 230 additional pages. The Eastern Orthodox Bible includes the 12 of the Apocrypha while adding two additional books, Second Esdras and Third Maccabees, and deleting the Book of Revelation. The Russian Orthodox adds Third Esdras to the Eastern Orthodox Bible. Throughout the Christian era, numerous lists and collections of writings have been advanced as canonical by different groups of Christian believers. (Robinson, S., pp. 52-5; Peterson and Ricks, pp. 118-21) The oldest New Testament collection, the Codex Sinaiticus from the fourth century, contains two books not included in any of the Christian Bibles, the Shepherd of Hermas and Barnabas. (Ross, pp. 59-60)

All of these different canons of scripture raise the question as to which members of the Christian community are adding to or deleting from the Bible and which have the complete and closed collection of writings. From the perspective of Roman Catholics, the Protestants have deleted 230 pages. If one accepts the Protestant Bible, then the Eastern Orthodox Christians have added 14 books while deleting the very book that carries the injunction against adding to or deleting from it. This may be the ultimate irony in the claim of Bible completeness. Major members of the Christian community cannot agree on which books are included in and excluded from the closed canon of scripture.

Prophecies Concerning Other Books To Come Forth

An additional challenge to the notion of a closed canon of scripture is raised by prophecies in the Bible foretelling inspired books to come forth in the latter days. For example, Isaiah spoke of a marvelous work and a wonder brought to pass after the Lord's people had fallen into apostasy and embraced the precepts of men. This great work would be preceded by the coming forth of a book.

> And the vision of all is become unto you as the words of a book that is sealed, which men deliver to one that is learned, saying, Read this, I pray thee: and he saith, I cannot; for it is sealed: And the book is delivered to him that is not learned, saying, Read this, I pray thee: and he saith, I am not learned. (Isa 29:11-12)

In recorded history related to the Bible, there is no event which parallels and fulfills this prophecy of Isaiah. However, the Book of Mormon, published in the early years of the restoration, was translated by the power of God from a set of plates, a portion of which were sealed. The prophecy of Isaiah was fulfilled in its specifics by a learned man, professor Charles Anton of Columbia University, who complained he could not translate a sealed book when informed of the sealed portion of the plates. (JS-H 1:64) The Prophet Joseph Smith was the unlearned man equally unable to read the book, lacking formal training in all but the most rudimentary scholarship of his day. However, provision was made by the Lord for his prophet to translate this sacred record. The Book of Mormon, not the Bible, qualifies in every way as the book foretold by Isaiah which would usher in the beginning of a marvelous work and wonder.

In the same vein, the prophet Ezekiel wrote of two books to issue forth from two different peoples. Anciently, books were recorded on scrolls which were wrapped around poles or 'sticks.' Ezekiel refers to two sticks, or in other words, two books that would come together and be one in the hand of the faithful.

The word of the Lord came again unto me, saying,

Moreover, thou son of man, take thee one stick, and write upon it, For Judah, and for the children of Israel his companions: Then take another stick, and write upon it, For Joseph, the stick of Ephraim, and for all the house of Israel his companions:

And join them one to another into one stick; and they shall become one in thine hand. (Ezek 37:15-17)

At first glance, one might suspect Ezekiel foresaw the coming together of the Old and the New Testament. Certainly, they have become one in the hands of Christians throughout the earth. However, both of those records are from the same people, Judah and his companions. Ezekiel prophesied that the second book would issue forth from Joseph and his descendants.

Again, the Book of Mormon fits Ezekiel's prophecy perfectly. It is a record of the descendants of Joseph who came to the American continent and established a thriving civilization. The Book of Mormon records inspired prophecies and revelations given to prophets on this continent regarding the mission and ministry of Jesus Christ among the Jewish people. Most significantly, it reports the visit of the resurrected Lord to the descendants of Joseph on the American continent.

The Book of Mormon, the stick of Joseph, is one with the Bible, the stick of Judah, in bearing witness to the world that Jesus is the Christ; that he was born into mortality, he lived a perfect life, he suffered for the sins of the world, he died on the cross for all mankind, and he resurrected into eternal glory. As foretold in the Bible, these two books are one in the hands of those who bear witness to the mission and divinity of Jesus Christ. The Bible prophesies of additional canons of scripture.

Since the Bible does not preclude additional scripture, how do other Christians determine when sufficient scripture has come forth? The words of the Lord recorded in the Book of Mormon place this issue squarely before other Christians:

Wherefore murmur ye, because that ye shall receive more of my word? Know ye not that the testimony of two nations is a witness unto you that I am God . . . Wherefore I speak the same words unto one nation like unto another. And when the two nations shall run together the testimony of the two nations shall run together also . . .

Wherefore, because that ye have a Bible ye need not suppose that it contains all my words;

neither need ye suppose that I have not caused more to be written. (2 Ne 29:8, 10)

As indicated by the Apostle Peter, inspired scripture comes forth from holy men or prophets. (2 Pet 1:21) As long as God's prophets are on the earth, new scripture will continue to be added to sacred writ, and the canon of scripture will never be complete.

THE REAL ISSUE:
LIVING PROPHETS AND MODERN REVELATION

At last, we come to the real issue dividing Latter-day Saints and other Christians with regard to the inerrancy and completeness of the Bible. The bold doctrine of living apostles and prophets capable of providing authoritative interpretation of the Bible and adding to the canon of scripture lies at the heart of the disagreement and is categorically rejected by other Christians.

According to the teachings of many Christian denominations, living apostles and prophets are unnecessary because the Bible provides answers and direction to the lives of its members and to the church as a whole. As discussed above, this position insists that all revelation required to direct the affairs of God's kingdom on earth is provided within the pages of the Bible and can be accessed through inerrant inspiration poured out on those who search God's word. (Marty, p. 117; Gibbs, p. 12; Scott, pp. 95-99, Ankerberg, p. 88)

Inspired authors of the Bible and the Savior himself recommended personal study of sacred writ, but nowhere in the Bible do they endorse relying solely on interpretation of scriptures. One of the reasons for this seems to be a recognition of potential abuses arising from personal interpretations of sacred writ. For example, Peter points to the writings of his fellow apostle, Paul, as sometimes ". . . hard to be understood, which they that are unlearned and unstable wrest, as they do also the other scriptures, unto their own destruction." (2 Pet 3:16) Perhaps, Peter foresaw with prophetic insight an unstable wresting of Paul's writings to produce the doctrine of salvation by grace alone which ignores a body of scripture requiring works of faith and righteousness to qualify for salvation. Paul expressed his own concerns about private interpretations of scripture and wrote unflatteringly of those "which corrupt the word of God." (2 Cor 2:17)

Potential problems associated with relying solely on interpretations of the Bible should be apparent when Satan himself quoted the written word to tempt the Savior of the world. "If thou be the Son of God, cast thyself down: for it is written, He shall give his angels charge concerning thee: and in their hands they shall bear thee up, lest at any time thou dash thy foot against a stone." (Matt 4:6)

The danger of relying on the written word alone is also evident in events which overtook the Scribes and Pharisees of Judaism. These were the Biblical scholars of their day, searching scripture and expounding interpretations of the written canon. However, they erred in rejecting living prophets, and they failed to recognize the Messiah in their midst. This is a pattern that promises to repeat itself.

APPROPRIATE ROLE OF SCRIPTURES AND ONGOING REVELATION

The appropriate role of scripture as defined in the Bible is to edify, to instruct and, most importantly, to testify of Jesus Christ. Paul taught:

> Whatsoever things were written aforetime were written for our learning, that we through patience and comfort of the scriptures might have hope. (Rom 15:4)

> All scripture is given by inspiration of God, and is profitable for doctrine, for reproof, for correction, for instruction in righteousness,

> That the man of God may be perfect, thoroughly furnished unto all good works. (2 Tim 3:16-17)

These passages suggest great blessings for those who heed the Lord's counsel, "Search the scriptures." (John 5:39)

However, there is no evidence in the Bible that written scripture alone was ever intended to take the place of living apostles and prophets. Quite the opposite. Inspired accounts of the Bible make clear that followers of Christ looked first to living apostles and prophets and then searched the written record for additional insight in deliberating on important issues.

For example, when Paul and Barnabas were confronted by those who taught circumcision as essential to salvation, they traveled to Jerusalem seeking the counsel of the apostles. This was a hotly contested issue with strong feelings on both sides.

> And when there had been much disputing, Peter rose up, and said
> unto them, Men and brethren, ye know how that a good while ago God
> made choice among us, that the Gentiles by my mouth should hear the
> word of the gospel, and believe.
>
> And God, which knoweth the hearts, bare them witness, giving
> them the Holy Ghost, even as he did unto us. (Acts 15:7-8)

Peter then renounced compliance with specific requirements of the
Mosaic law as a condition of faithfulness in the church.

The basis for Peter's pronouncement was, first, a direct revelation
from God received by a living apostle and, second, evidence of God's
confirmation of this revelation by pouring out the Holy Ghost on gen-
tiles who had embraced the gospel and been baptized. According to
Luke's account, Paul and Barnabas then arose, corroborating the words
of Peter by pointing to miracles and spiritual gifts received in the lives
of gentile converts.

Then James addressed the assembled parties. In his comments, he
referred to "the words of the prophets, as it is written," suggesting some
instruction should be given to the new converts. "But that we write unto
them, that they abstain from pollutions of idols, and from fornication,
and from things strangled, and from blood." (Acts 15:20) These
instructions were approved by those assembled and were sent throughout the church.

This episode from the Bible provides great insight into the deliberations of early church leaders. The apostles were looked to as the chosen leaders of Christ's church. The apostles relied primarily on revelation given to them by the Lord. The written word and evidence from
the Spirit's workings within the church were examined to support or
confirm the inspiration of the apostles, but these secondary sources
were not determining factors. Most Christians want to rely on the latter two methods while rejecting the primary source used to direct
Christ's church: ongoing revelation.

Even among those who acknowledge spiritual gifts of prophecy
today, most insist that all new inspiration harmonize with the record of
the Bible, according to their particular interpretation. (Connelly, p. 33,
Reid, ed., pp. 948-9; *Presbyterians and Mormons*, pp. 8-9) But this
was not a restriction adhered to by living apostles and prophets of the
early church. They relied on personal revelation from Christ to guide
his church and its members.

When apostles and prophets turned to written scripture, they did so with prophetic discernment granted to them as chosen leaders of Christ's church. Their deliberations were not based on private interpretations of the scriptures. Rather, they approached the scriptures with the more sure word of revelation which accompanied their calling. The Apostle Peter counseled the saints to place their trust in "the more sure word" of living apostles and prophets and admonished against relying on individual interpretations of scripture.

> We [the apostles] have a more sure word of prophecy; whereunto ye do well that ye take heed, as unto a light that shineth in a dark place, until the day dawn, and the day star arise in your hearts;
>
> Knowing this first, that no prophecy of the scripture is of any private interpretation. (2 Pet 1:19-20)

FALSE PROPHETS AND TRUE PROPHETS

Despite evidence that God reveals his will through living apostles and prophets, many Christians reject the notion of prophets on earth today. There are good reasons for caution and skepticism. For example, unflattering accounts of David Karesh, Marshall Applewhite and Jim Jones cast a dark shadow over all claiming direct access to God and his will. In addition, the Bible warns of false prophets who will deceive many in the last days. (Matt 7:15; Matt 24:11, 24; Isa 30:10; 1 John 4:1; 2 Pet 2:1)

At the same time, warnings about false prophets seem to imply a continuing presence of true prophets. If authors of the Bible had intended to declare true prophets a thing of the past, they would have warned against anyone claiming to be a prophet. Such a blanket statement is not found in the Bible, suggesting the appearance of true prophets, as well as false prophets, in the last days.

The Savior made specific reference to the acid test for discerning between a true prophet and a false one. After counseling his followers, "Beware of false prophets" (Matt 7:15), Jesus alludes to true prophets in the future.

> Ye shall know them by their fruits . . . every good tree bringeth forth good fruit; but a corrupt tree bringeth forth evil fruit . . .
>
> Wherefore by their fruits ye shall know them. (Matt 7:16, 17, 20)

ATTACKS ON THE CHARACTER
OF THE LORD'S ANOINTED

Claiming to apply the Lord's test of a true prophet, critics of the LDS faith have attempted to paint the prophet of the restoration, Joseph Smith, as a master manipulator who went about deceiving his followers to serve his personal interests. Some may be inclined to believe these allegations because such an image is consistent with the behavior of others who have come in the name of religion.

However, one should use caution in applying a sweeping condemnation to all claiming to be sent by the Lord. Similar charges were flung at the Savior and his prophets throughout all generations. For example, Jesus was accused by the religious leaders of his day of having a devil (John 8:48-52; Matt 11:22-28; Mark 3:21-27), associating with sinners and women with sullied reputations (Matt 9:10-11; Mark 2:16-17; Luke 7:37-50), being a blasphemer (Mark 2:7-8; John 7:27-30), breaking the Sabbath (John 5:1-16), and fostering a disregard for the commandments of God (Matt 15:1-2; Mark 7:1-5).

The Savior prophesied that those who followed him would be persecuted even as he was persecuted. "Blessed are ye, when men shall hate you, and when they shall separate you from their company, and shall reproach you, and cast out your name as evil, for the Son of man's sake." (Luke 6:22) "The servant is not greater than his lord. If they have persecuted me, they will also persecute you." (John 15:20)

The pattern of persecuting true prophets repeats itself in every generation. The major source of persecution is typically the established religions of the day. "The time cometh, that whosoever killeth you will think that he doeth God service." (John 16:2) Stephen, confronting the religious leaders of his day, asked, "Which of the prophets have not your fathers persecuted?" (Acts 7:52)

The prophet Joseph Smith never claimed to be perfect. He was certain of his calling as the Lord's anointed prophet. At the same time, he was aware of his own human limitations and weaknesses, claiming only to be much better than his enemies portrayed him. Fortunately for Joseph Smith and every other prophet of the Lord, Jesus did not say that a prophet is perfect and without defect.

Those who would reject the prophet Joseph because of his humanity will be hard pressed to articulate a standard of personal conduct embracing prophets of the past but spurning this modern prophet of the restoration. Moses killed a man. (Ex 2:11-12) The Apostle Peter denied the Savior thrice. (Matt 26:69-75) Saul, later known as the Apostle Paul, hunted the saints and held the cloak of those who stoned Stephen. (Acts 9:1-2; Acts 7:57; 8:4) King David committed adultery and then had the husband of his mistress killed. (2 Sam 11:2-17) Solomon turned to idolatry at the prompting of his foreign wives and concubines numbering at least one thousand. (1 Kgs 11:1-8) All of these imperfect men have left inspired writings comprising portions of the Bible. Despite weaknesses and mistakes, we accept them as the Lord's chosen servants.

Other examples of human weaknesses displayed by the Lord's prophets include: Noah drank wine in excess (Gen 9:21-23), Abraham allowed mistreatment of Hagar by Sarai (Gen 16:6), Jacob obtained his brother's birthright by means of deception (Gen 27:11-35), Moses displayed occasional anger and arrogance (Ex 5:22-23, 32:19), James and John sought advancement over fellow apostles (Mark 10:35-38), Paul took delight in his confrontation with Peter (Gal 2:11-14), and both Peter and Paul displayed pride-filled impudence and combativeness (Matt 16:21-23; John 13:8-9; 18:10-11; Acts 15:36-39).

These examples should not be construed as justification for every cad or charlatan claiming to be a prophet. However, they illustrate an insidious pattern too often repeated in ecclesiastical history. It has always been easier to overlook the foibles of ancient prophets and fixate on imperfections of living prophets. In so doing, one would do well to heed the words of the Savior:

> Woe unto you . . . because ye build the tombs of the prophets, and garnish the sepulchres of the righteous,
>
> And say, If we had been in the days of our father, we would not have been partakers with them in the blood of the prophets.
>
> Wherefore ye be witnesses unto yourselves, that ye are the children of them which killed the prophets.
>
> Fill ye up then the measure of your fathers. (Matt 23:29-32)

True prophets seldom conform to the expectations of the established religious and political order. One should use extreme caution not to substitute subjective standards in judging those who come in the name of the Lord. The Savior suggested a more certain test. A true prophet will bring forth good fruit.

FULFILLMENT OF PROPHECIES DOCUMENTED

Certainly, one of those good fruits is the fulfillment of prophecies propounded by a prophet. A great irony in all of the infamy thrown at the prophet Joseph Smith is that perpetrators unwittingly fulfill one of his most extraordinary prophecies. Joseph was instructed by an angel of the Lord at the very beginning of events ushering in the restoration of the gospel, "God had a work for me to do; and that my name should be had for good and evil among all nations, kindreds, and tongues, or that it should be both good and evil spoken of among all people." (JS-H 1:33)

This is an amazing prophecy by an obscure farm boy of seventeen, lacking formal education and dwelling in the backwaters of upstate New York. Few prophecies by any prophet in recorded history seemed less plausible when pronounced than this prophecy by young Joseph. Yet, established religions of our day cannot leave the legacy of this man alone after more than one hundred and seventy-five years. Even today, this prophecy continues to be realized as the restored gospel of Jesus Christ reaches every corner of the earth, "among all nations, kindreds, and tongues." In each land where this message is taught, the outcome is the same. The name of Joseph Smith is "had for good and evil," as foretold.

This is one of many pronouncements by the prophet Joseph Smith which have been subsequently fulfilled. A few of his more prominent and better documented prophecies include:

- prophecy on wars in which the American Civil War was prophesied to commence in South Carolina with Great Britain and other nations being called upon to take sides in the conflict, and foretelling this war to be the beginning of an era of wars that would eventually escalate into World Wars involving all nations (D&C 87);
- revelation regarding laws of health, generally known as the Word of Wisdom, in which the saints are forewarned about the pernicious effects of alcohol, tobacco, coffee and tea and the designs of conspiring men in the last days to promote habitual use and dependency on these and other substances, also counsel given regarding appropriate diet emphasizing the benefits of natural grains, fruits, and vegetables and moderation in all things (D&C 89);

- prophecy about then-Judge Stephen A. Douglas of Illinois, fore-telling his success in attaining prominent political positions and eventually aspiring to the Presidency of the United States, promising him that if he ever turned his influence against the Latter-day Saints, he would experience defeat and know the chastisements of God (Burton, audio-tape);
- prophecy that the saints would eventually remove to the Rocky Mountains and build up flourishing centers of commerce and industry; that temples would cover the land and that the restored gospel of Jesus Christ would go forth from the everlasting hills to reach every nation, tongue and people (*Ibid*).

In each case, these prophecies by the prophet Joseph Smith were fulfilled in dramatic fashion. Literally, hundreds of prophecies and revelations given through Joseph Smith have been and continue to be fulfilled as the Lord's kingdom rolls forth in preparation for the Savior's second coming. (See Crowther, PJS)

UNFULFILLED PROPHECIES AND GROWING FROM GRACE TO GRACE

One might appropriately ask, have all of Joseph Smith's pronouncements been fulfilled? Are there prophecies that subsequent events did not fully exonerate?

This is a more difficult question to answer with certitude. Certainly, detractors of the church would claim Joseph Smith erred in some of his prophetic utterances. (Reed and Farkas, pp. 101-4; Ankerberg, pp. 343-54) Far too often such claims are based on representations from questionable sources who can be suspected of less than honorable motives. In many other cases, expectations of timing have to be clarified. For example, the saints were commanded to establish Zion in Independence, Missouri, but were later driven out of that state by mobs and an extermination order of the then-governor, Lilburn Boggs. Latter-day Saints believe Joseph Smith's prophecy awaits fulfillment at a future time.

Many Christians arguing for biblical inerrancy insist on a perfect track record of fulfilling prophetic utterances. (Ankerberg, p. 50) The argument goes something like this: If a single prophecy is shown to be in error, then the prophet is to be rejected because true prophets never prophesy in error. (Ankerberg, pp. 341-3)

This is an assertion not supported by the Bible. The Lord is more tolerant with his human emissaries. "When a prophet speaketh in the name of the Lord, if the thing follow not, nor come to pass . . . the prophet hath spoken it presumptuously." (Deut 18:22) The Lord does not condone such behavior, but he does not reject his prophets, even when they are less than perfect.

Certainly, there are examples in the scriptures of unfulfilled prophecies and "presumptuous" utterances by prophets and apostles of the Lord Jesus Christ. For instance, Jonah prophesied to the inhabitants of Ninevah, "Yet forty days, and Ninevah shall be overthrown." (Jonah 3:4) The king and his nobles repented, and the Lord saw fit to preserve the people. "But it displeased Jonah exceedingly and he was very angry." (Jonah 4:1) Jonah felt he had been discredited in the eyes of this people because the words of his prophecy were not fulfilled. He pleaded, "O Lord, take, I beseech thee, my life from me; for it is better for me to die than to live." (Jonah 4:3)

Jonah endured a trial of his faith. He learned a very poignant lesson. A prophet's decrees can be altered by the Lord in response to the choices of God's children, even after the words have gone forth from his servant's mouth. It is in the providence of God to give decrees and to rescind them, in his divine wisdom. In a similar manner, the children of Israel were promised, "And ye shall be unto me a kingdom of priests, and an holy nation," (Ex 19:5-6, 22:31; Ex 28) but later the priesthood was entrusted only to the tribe of Levi.

Another example is found in the prophecies of Jeremiah. It is difficult to imagine that Zedekiah felt fully satisfied at the end of his life with the prophecy of Jeremiah promising:

> Thou shalt not die by the sword:
> But thou shalt die in peace . . . so shall they burn odours for thee;
> and they will lament thee. (Jer 34:4-5)

Later, the Bible records:

> the king of Babylon slew the sons of Zedekiah before his eyes . . .
> Then he put out the eyes of Zedekiah; and the king of Babylon
> bound him in chains, and carried him to Babylon, and put him in
> prison till the day of his death. (Jer 52:10-11)

The prophecy of Nathan to King David provides yet another example. David had expressed a desire to build a house of God. Nathan informed him:

> I will set up thy seed after thee, which shall proceed out of thy bowels . . .
>
> He shall build an house for my name, and I will stablish the throne of his kingdom forever. (2 Sam 7:12-13; see also verses 4-17)

Later, David's heirs were deposed by Babylonians, and though the Savior eventually descended through the Davidic line, descendants of David and his son, Solomon, preside over no earthly kingdom to this day.

Perhaps statements of Paul regarding women and marriage belong in the category of presumptuous utterances. It is certain that few Christian denominations today are exhorting their members to adhere to Paul's counsel, "Let your women keep silence in the churches: for it is not permitted unto them to speak; but they are commanded to be under obedience, as also saith the law." (1 Cor 14:34) Likewise, "Let the woman learn in silence with all subjection. But I suffer not a woman to teach, nor to usurp authority over the man, but to be in silence." (1 Tim 2:11-12) Similarly, few espouse Paul's views regarding marriage, "But if they cannot contain, let them marry: for it is better to marry than to burn." (1 Cor 7:9)

Some will rush to Paul's defense, suggesting these statements are merely a reflection of his culture and his time. However, these teachings are contained in sacred canon. In addition, Paul invokes "the law," to add credence to his statement on women. Surely the Lord, comprehending the end from the beginning, foresaw these writings passed down to later generations when Paul's counsel appears strange and somewhat less than inspired. Did Paul write presumptuously?

God makes provision for his imperfect servants. There is a pattern recorded in scripture suggesting the Lord's prophets grow in understanding and knowledge, even as they perform God's work. In other words, they grow from grace to grace. They learn line upon line, precept upon precept. This, too, provides insight into the human, yet divine, process by which the Lord works through his living apostles and prophets.

For example, some of the early apostles and disciples of Christ expected his second coming to occur within a short period of time after his ascension. In his initial epistle to the Thessalonians, Paul records:

> For the Lord himself shall descend from heaven . . . and the dead in Christ shall rise first:
>
> *Then we which are alive and remain* shall be caught up together with them in the clouds, to meet the Lord . . . (1 Thes 4:16-17; emphasis added)

This passage seems to suggest Paul expected many alive when he penned this epistle, including himself, to be dwelling on earth at the Savior's triumphant return. Some Bible scholars believe one reason for Paul's counsel to avoid marriage was his conviction that the Savior would soon return, bringing this earth to its foreordained end. (Placher, p. 34) This notion finds strong support in the words of Paul:

> But this I say, brethren, the time is short . . .
> for the fashion of this world passeth away." (1 Cor 7:29,31)

By the time of his second epistle to the Thessalonians, Paul appears to have received additional understanding on this important subject:

> Now we beseech you, brethren, by the coming of our Lord Jesus Christ, and by our gathering together unto him,
>
> That ye be not soon shaken in mind, or be troubled, neither by spirit, nor by word, nor by letter as from us, as that the day of Christ is at hand.
>
> Let no man deceive you by any means: for that day shall not come, except there come a falling away first." (2 Thes 2:1-3)

Finally, toward the end of his ministry, Paul leaves no doubt that he will not live to see either the second coming of Christ or the falling away of which he prophesied in the second epistle to the Thessalonians. Speaking to elders of the church in Ephesus, Paul counseled:

> Take heed therefore unto yourselves, and to all the flock . . .
>
> For I know this, that after my departing shall grievous wolves enter in among you, not sparing the flock.
>
> Also of your own selves shall men arise, speaking perverse things, to draw away disciples after them.
>
> Therefore, watch, and remember, that by the space of three years I ceased not to warn every one night and day with tears. (Acts 20:28-31)

In the pattern of Paul, and presumably all other prophets, Joseph Smith grew in his capacity as a prophet to comprehend more fully the mind of God. Toward the end of his life, Joseph instructed the saints with greater clarity and boldness. To any extent Joseph Smith prophesied imperfectly, he was not the first of the Lord's anointed to err and be corrected. God provides his servants with additional knowledge and teaches them poignant lessons even as they bring forth his work and his word.

The track record of the prophet Joseph Smith related to fulfillment of prophecy is astonishing. Those who seek to discredit him and his work should take pause, lest they act "presumptuously" in following a pattern all too common among those who refuse to see living prophets of God with their eyes and hear them with their ears.

BY THEIR FRUITS: THE TESTIMONY OF JESUS CHRIST

If prophets are human and grow in their capacity as prophets, then how can the honest in heart recognize a true prophet? What is the fruit by which one is able to discern with certainty a true prophet from a false one? The answer to this question is manifest in the fruit brought forth when a prophet functions as a prophet; when a prophet issues the pronouncement, "Thus saith the Lord." This fruit includes both the written canon of the prophet as well as the results of his teachings in the lives of those who follow his counsel.

In addition to the Bible, which is regarded as the first and foremost volume of their scriptures, official teachings of The Church of Jesus Christ of Latter-day Saints are included in three other canons of scripture, namely the Book of Mormon, A Second Testament of Jesus Christ; the Doctrine and Covenants; and the Pearl of Great Price. Each of these volumes contains significant teachings "profitable for doctrine, for reproof, for correction, for instruction in righteousness." (2 Tim 3:16)

The *Book of Mormon, A Second Testament of Jesus Christ*, is exactly what it purports to be. It is a second witness, complementing the testament of the Holy Bible in declaring to the world that Jesus is the Christ.

The Book of Mormon is an ancient record of people who left Jerusalem about 600 BC and came to the American continent. They brought with them sacred records including a significant portion of what is found in the Old Testament. After arriving, the people split into two factions, the Nephites and the Lamanites. The Nephites taught their posterity the teachings of prophets, foretelling the coming of a Messiah to be born near Jerusalem. This Messiah would teach his people and would be rejected by many, suffering and dying for the sins of mankind. On the third day, he would resurrect from the dead. Significant manifestations were prophesied in advance for those on the American continent, marking the birth and death of the Messiah.

Among these manifestations, the culminating event was the personal visit of the resurrected Lord to the Nephite and Lamanite nations. During his mortal ministry, the Savior told his apostles he would visit other people. "And other sheep I have, which are not of this fold: them also I must bring, and they shall hear my voice; and there shall be one fold, and one shepherd." (John 10:16) Following his post-resurrection ministry in the old world, Jesus Christ appeared in person to his "other sheep" on the American Continent, giving them ordinances of salvation, organizing his church and blessing the assembled believers.

The Book of Mormon is rich in doctrine and spiritual insight. It clarifies important teachings in the Bible regarding the fall and atonement, resurrection and the final judgment, the apostasy and restoration of the gospel in the last days, the moral agency of man, the proper manner of baptism, the gathering of Israel, what it means to be born again, to exercise faith, to repent of sins, to be edified by the gifts of the spirit, and to practice true charity, to name just a few.

The *Doctrine and Covenants* contains many of the revelations and instructions given to the prophet Joseph Smith in bringing about the restoration of the gospel. It speaks to principles of organization and priesthood in re-establishing God's kingdom on earth. It prophesies many events that will come to pass as the world draws near the second coming of the Lord. It provides additional insights into the most transcendent of all events, the atonement and resurrection of Jesus Christ. It teaches of the establishment of Zion as a gathering place for the saints and for the tribes of Israel. It contains teachings and counsel regarding prayer, fasting, tithes and offerings, a law of health, eternal marriage, and moral conduct. It records sacred visions and visitations by the resurrected Lord and his ministering angels in restoring priesthood powers to the earth. Above all else, it is a modern-day witness of Jesus Christ, that he lives and is eternally involved in the work of salvation among the children of man.

The *Pearl of Great Price* consists of two parts. One portion is an inspired translation of ancient writings of Moses and Abraham regarding the creation of the earth and related events. The second part of this canon contains words of the prophet Joseph Smith describing important events in the restoration of Christ's church in these latter days and a concise statement of central tenets of the church.

Taken as a whole, these four volumes of scripture provide valuable instruction and doctrine to followers of Jesus Christ. Most importantly, they witness to all nations, kindreds, tongues and people in all generations of time that Jesus of Nazareth is the Son of the Living God, the promised Messiah, the Savior of the world.

Two examples, one from the Book of Mormon and one from Doctrine and Covenants, provide ample evidence of the power and divine purpose of these additional scriptures. The first is an account taken from the Book of Mormon recording the appearance of the resurrected Christ to inhabitants of the American continent:

> And now it came to pass that there were a great multitude gathered together . . .
>
> while they were thus conversing one with another, they heard a voice as if it came out of heaven . . .
>
> And again the third time they did hear the voice, and did open their ears to hear it . . .
>
> and it said unto them:
>
> Behold my Beloved Son, in whom I am well pleased, in whom I have glorified my name—hear ye him. And it came to pass, as they understood they cast their eyes up again toward heaven; and behold, they saw a Man descending out of heaven; and he was clothed in a white robe; and he came down and stood in the midst of them; and the eyes of the whole multitude were turned upon him . . .
>
> And it came to pass that he stretched forth his hand and spake unto the people saying:
>
> Behold I am Jesus Christ whom the prophets testified should come into the world.
>
> And behold, I am the light and the life of the world; and I have drunk out of that bitter cup which the Father hath given me, and have glorified the Father in taking upon me the sins of the world, in the which I have suffered the will of the Father in all things from the beginning . . .

Arise and come forth unto me, that ye may thrust your hands into my side, and also that ye may feel the prints of the nails in my hands and in my feet, that ye may know that I am the God of Israel, and the God of the whole earth, and have been slain for the sins of the world. (3 Ne 11:1-14)

A second passage, from Doctrine and Covenants, contains the testimony of Joseph Smith and Sidney Rigdon, two of the early leaders in the restored church. Together, Joseph and Sidney beheld a glorious vision of Jesus Christ and the three degrees of heaven.

The Lord touched the eyes of our understandings and they were opened, and the glory of the Lord shone round about.

And we beheld the glory of the Son, on the right hand of the Father and received of his fullness;

And saw the holy angels, and them who are sanctified before his throne, worshiping God, and the Lamb . . .

And now, after the many testimonies which have been given of him, this is the testimony, last of all, which we give of him: That he lives!

For we saw him, even on the right hand of God; and we heard the voice bearing record that he is the Only Begotten of the Father—

That by him, and through him, and of him, the worlds are and were created, and the inhabitants thereof are begotten sons and daughters unto God. (D&C 76:19-24)

John the Revelator proclaimed, "the testimony of Jesus . . . is the spirit of prophecy." (Rev 19:10) By this divine standard, Joseph Smith qualifies unquestionably as a true prophet of God.

As one LDS leader has observed, the passion of those who attack the prophet of the restoration would be understandable if Joseph Smith had declared he was the Christ or another was the Christ or that there never would be a Christ. But from beginning to end, the testimony of Joseph Smith was always the same: Jesus is the Christ, the Son of God. His message was that of a true prophet. (paraphrase from Brown, audio-tape)

WITNESSES TESTIFY OF A TRUE PROPHET

Another indication that Joseph Smith is a true prophet is that others shared his experiences and bore witness of important events related to the restoration of the gospel. The open vision received by Joseph Smith and Sidney Rigdon, cited above, is an example of how the Lord provided witnesses to testify of the prophet Joseph Smith and his works. None of the seminal events related to the restoration of the gospel was performed in darkness or secrecy. Each significant occasion was witnessed by others, consistent with the law of witnesses set forth in the Bible: "In the mouth of two or three witnesses shall every word be established." (2 Cor 13:1)

On the occasion of the glorious vision described above, Sidney Rigdon saw all that the prophet beheld and recorded. In addition, at least five others were present in the room with Joseph and Sidney. They did not see the vision, but they witnessed the appearance of the two who did. One of those present left this account: "Joseph wore black clothes but at this time seemed to be dressed in an element of glorious white, and his face shown as if it were transparent." (Lundwall, p. 11)

Nor was this experience an isolated one. At the time Joseph Smith received the prophecy concerning relocation of the saints to the Rocky Mountains, the prophet was in the company of several others. Anson Call leaves his eyewitness account,

> I had before seen him (Joseph) in vision, and now saw while he was talking his countenance change to white; not the deadly white of a bloodless face, but a living, brilliant white. He seemed absorbed in gazing at something at a great distance, and said: 'I am gazing upon the valleys of those mountains.' This was followed by a vivid description of the scenery of these mountains, as I have since become acquainted with it . . . Pointing to me, he said: 'There is Anson, he shall go and shall assist in building up cities from one end of the country to the other.' (Roberts, CHC, Vol. II, pp. 181-2)

Likewise, important events attendant to the coming forth of the Book of Mormon and the restoration of the priesthood of God were shared by others who recorded their witnesses. The ancient plates from which the Book of Mormon was translated were seen by three special witnesses who also heard the voice of God bearing record to the truthfulness of the record and its translation. At a later time, eight others handled the plates and examined their markings. The written testimonies of the three special witnesses and of these eight other witnesses are recorded on the first few pages of the Book of Mormon. The restoration of the Aaronic and Melchizedec priesthood and the long-awaited visit of

Elijah, as prophesied by Malachi and the Savior, were witnessed by Oliver Cowdery, an early convert and the scribe who recorded most of the Book of Mormon as Joseph Smith translated it.

Because of the collapse of the Kirtland Safety Society, as part of the national financial panic of 1837, several of those who witnessed these sacred events fell away from the church. Some later reconciled with the prophet and the church while others remained apart until their death. However, in no case, did any of these important witnesses of the restoration ever deny their solemn testimony of events shared with the prophet. (see Anderson; also Cook)

The testimonies of these witnesses provide unassailable evidence of the veracity of Joseph Smith's work. The good fruits of a true prophet are attested to by the mouth of two or more witnesses.

COMMON SENSE TESTIFIES OF A TRUE PROPHET

A casual reading of the canon of scripture introduced by the prophet Joseph Smith is sufficient to convince many that a man with his limited schooling could not have produced these works without divine guidance. This insight is particularly apparent with regards to the Book of Mormon.

The Book of Mormon is a volume of approximately 275,000 words, recorded in little more than two months. Joseph Smith received ancient plates of gold from an angel of God. By divine providence, Joseph Smith was given power to translate a portion of these plates into the Book of Mormon. While the exact process of translation is not fully understood, it is clear Joseph Smith dictated the entire volume to a scribe, primarily Oliver Cowdery, from behind a suspended sheet without notes or outlines and without source materials. This work was recorded just as it flowed from the lips of the prophet, with virtually no revisions or refinements.

Given the method by which it was produced, one might expect a meandering account of confusion and obvious contradictions. Instead, this inspired record is remarkably coherent and easy to read. The solemn account follows a tight story line, avoiding tangents and digressions even when events are overlapping and timelines are complicated.

Interwoven through the pages of the Book of Mormon are distinctive characteristics including:

- 55 chapters on visions and prophecies;
- 71 chapters expounding doctrine and exhortation;
- 21 chapters recording the ministry of Christ among the ancient inhabitants of America;
- original Hebrew literary forms including figures of speech, metaphors, similes, narration, epic, lyric, oratory, allegory, epistles, logic and parables, to name just a few; (Brown, audio-tape)
- at least 25 forms of poetic parallelism, the most prevalent pattern in Hebrew scripture, including extensive use of chiasmus, the most complex and beautiful form. When the Book of Mormon was translated, western scholarship was ignorant regarding the structure and prevalence of chiasmus in Hebrew literature (Morgan, pp. 181-2)

Since its publication, non-Mormon scholars of the Bible have poured over the pages of this book searching for teachings not in strict harmony with other scripture. These efforts have proven futile, producing nothing to contradict the claim of the Book of Mormon as a second testament of Jesus Christ and a companion volume to the Holy Bible.

The question that has occupied the minds of believers and skeptics alike, when confronted with such intelligent material, is this: Could Joseph Smith have written this book? In response, historically, both Latter-day Saints and detractors of all types have tended to agree that a young man of Joseph Smith's limited educational background could not have conceived and brought forth the Book of Mormon on his own.

When the Book of Mormon was published, Joseph Smith was 23 years old. Even by standards of rural America in the early eighteenth century, Joseph Smith's education was rudimentary, at best. His mother has indicated that Joseph was not naturally drawn to books and learning in his early years. (L. M. Smith, p. 82) At the time of publication, Joseph had shown no inclination toward the difficult mental discipline required to produce anything resembling the Book of Mormon. It was the conclusion of contemporaries who knew the young man personally that Joseph Smith could not have accomplished this feat without the aid of an external source.

Emma Smith, the prophet's more-educated wife and early scribe in the work of translation, left her own reflections on the role of her husband in bringing forth the Book of Mormon:

No man could have dictated the writing of the manuscripts unless he was inspired; for, when acting as his scribe, [Joseph] would dictate to me hour after hour, and when returning after meals, or after interruptions, he would at once begin where he had left off, without either seeing the manuscript or having any portion of it read to him. This was a usual thing for him to do. It would have been improbable that a learned man could do this, and for one so ignorant and unlearned as he was, it was simply impossible. (Morgan, pp. 184-5)

Different possibilities have been advanced by various parties to provide an explanation that does not depend on divine intervention as claimed by Joseph Smith. Skeptics have put forth theories ranging from plagiarism to secret manuscripts from other sources to ghost writers. (Brodie, pp. 68-9; Scott, pp. 30, 75) Of these, an alleged conspiracy involving Joseph Smith and Sydney Rigdon plagiarizing a manuscript authored by Solomon Spalding has received the most publicity. With time, each alternative explanation has proven false or faded away, lacking factual substance to support the allegations. (*Ibid.*, also Morgan, pp. 87-9)

In recent years, critics have been forced to change direction, ascribing genius-like qualities to young Joseph. (Brodie, pp. 68-9). It is important to recognize this for what it is. After years of charging conspiracy and duplicity, those seeking alternative explanations are, in effect, acknowledging that skeptics and scholars have exhausted other rationalizations without success. Faced with the choice of accepting Joseph Smith's account, and therefore the divinity of this work, they have retreated to the ultimate secular miracle, "genius." They cannot explain how the Book of Mormon could have been produced by one so poorly prepared as Joseph Smith, but they insist on a natural explanation. Not having a clue what it is, they call it genius of the man.

Each reader must draw his or her own conclusion as to whether the intellect of Joseph Smith, alone, can account for the Book of Mormon. As one studies this book, what becomes apparent is a clarity of doctrine and spiritual insight unsurpassed by any other volume of scripture, including the Bible. The following passages are worthy of special attention:
- the ministry of Jesus Christ among the ancient inhabitants of America (3 Ne 11-26);

- the vision of Nephi regarding the birth and divine mission of Jesus Christ and prophecies concerning latter-day events (1 Ne 11-14);
- teachings on moral agency and joy as the divine purpose of our existence (2 Ne 2);
- a psalm of repentance and redemption (2 Ne 4);
- an exposition of the atonement (2 Ne 9);
- a discourse on service and charity, atonement and redemption (Mos 2-4);
- doctrine regarding being born again (Alma 5, 36);
- an exposition of faith (Alma 32; Ether 12);
- an exposition of the fall, atonement and resurrection (Alma 40-42); and
- an epistle on faith, hope and charity (Moroni 7)

In reading these passages, common sense has convinced many approaching this book with an open mind that no man could have written these things, least of all the 23-year-old, then semi-literate Joseph Smith. More importantly, the spirit of God continues to touch the honest in heart with a deep conviction that the prophet Joseph did not and could not have written this book without guidance from on high. The Book of Mormon is a work of divine providence.

The same is true of the Doctrine and Covenants and the Pearl of Great Price. For example, Section 93 of Doctrine and Covenants is among the most profound statements of theology and science ever produced. In these inspired verses, the Lord revealed through the prophet Joseph Smith the following truths:

- Truth is knowledge of things as they are, and as they were, and as they are to come; (verse 24)
- Jesus did not receive a fullness of glory at mortal birth, but grew from grace to grace, until he received a fullness of glory; after his death and resurrection, he received all power both in heaven and on earth and the glory of the Father is with him forever; (verses 11-17)
- By a similar process of growing from grace to grace, man can receive a fullness of glory as did the Son; (verses 19-22)
- Man was in the beginning with God; (verses 23, 29)

- Intelligence and physical matter do not issue forth from nothing, rather they are eternal; they have always existed and they will always exist in the future; (verses 29, 33)
- All truth and eternal law are independent in the sphere in which God has placed them; that is, they function without intervention or coercion; (verse 30)
- All intelligence endowed with moral agency is also granted independence to act for itself; this allows man to choose life or condemnation as an accountable being; (verses 30-31)
- Man is comprised of spirit and physical matter (element); only when spirit and element are inseparably connected, as in the resurrection, can man receive a fullness of joy and be like his Father in Heaven; (verses 33-34)
- Every spirit of man was innocent in the beginning; because God redeemed man from the fall, man became again innocent before God; (verse 38)
- Satan seeks to deprive man of light and truth by persuading him to disobey commandments that make us more like our Savior and Father in Heaven; if we succumb to the influences of Satan, it is because we choose to follow him, and not because we are impure from the beginning. (verses 38-39)

Whether one embraces the specific doctrines of Section 93 or not, it is apparent these verses deal with weighty matters of eternal significance. Through the centuries since Christ, some of the best minds of the western world have grappled with these issues, including Saint Augustine, Thomas Aquinas, Martin Luther, and John Calvin. Despite training and devoted scholarship, none has been successful in producing a statement of doctrine as coherent and profound as Section 93. History witnesses that no man could have produced these sacred writings of inspired insight, least of all, the young Joseph Smith.

This points to another amazing fact regarding the teachings of the Latter-day Saints. Without theologians and without councils and synods, doctrines of the Latter-day Saints have remained consistent and free of major revisions from the early years of the restoration. This is a fact commented on by scholars of religion and is most striking in its contrast to both Catholic and Protestant doctrines which have undergone dramatic changes over the same time period.

For example, in the early 1900's, a renown German scholar, Eduard Meyer, visited Salt Lake City, Utah, for the period of a year to study this new religion, frequently referred to as Mormonism. Meyer was a scholar of ancient religions. He hoped to understand how a new religion gets established by studying The Church of Jesus Christ of Latter-day Saints while still in its infancy. Meyers was a man of immense scholarship who belonged to no religious community. As such, he was impartial and free from prejudice to pursue his objective study of the Mormons.

What Eduard Meyer observed convinced him that, above all else, the doctrine of Latter-day Saints was consistent. In his own words, the doctrine was "absolutely literal, sober and logical." (Nibley, NMTAH, p. 47) He noted striking parallels between the teachings and customs of Latter-day Saints and those of Christ's church as recorded in the Bible. (*Ibid.*, p. 19) He remarked how science had substantiated many specifics of Latter-day Saint teachings (*Ibid.*, p. 47), and he concluded the prophet Joseph Smith must have had an actual vision at the beginning of his ministry. (*Ibid.*, p. 29)

Eduard Meyer's observations are cited to illustrate a single point. The teachings of Joseph Smith have not evolved to fill obvious holes in logic and reason over the 150 years since his death. This remarkable feat is unparalleled by all Christian writers and theologians since the times of the New Testament. Common sense suggests this is no mere coincidence.

Finally, in the computer age using unbiased word-print analysis, scholars have demonstrated Joseph Smith is not the original author of these inspired writings. By comparing the writings of Joseph Smith and other early church leaders to passages from the Book of Mormon, statisticians have concluded the Book of Mormon was written by several authors, all having distinctively different styles from each other and from the personal writings of Joseph Smith or his early followers. Specifically:

> Within the first two books are more "eth" suffixes than any subsequent book; within the book of Mosiah are 559 words not found in the preceding 144 pages, and 203 of them are not used anywhere else in the following 324 pages; in Alma's book alone are 675 words found nowhere else in the Book of Mormon; Alma is located approximately midway through the book, yet more words are introduced there than in

any other book before it (most words in novels are introduced toward
the beginning); Moroni, the last author, introduces the second highest
number of words. The Book of Mormon has 5,665 different words, the
Bible approximately 6,000, but the Book of Mormon is less than half
the size of the Bible; the word "and" occurs about 6 percent of the time
in the Bible and the Book of Mormon, but only about 3.5 percent in
Joseph Smith's own prose. (Morgan, pp. 182-3)

These facts defy even the label of genius. Either Joseph Smith was
the translator of ancient prophets' writings, as he claimed, or the world
of skeptics will have to concoct yet another theory to explain this marvelous work and wonder.

THE SPIRIT TESTIFIES OF A TRUE PROPHET

More important than the intellectual witness of sense and reason, a
spiritual witness is promised to the honest in heart who read and study
the words of scripture brought forth by the prophet Joseph Smith.
Visiting a gathering of Latter-day Saints on any given Sunday, one is
almost certain to hear the solemn witness of individuals testifying their
souls have been touched by the Holy Spirit concerning the divine mission of Joseph Smith and sacred truths revealed through him.

These are fruits of a true prophet. The Holy Ghost is poured out on
those seeking truth and willing to follow their Savior Jesus Christ in
being baptized by one having authority. These are the saints of God
who hear the voice of the good shepherd and strive to walk in his path
of righteousness. They are not perfect, but they are striving to be more
Christ-like. They come from different backgrounds, cultures, ethnic
groups, political persuasions, economic stations and educational prepa-
rations. Each has a unique personality and defining idiosyncrasies.
However, all share one thing in common. The Spirit has touched the
soul of each faithful Latter-day Saint, testifying to him or her that God
lives, Jesus is the Christ, Joseph Smith is the prophet of the restoration
and The Church of Jesus Christ of Latter-day Saints is led by a living
prophet today. This is not a witness based on tradition or birth. Those
born into The Church of Jesus Christ of Latter-day Saints are taught
that they cannot live on borrowed light. They must receive a personal
witness of the Spirit.

The experience described by many Christians when they are made
aware of the grace of Jesus Christ is similar to the witness of the Spirit

regarding the truths of the restored gospel. Jesus is the way, the truth and the life. No one will approach the throne of God without Jesus Christ. But the truths of the gospel encompass all truth including the divine mission of Joseph Smith and the restoration of all things, foretold by ancient prophets.

The same Spirit convincing all true Christians that Jesus is the Christ will testify to the honest in heart that Joseph Smith is the prophet of the Lord who brought forth the Book of Mormon, Doctrine and Covenants and the Pearl of Great Price through the power of God as further witnesses of Jesus Christ. By that same Spirit, one can know that Jesus Christ has once again restored his true church, The Church of Jesus Christ of Latter-day Saints, led by living apostles and prophets today.

This inspiration and sure knowledge of the Spirit are promised to all who seek truth with a pure heart and real intent. In the final chapter of the Book of Mormon, the Lord leaves his promise concerning a spiritual witness:

> Behold, I would exhort you that when ye shall read these things . . . that ye would remember how merciful the Lord hath been unto the children of men, from the creation of Adam even down until the time that ye shall receive these things, and ponder it in your hearts.
>
> And when ye shall receive these things, I would exhort you that ye would ask God, the Eternal Father, in the name of Christ, if these things are not true; and if ye shall ask with a sincere heart, with real intent, having faith in Christ, he will manifest the truth of it unto you, by the power of the Holy Ghost.
>
> And by the power of the Holy Ghost ye may know the truth of all things. (Moroni 10:3-5)

This was the experience of young Joseph Smith. He searched for truth, attending various Christian denominations and attempting to understand their teachings. He concluded that he could not make a determination as to which church was true because each church interpreted the scriptures so differently. One day while studying the Bible, he read a passage in James, chapter one, verse five, exhorting him to pray to God for all wisdom. This he did, and received the first of many visions and revelations, ushering in the restoration of the gospel of Jesus Christ.

The promise at the end of the Book of Mormon is an assurance that Joseph Smith's experience was not so unique. By the witness of the Spirit, one can come to know as Joseph did. There may not be open visions, but the witness of the Spirit comes with power and certainty. God is no respecter of persons. (Acts 10:34) By following an invitation of the Spirit to ask God, it is possible to know the truth of all things.

When the Spirit has touched one's soul, there is no question about the reality of revelation. There is a quiet confidence whispering, "Be still and know that I am God." All things are provided for in the providence of our Lord. He will not leave his children to grope in personal interpretations of his recorded word. Rather, he will give us light and knowledge to manage our lives through personal revelation, and he will bring forth his kingdom through revelation to his servants, living apostles and prophets. This has always been his way. So it is even now and will be until he returns to reign in glory and righteousness with the meek and the godly.

We can feel his peaceful certitude. We can experience his grace. And by that same Spirit, we can know the truth of all things. His promises are certain. "Knock and it shall be opened unto you." (Matt 7:7)

Author's Epilogue

In researching and writing this book, I have found myself engaged in a labor of love. Over the last four years, I have read the works of more than 100 non-LDS scholars, writers and theologians. I have participated in scores of conversations with Christians from diverse denominations, attempting to understand their teachings and beliefs. Traveling in conjunction with my profession, I have listened to hundreds of hours of Christian radio broadcasts from many regions of this great country.

Reflecting on the cumulative effect of these activities, I am convinced that members of the Christian community worship the same God, accept the same Christ and experience the same Holy Spirit. Those who would justify the superiority of their own beliefs by attributing satanic influences or deceiving angels of light to others do a disservice to the larger body of Christ and demonstrate more intolerance than insight.

From the beginning of my journey in writing this book, I have asked myself a simple question: Do differences in professions of faith really matter? I have reflected on this question many times in the last four years. At this point, my conclusion is quite clear. I am inclined to believe that greater degrees of light and truth really do make a difference in our mortal lives and in eternity. I am aware that many will insist otherwise, and therefore, I feel compelled to share some reasons for my conclusion.

In a very practical sense, I believe it matters whether one conceives of God as an incomprehensible, spirit essence, radically and eternally different from man, rather than as the literal Father of our spirits in whose image we all are created. Many have despaired and lost hope in ever relating to a Trinity completely removed from human sensibilities. At the same time, it seems so reasonable and attainable to exercise faith in a loving, personal Being from whom we all inherited spiritual qualities and traits. Greater truth is found in this simpler, more approachable Deity.

I believe it makes a difference to know that we must do our small part in working out our salvation with fear and trembling before God. Extremes of all grace or all works cannot inspire sufficient faith to sustain us in challenges and trials. Only those who possess promises within the new covenant can attain a hope sufficient to purify themselves. "And every man that hath this hope in (Christ) purifieth himself, even as he is pure." (1 John 3:3) A balance is then struck between the finished work of the atonement and our small part to receive the mediation of our Savior.

I believe it matters when we know we are children of God, eternal beings like our Father; to know we lived with God before this mortal life and chose to enter this world with foreknowledge of our circumstances and possibilities for progression. Man is not created from nothing, ex nihilo, to serve an end knowable only to God. Rather, our lives have purpose. Each of us is here on a mission to grow through experience and assist others in their struggles. We must be tested and tried to become all we desire to be; all we are capable of becoming by right of our noble birthright as children of God and new creatures in Christ.

I believe it makes a difference to know that everyone who ever will live or ever has lived on this earth will have an opportunity, in this life or the next, to hear the gospel of Jesus Christ and accept or reject it for themselves. A just God worthy of our complete devotion would not bring the majority of humankind into existence, ex nihilo, and then banish them to an eternity in hell for reasons completely beyond their control. Only if all receive the same opportunity can we "be judged according to men in the flesh" (1 Pet 4:6), fully accountable for our choices before the supreme judge whose justice and mercy are perfect. Likewise, many grades of valiancy and faithfulness evinced by the children of men suggest multiple mansions and degrees of glory in the world to come. Our choices really do matter.

I believe it makes a difference that Christ organized his church with divine wisdom and insight, providing for unity of the faith. Only Jesus Christ, the chief cornerstone, can lead his church, and, in all generations of time, he has directed his kingdom through properly ordained apostles and prophets. The edifice of the church rests upon a sure foundation of ongoing revelation between Christ and his anointed, ensuring that "the gates of hell shall not prevail against it." (Matt 16:18) Authority to act in the name of God with the "keys of the kingdom" to "bind on earth" those things that "shall be bound in heaven" (Matt 16:19) is found with true apostles and prophets of Jesus Christ. As evident throughout the Christian community, the alternative is fragmentation and division. These things are not of God.

Finally, it makes a difference to know where the Oracle of God is found on earth today. Through his chosen servants, Jesus Christ will reveal his will and administer his kingdom. This work will be accompanied by a disproportionate outpouring of the Spirit; and where there is more of the Holy Spirit, there will be more enlightenment; and where there is more enlightenment, there will be more knowledge and truth; and where there is more knowledge and truth, there will be greater faith which brings forth an increase of spirit, of light and of truth, growing unto the perfect day in the Lord Jesus Christ.

As a Latter-day Saint, "I count not myself to have apprehended" (Philip 3:13), but I press forward with hope in Christ, striving to be found in the light of the Spirit which will change me and mold me in the image of my Master. After four years of diligently studying the tenets of other Christian denominations, my faith is increased and my witness is more sure. The Church of Jesus Christ of Latter-day Saints has access to the Spirit in greater abundance, and therefore, more light, more knowledge, and more truth. It also has the binding power of priesthood authority, ushering us into a new covenant of life and mercy. This solemn witness I bear to all who will hear, inviting them to partake of the fullness of Christ in greater abundance as a member of his true church.

Appendix One:
Materials Given to Marianne by Betsy

HOW DO MORMON TEACHINGS DIFFER FROM CHRISTIAN TEACHINGS?

Because Mormon theology is Mormon and not Christian, it is easy to compare the beliefs of Mormonism with the beliefs of Christianity. As an introduction to this section, we offer the following chart contrasting basic Mormon and Christian teachings.

Mormonism	Christianity
Bible	
Unreliable	Reliable
Incomplete as it is	Complete as it is
Adds new revelations to God's Word	Rejects new revelations
Unbiblical theological presupposition in interpretation	Normal hermeneutic utilized in interpretation
God	
Tritheism/polytheistic	Trinity/monotheistic
Physical (evolved man)	Spirit
Finite	Infinite
Morally questionable	Creator of matter from nothing
Sexual polygamist	Nonsexual
Jesus	
A god	God
Created	Eternal
Earned salvation (exaltation to Godhood)	As eternal God neither salvation nor exaltation required
Not virgin born	Virgin born
Polygamist	Unmarried
Salvation	
By works	By grace
Denies biblical atonement	Affirms atonement
Possible after death	Impossible after death
Death	
"Purgatorial"; Three celestial kingdoms; almost universalistic	Eternal heaven or hell; no purgatory; not universalistic

For anyone to maintain that Mormonism and Christianity teach the same thing is logically, historically and doctrinally an indefensible position.

2 Corinthians 11:13-15
Church of Jesus Christ and the Latter Day Deceived

QUESTIONS ABOUT THE MORMON CHURCH

Pagan • Polytheism • not Christian • occultic beliefs • blasphemy

1. What is Mormonism and why is it important?

A cult, attractive on the outside, evil on inside, growing in numbers, one of the leading non-Christian religions in U.S. 7,000,000 worldwide, hope to double by 2000 AD. Power and influence.

2. How did Mormonism begin?

Joseph Smith, 1820, God and Jesus appeared to Smith telling him the Bible was a lie, and Smith should reorganize the Christian religion. 1823—angel revealed gold plates, the Book of Mormon—historical record of ancient Jewish tribe—migrated to America—to historical record as proof: 135 revelations.

3. Is Mormonism a Christian religion?

No! Anti-Christian, unbiblical, rejects Biblical definition of Christian. Mormons: Christianity is a false and damnable apostate religion. God, one of many, self-progressing, bodily deities, formally a man, finite. Jesus not of a virgin, spirit children of Elohim. Denies true meaning of Biblical terms.

4. What does Mormonism teach about God?

Believe in God and the Bible and the Holy Trinity—untrue— church accepts and teaches polytheism, Father, Son & Holy Ghost are three separate God's, many others also—those who are exalted become God's—rule their own world [Isaiah 43:10] "Before me there was no God formed and there will be none after me." Each god is evolving, self-progressing. Bible: God is an infinite being—unchanging from now until eternity. God is spirit, not man. [John 4:24]

5. *What does Mormonism teach about Jesus Christ?*

He was an exalted God, evolved to today—created being—first and foremost of many spirit children who were of God's; Jesus & Lucifer blood brothers—Jesus had many wives and children, earned his salvation & godhood.

6. *What do Mormons teach about salvation and life after death?*

Based on works, you must earn it—different kinds of salvation: General for everyone—on grace, resurrected & immortal—in determined heaven [Eph. 1:7—redemption through Christ; also Gal 1:6-8]; on works, individual determines which of 3 heavens you go to: lowest telestial kingdom, wicked excluded from presence of God; terrestrial, luke warm Mormons and good non-Mormons; celestial, complete obedience to Mormon gospel—3 kingdoms: within top one, you become a god and have a world.

[Author's Note: This material consisted of a handwritten test. Those portions in italicized script represent Betsy's answers and comments, based on her learning from the pastor's teachings. Punctuation has been altered in some cases to make it more comprehensible. Original copies are in the possession of the author.]

Appendix Two:

My Letter to Marianne and Her Christian Friends

February 17, 1992

Dear Marianne:

Thank you for sharing with me the materials you received from your friend, Betsy. After studying them, I am left with a feeling of sadness that any religious leader would publish such misleading half-truths about the beliefs of others. There is no intent to inform or educate in these materials but only to condemn what they do not understand and are afraid to learn about.

They claim Mormons are not Christians. The name of our church proclaims our devotion to Jesus Christ, The Church of Jesus Christ of Latter-day Saints. What they are really saying is that their interpretation of Christianity is not the same as ours.

If a Christian is one who accepts Jesus Christ as his or her personal Savior believing He is the Son of God, that His mortal life was lived perfectly, that He is the embodiment of love, mercy, light and truth, that He is the Redeemer of mankind through His personal act of the atonement, that only through Him can mankind be reconciled with God and enter into His presence after death, that He resurrected from the grave and opened the way for the resurrection of all mankind, that He lives today and is involved in our daily existence; if this is what it means to be a Christian, then members of The Church of Jesus Christ of Latter-day Saints qualify as Christians in every sense of the word.

If being a Christian means accepting the interpretations of some Christian denominations regarding the Trinity (God is three-in-one) or their beliefs about how grace is received, then members of The Church of Jesus Christ of Latter-day Saints will be excluded under their narrow definition. We do not accept these doctrines. We do not believe they are consistent with a comprehensive study of the Bible. Rather, they are based on the traditions of man speculating without prophetic powers and on selected passages from the Bible that seem to support their position while ignoring or minimizing other passages that clearly contradict these teachings.

Betsy and her pastor claim their beliefs about Jesus Christ and His eternal truths are derived from the Bible as recorded by holy prophets of God. Their claim to be able to interpret the Bible correctly is just as valid as hundreds of other Christian churches who claim to practice true religion as taught in the Bible. These churches, while sincere and well-meaning, cannot agree among themselves about basic doctrines such as:

- how to perform proper baptisms
- whether baptism is necessary for salvation
- whether there is a need for God's priesthood to perform ordinances of salvation
- who holds the priesthood
- who can be ordained to the priesthood (men, women, homosexuals, etc.)
- how Christ's church is to be organized
- who is to lead Christ's church
- the physical nature of God (one personage or three)
- the role of grace and of works in securing salvation

This is just a partial list. The different interpretations are so diverse on subjects of fundamental importance that they cannot be reconciled. The result is hundreds of different Christian denominations, each teaching its own brand of Christianity.

An honest study of the evolving doctrines of these churches will reveal that their beliefs today are significantly different from those of fifty or one hundred years ago. For them, revelation has ceased but their doctrines continue to change and modify.

Many of the leaders of these Christian denominations will try to minimize the differences among the various factions and may pretend they are inconsequential, but the differences dividing these churches are real and are not likely to be reconciled. Quite the opposite, they will continue to lead to more fragmentation and further splintering as special interest groups select passages from the Bible to support their preconceived ideas and preferences.

God is not the author of such confusion; man is. God did not leave man to seek out interpretations of past writings as the sole source of light and truth. This is the mistake made by some Jews in the time of Christ. Christian churches are following an equally slippery path today.

In the days of Jesus' mortal ministry, many proudly proclaimed, "We have the complete word of God. We are the descendants of Abraham and Moses. We have no need for a new revelation." They contended with the Savior about interpretations of scripture while rejecting the additional light of truth and salvation.

In our day and age, Christian leaders repeat these errors of the past. They claim revelation ceased with the apostles, that the Bible is complete, that it contains the fullness of Jesus Christ's ministry. In so doing, they reject the revealed word of God through modern prophets and use their interpretations of biblical passages to shield them from the light of continuing revelation. They ignore the more sure word of prophecy to be restored in the latter days as foretold in the Old and New Testaments (Daniel 2:44-45; Acts 3:19-21).

They claim the Bible teaches there is to be no more revelation, and they cite the Book of Revelation 22:18 which says, "For I testify unto every man that heareth the words of the prophecy of this book, if any man shall add unto these things, God shall add unto him the plagues that are written in this book."

This passage was written in reference to the Book of Revelation and not to the Bible as a whole. How do we know this? *First*, there is a similar phrase found in Deuteronomy 4:2. If we are to accept their interpretation of Revelation 22:18, then everything written after Deuteronomy should not be accepted as revelation from God based on the same reasoning.

Second, Bible scholars, including those in Betsy's church, generally agree the Book of Revelation was written by the apostle John several years before the fourth gospel and the three general epistles attributed to him. Based on their interpretation, John violated his own admonition against adding to the closed canon of scripture. This would render his later writings invalid as revelation from God.

In addition, the Bible refers by name to numerous books of holy scripture which are not found in our Bible today (Book of Covenant, Ex 24:7; Book of Nathan, 2 Chron 9:29; a third epistle to the Corinthians, 1 Cor 5:9, just to mention a few of at least 17 references). The Bible even quotes verbatim other prophecies not found elsewhere in its own pages (Matt 2:23; Jude 1:14-15). The Bible also refers to other books that will come forth in the last days (Ezekiel 37:15-20; Isaiah 29:4-12) and revelations that will be poured out upon the people prior to the second coming of Christ (Joel 2:28-32; Rev 14:6-7). If the Bible is the end of revelation, it has a great defect in that it does not claim so within its pages.

Betsy's pastor would have her believe their interpretation of the Bible is the true interpretation of God's word. To establish the correctness of their position, they often resort to citing passages of scripture that support their ideas. Their recitation of scripture is a selective one and does not include those passages that contradict or cast doubt on their interpretations. Let me give you a couple of examples.

Betsy's church teaches God is Spirit, an infinite and eternal three-in-one being who is the Father, the Son and the Holy Ghost, all at once but manifesting itself in different ways and at different times; a spiritual essence without body parts or form that cannot be comprehended by man's finite mind. This bewildering doctrine does not come from the Bible but from a series of councils convened during the fourth, fifth and sixth centuries, AD. The first of these councils is referred to as the Nicene council. The purpose of this gathering was to clarify teachings from remnants of the Christian church regarding the nature and attributes of God. To support their ideas of God and His truths, these men often referred to passages in the Bible such as "God is a spirit . . ." (John 4:24) and "there is one God; and there is none other but he." (Mark 12:32)

However, these well-intentioned men failed to account for all of the Biblical passages that seem to contradict their interpretation. For instance, many passages suggest that God has a form similar to man and that the Father and the Son are separate and distinct beings.

The patriarch, Jacob, left his witness that he beheld God and that God possesses features similar to man. "I have seen God face to face . . ." (Gen 32:30). Also, "the Lord spake unto Moses face to face, as a man speaketh unto his friend." (Gen 33:11) The writer of

Genesis informs us, "God created man in his own image" (Gen 1:25,27). The writer of the Book of Acts records that Stephen saw the heavens open, "and the Son of man [Jesus] standing on the right hand of God," separate and distinct beings (Acts 7:55-56). There are more than thirty passages in the Bible that refer to physical shape, form and body parts of God. There are numerous passages establishing the Father and the Son as distinct and separate beings, and yet these scriptures are ignored or trivialized to rationalize the concept of Trinity passed down by tradition from the Nicene council.

Another significant example is the age-old controversy over whether salvation is secured by grace or works. Betsy's religion affirms, "by grace are ye saved through faith; and that not of yourselves: it is the gift of God. Not of works, lest any man should boast." (Eph 2:8) And, "we believe that through the grace of the Lord Jesus Christ we shall be saved . . ." (Acts 15:11)

However, a recitation of these passages is incomplete and fails to account for the Savior's teachings, "Not every one that saith unto me, Lord, Lord, shall enter into the kingdom of heaven; but he that doeth the will of my Father which is in heaven." (Matt 7:21) Twice the Savior was asked, "What shall I do that I may have eternal life?" Both times, Jesus replied, "if thou wilt enter into life, keep the commandments." (Matt 19:16, Luke 10:25; Luke 18:18) John the Revelator saw the final judgment scene and testified, "the dead were judged out of those things which were written in the books, according to their works." (Rev 20:12)

We believe the Bible is true and is intended to be taken literally when it teaches that mankind is saved through the grace of Jesus Christ *and* according to the works of each individual while on earth. We believe that the Bible means what it says and says what it means when stating that God is *both* spirit and body, and that the Father, the Son, and the Holy Ghost are separate and distinct beings, but one God with perfect unity in purpose and attributes.

This is not polytheism. This is monotheism that includes the Father, the Son, and the Holy Ghost without resorting to a mass of confusion that goes by the name of the doctrine of Trinity.

Betsy and her pastor are welcome to believe otherwise and continue to adhere to their interpretation of the passages of the Bible with which they feel comfortable. But if they would follow the example of

Christ, they should not be so narrow and dogmatic as to label anyone who does not agree with them as non-Christian and their beliefs as non-Biblical. We respect their tenets and hope they will accord us the same respect.

Our church and its teachings are true because The Church of Jesus Christ of Latter-day Saints is the only church led by Jesus Christ himself through living apostles and prophets. As an inspired writer in the Bible stated, "Surely the Lord God will do nothing, but he revealeth his secret unto his servants the prophets." (Amos 3:7)

This is the way Christ organized His church while on earth. It continued after his ascension into heaven and was intended to continue as long as Christ's true church remained on the earth. Paul writes that as members of His church we are "fellowcitizens with the saints and of the household of God, And are built upon the foundation of the apostles and prophets, Jesus Christ himself being the chief corner stone." (Eph 2:19-20) Paul goes on to explain that the Savior organized His church with apostles and prophets and other offices of the priesthood, "For the perfecting of the saints, for the work of the ministry, for the edifying of the body of Christ: Till we all come in the unity of the faith and of the knowledge of the Son of God, unto a perfect man, unto the measure of the stature of the fulness of Christ: That we henceforth be no more children, tossed to and fro and carried about with every wind of doctrine . . ." (Eph 4:11-14)

One of the clear indications that we need living apostles and prophets is the lack of unity and the fragmentation in the Christian community today. The obvious question is why don't these Christian churches have apostles and prophets as established in Christ's church? Who authorized them to change the organization of the church that Jesus Christ set up and that Paul indicated was intended to continue? Where in the Bible these churches accept does it authorize the changes other churches have introduced? Keep in mind, according to these churches, revelation ceased with the Bible and new revelation is to be rejected. Yet the founders of these denominations obtained the wisdom or insight or some other basis for changing the organization of the church Jesus Christ established and the apostles labored to perpetuate after the ascension.

Because our church is built upon the only sure foundation of apostles and prophets, Jesus Christ himself, being the chief cornerstone, we do not need to misinform our members about other churches and their beliefs. We are not afraid to explore other religions. Joseph Smith visited other churches as a youth and studied their teachings. He found much good in them, but he also found contradiction and confusion despite the claim that each was based on the teachings of the Bible. Joseph Smith found truth only after he followed the admonitions of James and asked the Lord for wisdom (James 1:5-7).

If Betsy and her family want to know the truth of this church, they will accept an invitation to learn about our faith from a member of our church and not from their pastor who can only expose them to half-truths. If they are honest in heart and sincerely seeking truth, they will realize the promises of the Lord and gain a personal testimony of the restored gospel of Jesus Christ. This will require them to study the teachings of our church and ask the Lord if the teachings of The Church of Jesus Christ of Latter-day Saints are true.

We would be delighted to host Betsy and her family in our home if they are interested in understanding our beliefs. The choice is theirs. We can do no more than offer to share these truths which we hold so dear.

> With love and admiration,
> Dad

Bibliography

Anderson, Richard Lloyd. *Investigating the Book of Mormon Witnesses.* Salt Lake City, UT: Deseret Book Company, 1981.

Andrus, Hyrum L. *Doctrines of the Kingdom.* Volumes 1-3. Salt Lake City, UT: Bookcraft, Inc., 1973

Ankerberg, John & Weldon, John. *Everything You Ever Wanted to Know About Mormonism.* Eugene, OR: Harvest House Publishers, 1992.

Averill, Lloyd J. *Religious Right, Religious Wrong: A Critique of the Fundamentalist Phenomenon.* New York, NY: Pilgrim Books, 1989.

Barth, Karl. *Church Dogmatics, The Doctrine of Creation*, Volumes 1 through 4. Edenburgh: T & T Clark, 1969.

Barth, Karl. *The Teaching of the Church Regarding Baptism.* Translated by Payne, Ernest A. London: SCM Press, 1948.

Barker, James L. *Apostasy from the Divine Church.* Salt Lake City, UT: Bookcraft, 1960.

Berkhof, Louis. *The History of Christian Doctrines.* Grand Rapids, MI: Baker Book House, 1975.

Berkhof, Louis. *Systematic Theology.* Grand Rapids, MI: Eerdman's, 1939.

Bernstein, Father A. James. "Which Came First: The Church or the New Testament." *The Christian Activist.* Volume 9, Fall/Winter, 1996.

Bertrand de Margerie, J. D. *The Christian Trinity in History.* Still River, MA: St. Bede's Publications, 1982.

Bickerstelk, Edward. *The Trinity.* Grand Rapids, MI: Kreigel Publications, 1980.

Bloesch, Donald. *Essentials of Evangelical Theology: Volume I, God, Authority and Salvation.* San Francisco, CA: Harper & Row Publishers, 1978.

Bonhoeffer, Dietrich. *The Communion of Saints.* New York, NY: Harper & Row Publishers, 1963.

Bray, Gerald. *The Doctrine of God.* Downers Grove, IL: InterVarsity Press, 1993.

_____, *The Book of Mormon.* Smith, Joseph Jr., translator, Salt Lake City, UT: The Church of Jesus Christ of Latter-day Saints, 1981.

Bowman, Robert M., Jr. *Orthodoxy and Heresy*. Grand Rapids, MI: Baker Book House, 1992.

Brodie, Fawn M. *No Man Knows My History*. New York, NY: Alfred A. Knopf, 1985.

Brown, Hugh B. "Profile of A Prophet." Audio-tape, Salt Lake City, UT: Covenant Recordings, 1979.

Bruce, F. F. *History of the Bible in English*. 3rd Edition, New York, NY: Oxford University Press, 1978.

Burton, Alma P. "The Divine Mission of the Prophet Joseph Smith." Audio-tape, Salt Lake City, UT: Covenant Recordings, 1980.

Cantelon, James. *Theology for Non-Theologians*. New York, NY: Macmillan Publishing Company, 1988.

_____, *Catholic Encyclopedia*, Vol. IV., New York, NY: Robert Appleton, 1908.

_____, *Catholicism*. McBrien, Richard P., general editor, Minneapolis, MN: Winston Press, 1980.

Chafer, Lewis Sperry. *Major Bible Themes*. revised by Walvoord, John F., Grand Rapids, MI: Academie Books, 1974.

Connelly, Douglas. *After Life*. Downers Grove, IL: InterVarsity Press, 1995.

Cocoris, G. Michael. *Evangelism: A Biblical Approach*. Chicago, IL: Moody Press, 1984.

Cocoris, G. Michael. *Lordship Salvation: Is It Biblical?*. Dallas, TX: Redencion Viva, 1983.

_____, David Whitmer. *Interviews*. Cook, Lyndon W., ed., Orem, UT: Grandin Book Company, 1993.

Crowther, Duane S. *Life Everlasting: A Definitive Study of Life After Death*. Bountiful, UT: Horizon Publishers, 1997.

Crowther, Duane S. *The Prophecies of Joseph Smith: Over 400 Prophecies By and About Joseph Smith and Their Fulfillment*. Bountiful, UT: Horizon Publishers, 1983.

Decker, Ed & Hunt, Dave. *The God Makers*. Eugene, OR: Harvest House Publishers, 1984.

_____, *Dictionary of Christianity in America*. Reid, Daniel C., et. al., editors, Downers Grove, IL: InterVarsity Press, 1990.

_____, *The Doctrine and Covenants*. Salt Lake City, UT: The Church of Jesus Christ of Latter-day Saints, 1981.

Dunnett, Walter M. *The Priesthood of the Believer and Its Expression in the Life of the Church* (A Thesis). Wheaton, IL: Wheaton College, 1953.

_____, Eerdmans' *Handbook to Christian Belief*. Keeley, Robin, et. al., consulting editors, Grand Rapids, MI: Wm. B. Eerdmans Publishing Company, 1982.

_____, Eerdmans' *Handbook to the World's Religions*. Beaver, R. Pierce, et. al.. consulting editors. Grand Rapids, MI: Eerdmans Publishing Company, 1994.

_____, *Encyclopedia of American Religions: Religious Creeds*, First Edition. Melton, J. Gordon, editor, Detroit, MI: Gale Research Company, 1988.

Erickson, Millard J. *God in Three Persons*. Grand Rapids, MI: Baker Books, 1995.

Evans, Rob L. & Berent, Irwin M. *Fundamentalism: Hazards and Heartbreaks*. LaSalle, IL: Open Court Publishing Company, 1988.

Evans, Tony. *The Promise, Experiencing God's Greatest Gift, The Holy Spirit*. Chicago, IL: Moody Press, 1996.

Evenson, Darrick T. *The Gainsayers*. Bountiful, UT: Horizon Publishers and Distributors, 1989.

Gibbs, Alfred P., *et. al. What Christians Believe*. Chicago, IL: Moody Press, 1951.

Godsey, John D. *The Theology of Dietrich Bonhoeffer*. Philadelphia, PA: The Westminster Press, 1958.

Graham, Billy. *My Answer*. Garden City, NY: Doubleday & Co., 1960.

Graham, Billy. *Peace with God*. Waco, TX: Word Books, Publisher, 1984.

Graham, Billy. *The Challenge*. Garden City, NY: Doubleday & Company, 1969.

Grosheide, F. W. *Commentary on the First Epistle to Corinthians*. Grand Rapids, MI: Eerdmans, 1953.

Harris, Murray J. *Jesus as God: The New Testament Use of Theos in Reference to Jesus*. Grand Rapids, MI: Baker Book House, 1992.

Hatch, Edwin. *The Influence of Greek Ideas on Christianity*. New York, NY: Harper & Row Publishers, 1957.

_____, *Harper-Collins Dictionary of Religion*. Smith, Jonathan Z., et. al., contributing editors, San Francisco, CA: HarperCollins Publishers, 1995.

Heppe, Heinrich. *Reformed Dogmatics*. Grand Rapids, MI: Baker Book House, 1950.

Hodges, Zane C. *The Gospel Under Siege*. Dallas, TX: Redencion Viva, 1981.

Hopkins, Richard R. *Biblical Mormonism*. Bountiful, UT: Horizon Publishers & Distributors, Inc., 1994.

Hordern, William E. *A Layman's Guide to Protestant Theology*. New York, NY: The Macmillan Company, 1968.

Howells, Rulon S. *His Many Mansions*. New York, NY: The Greystone Press, 1940.

Kaufman, Gordon D. *Systematic Theology: A Historicist Perspective*. New York, NY: Charles Scribner's and Sons, 1968.

Keller, Roger R. *Reformed Christians and Mormon Christians, Let's Talk*. United States: Pryor Pettengill, 1986.

Kelly, J. N. D. *Early Christian Doctrines*. New York, NY: Harper & Row Publishers, 1960.

Kendall, R. T. *Once Saved, Always Saved*. Chicago, IL: Moody Press, 1984.

Lawson, John. *Comprehensive Handbook of Christian Doctrine*. Englewood Cliffs, NJ: Prentice Hall, Inc., 1967.

Lee, Rex E. *What Do Mormons Believe?*. Salt Lake City, UT: Deseret Book Company, 1992.

Lewis, C. S. *Mere Christianity*. New York, NY: The Macmillan Company, 1971.

Little, Paul E. *Know What You Believe*. Wheaton, IL: Victor Books, 1984.

Lucado, Max, *In the Grip of Grace*. Dallas, TX: Word Publishers, 1996.

Lutzer, Erwin W. *How You Can Be Sure That You Will Spend Eternity with God*. Chicago, IL: Moody Press, 1996.

Lutzer, Erwin W. *One Minute After You Die*. Chicago, IL: Moody Press, 1997.

Lutzer, Erwin W. *The Serpent of Paradise*. Chicago, IL: Moody Press, 1996.

MacArthur, John F., Jr. *Faith Works: The Gospel According to the Apostles*. Dallas, TX: Word Publishing, 1993.

MacArthur, John F., Jr. *The Glory of Heaven*. Wheaton, IL: Crossway Books, 1996.

MacArthur, John F., Jr. *The Gospel According to Jesus*. Grand Rapids, MI: Zondervan Publishing House, 1988.

Macquarie, John. *Principles of Christian Theology*. New York, NY: Charles Scribner's and Sons, 1977.

Madsen, Truman G. *Eternal Man*. Salt Lake City, UT: Deseret Book Company, 1970.

Manson, T. W. *Ministry and Priesthood: Christ and Ours*. Richmond, VA: John Knox Press, 1957.

Marsden, George M. *Fundamentalism and American Culture*. New York and Oxford: Oxford University Press, 1980.

Martin, Ralph P. *The Worship of God*. Grand Rapids, MI: Eerdmans, 1980.

Martin, Walter. *Essential Christianity*. Ventura, CA: Regal Books, 1980.

Martin, Walter. *The Maze of Mormonism*. Ventura, CA: Regal Books, 1978.

Marty, Martin E. *Protestantism*. New York, NY: Holt, Rinehart and Winston, 1972.

McGrath, Allister. *Evangelism and the Future of Christianity*. Downers Grove, IL: InterVarsity Press, 1995.

McConkie, Bruce R. *Mormon Doctrine*. Salt Lake City, UT: Bookcraft, 1966.

McMurrin, Sterling M. *The Theological Foundations of the Mormon Religion*. Salt Lake City, UT: University of Utah Press, 1965.

Meeks, Wayne. *The First Urban Christians*. New Haven, CT: Yale University Press, 1983.

Mead, Frank S. *Handbook of Denominations in the United States*. revised by Hill, Samuel S., Nashville, TN: Abingdon Press, 1995.

Millet, Robert L. *By Grace Are We Saved*. Salt Lake City, UT: Bookcraft, 1989.

Murphee, Jon Tal. *A Loving God and A Suffering World*. Downers Grove, IL: InterVarsity Press, 1981.

Morgan, Willard. *From Critic to Convert*. Bountiful, UT: Horizon Publishers and Distributors, Inc., 1995.

_____, *The New Testament Student Manual*, Vol. 1. The Church of Jesus Christ of Latter-day Saints, 1974.

Nibley, Hugh. *Mormonism and Early Christianity*. Salt Lake City, UT: Deseret Book, 1987.

Nibley, Hugh. *"No Ma'am That's Not History."* Salt Lake City, UT: Bookcraft, 1946.

Nibley, Hugh. *Since Cumorah*. Salt Lake City, UT: Deseret Book Company, 1967.

Niebuhr, Reinhold. *The Nature and Destiny of Man*. New York, NY: Charles Scribner's & Sons, 1964.

Ogden, Greg. *The New Reformation, Returning the Ministry to the People of God*. Grand Rapids, MI: Ministry Resources Library, 1990.

_____, *One God in Trinity*. ed., Toon, Peter and Spiceland, James D., Westchester, IL: Cornerstone Book, 1980.

Payne, David F. "The Text and Canon of the New Testament." *The International Bible Commentary*. ed., F. F. Bruce, Grand Rapids, MI: Zondervan Publishing House, 1986.

_____, *The Pearl of Great Price*. Salt Lake City, UT: The Church of Jesus Christ of Latter-day Saints, 1981.

Peterson, Daniel C. & Ricks, Stephen D. *Offenders for a Word*. Salt Lake City, UT: Aspen Books, 1992.

Placher, William C. *A History of Christian Theology*. Philadelphia, PA: The Westminster Press, 1983.

_____, "Presbyterians and Mormons: A Study in Contrasts." Theology and Worship Ministry Unit, Presbyterian Church (U.S.A.), 1990.

Rahner, Karl. *Foundations of Christian Faith*. translated by Dych, William V., New York, NY: The Seaburg Press, 1978.

Rahner, Karl. *On the Theology of Death*. New York, NY: The Seaburg Press, 1973.

Rahner, Karl. *The Priesthood*. New York, NY: The Seaburg Press, 1973.

Rahner, Karl. *The Trinity*. New York, NY: Herder & Herder, 1970.

Reed, David A. and Farkas, John R. *How to Rescue Your Loved One from Mormonism*. Grand Rapids, MI: Baker Books, 1994.

_____, *Reflections on Mormonism: Judaeo-Christian Parallels*. ed., Madsen, Truman G. Provo, UT: Religious Studies Center, BYU, 1978.

Richards, Lawrence O. and Martin, Gib. *A Theology of Personal Ministry*. Grand Rapids, MI: Zondervan Publishing House, 1981.

Richards, LeGrand. *A Marvelous Work and A Wonder*. Salt Lake City, UT: Deseret Book Company, 1972.

Richardson, Cyril. The Doctrine of the Trinity. New York, NY: Abingdon Press, 1958.

Roberts, B. H. *A Comprehensive History of the Church*. Volumes 1-6. Provo, UT: Brigham Young University Press, 1965.

Roberts, B. H. *Mormon Doctrine of Deity*. Bountiful, UT: Horizon Publishers & Distributors, Inc., 1982.

Robinson, Stephen E. *Are Mormons Christians?*. Salt Lake City, UT: Bookcraft, 1991.

Robinson, William. *Completing the Reformation, The Doctrine of the Priesthood of All Believers*. Lexington, KY: The College of the Bible, 1955.

Ross, J. M. "Some Unnoticed Points in the Text of the New Testament." *Novum Testamentum*. Volume 25, 1983.

Rusch, William G. *The Trinitarian Controversy*. Philadelphia, PA: Fortress Press, 1980.

Scott, Latayne Colvett. *The Mormon Mirage*. Grand Rapids, MI: Zondervan Publishing House, 1979.

Smith, Huston. *The Religions of Man*. New York, NY: HarperCollins Publisher, Inc., 1986.

Smith, Joseph Jr. *History of the Church*. Volumes 1-6. Salt Lake City, UT: Deseret Book Company, 1978.

Smith, Joseph Jr. *Teachings of the Prophet Joseph Smith*. Smith, Joseph Fielding, compiler, Salt Lake City, UT: Deseret Book Company, 1970.

Joseph F. Smith. *Gospel Doctrine*. Salt Lake City, UT: Deseret Book, 1939.

Smith, Joseph Fielding. *Doctrines of Salvation*. Volumes 1-3. Bruce R. McConkie, compiler, Salt Lake City, UT: Deseret Book Company, 1955.

Smith, Lucy Mack Smith. *History of Joseph Smith*. Salt Lake City, UT: Bookcraft, n.d.

Smith, Wilbur M. *The Biblical Doctrine of Heaven*. Chicago, IL: Moody Press, 1968.

Swinburne, Richard. *The Christian God*. Oxford: Clarendon Press, 1994.

Stanley, Charles. *Eternal Security, Can You Be Sure?* Nashville, TN: Thomas Nelson Publishers, 1990.

Studer, Basil. *Trinity and Incarnation*. Collegeville, MN: The Liturgical Press, 1993.

Swindoll, Charles R. *Strengthening Your Grip*. Minneapolis, MN: Worldwide Publishing, 1982.

Talmage, James E. *Articles of Faith*. Boston, MA: University Press, 1959.

_____, *The Theology of Paul Tillich, Volume One*. Kegley, Charles W. And Bretall, Robert W., ed., New York, NY: The MacMillan Company, 1964.

_____, *Theological Foundations for Ministry*. Anderson, Ray S., ed., Grand Rapids, MI: William B. Eerdman's, 1979.

Thieme, R. B. *Apes and Peacocks or the Pursuit of Happiness*. Houston, TX: Thieme, 1973.

Tillich, Paul. *Systematic Theology, Three Volumes in One*. Chicago, IL: University of Chicago Press, 1967.

Tillich, Paul. *The Eternal Now*. New York, NY: Charles Scribner's & Sons, 1963.

Tillich, Paul. *The Shaking of the Foundations*. New York, NY: Charles Scribner's & Sons, 1948.

Timiadis, Emilianos. *The Nicene Creed, Our Common Faith*. Philadelphia, PA: Fortress Press, 1983.

Toon, Peter. *One Triune God*. Wheaton, IL: Victor Books, 1973.

Vine, W. E. *Vine's Expository Dictionary of Old and New Testament Words*. Old Tappan, NJ: Revell, 1981.

_____, *The Vision*. Lundwall, Nels B., compiler, Salt Lake City, UT: Bookcraft, n.d.

Wainwright, Arthur W. *The Trinity in the New Testament*. London: SPCK, 1962.

World Book Encyclopedia, Chicago, IL: World Book, Inc., 1985.

Index

Scripture Reference List